SOCRATES AMONG STRANGERS

SOCRATES AMONG STRANGERS

Joseph P. Lawrence

Northwestern University Press
Evanston, Illinois

Northwestern University Press
www.nupress.northwestern.edu

Printed in the United States of America

10 9 8 7 6 5 4 3 2 1

Library of Congress Cataloging-in-Publication Data

Lawrence, Joseph P., 1952– author.
    Socrates among strangers / Joseph P. Lawrence.
       pages cm
    Includes bibliographical references and index.
    ISBN 978-0-8101-3167-5 (cloth : alk. paper) — ISBN 978-0-8101-3169-9
(pbk. : alk. paper) — ISBN 978-0-8101-3168-2 (ebook)
    1. Socrates. 2. Philosophy, Ancient. I. Title.
    B317.L39 2015

                                                                    2015025326

To my students

Contents

Preface

I wrote the first draft of this book twenty years ago. The reason I did not see it through to publication at the time is because its integrity seemed compromised by a precarious fault line running through it. Having initially intended the book as a contribution to scholarly literature on Socrates, I was sidetracked when reality intervened in the form of the Kobe earthquake (January 17, 1995), which heavily damaged the house my family and I were living in, while leveling much of our immediate neighborhood. Scholarly detachment became difficult to maintain; philosophical calm, a virtue to be sought rather than exercised.

My wife and daughters and I soon found ourselves encamped in the university gymnasium with scores of our Japanese neighbors, enduring with them the drone of helicopters coming down to remove dead bodies. One of them was the body of a friend I had uncovered myself. A few days before the earthquake, we had dined at his house, which had collapsed completely. It is hardly surprising that when I returned to my writing (after a surreal four or five weeks), I found myself torn between the desire to write about Socrates and the desire to write about the Kobe earthquake. Had I elected to write about the earthquake, I knew my theme: I would have celebrated the remarkable calm that the people of Kobe and Nishinomiya maintained in the wake of the horrific event. It highlighted an aspect of Japanese culture I much admired. Instead of pursuing this theme, however, I chose to continue writing about Socrates, shifting the focus away from his argumentative strategies and toward the calm that he too is said to have mastered, maintaining it even while drinking his poison. This in itself is perfectly acceptable. Good scholars are permitted to work on topics that life itself places before them.

What scholarly convention does not permit, however, is any kind of sustained intrusion of one's person into one's work, whether in the form of personal narrative or, in my case, of earthquake memories. I was guilty of just that. Guilty, moreover, for no better or worse reason than that my own brush with death had placed me before a riddle that went right to the heart of the question I was asking about Socrates. On the one hand, as saturated as I was with the ideas of Socrates and Plato, my immediate response to the earthquake was far from cerebral. My wife described what came up out of me as a primordial scream, almost as if I had felt the need to compete with the roar of the earthquake itself. If so, it was a scream that came from a deeper place than either my mind or my will; it was not I, but my body that so screamed (*I* had been soundly asleep when the walls came down on us). This experience of a screaming body made me suspicious of the Socratic ideal of using philosophy to prepare oneself for death. That now appeared as wishful thinking, to be rejected as such. The mind simply has no control of such things. This is what I inferred from the first wave of fear that flowed over me.

On the other hand, the striking equanimity with which my Japanese neighbors greeted the same event indicated that what goes on in the mind might indeed matter. If "first waves" of fear are physiological, the waves that follow are very often psychological—evidence of what Socrates and Plato would have called a poorly attuned soul. A properly attuned soul is not so easily thrown off balance. In contrast to my neighbors, it seemed that I myself had some serious learning to do. When things settled down enough that I could return to my research and writing, I realized that it was no longer as an authority (a master of my discipline) that I wanted to pursue my work but as something fundamentally different: I was a person in desperate search of what I needed to know. This struck me with the force of a genuine philosophical discovery: it was in my need, not in my learning, that I encountered the Socrates I wanted to write about.

This is the place where the curious fault line began to show itself in my writing, for I found myself caught between my own deepest impulses and a scholarly ethos that demands that we speak from what we know, not from our aching need to know.[1] To speak of and out of one's need is to abandon the objective standpoint that constitutes the condition of good scholarship. More than that, it is unseemly, an affront to the very human desire to seek shelter in the security that objectivity provides. As proof of this, I confess that I experienced the tension that had infiltrated my writing, the distressing gap between knowledge and the human need to know, primarily in the form of insecurity ("do I really know what I am talking about?"). Even so, I was soon enough to learn that, experienced from the side of my readers, the same insecurity could be read as a sign of arrogance ("who does he think he is to write in this manner?"). It is a peculiar feature of the academic world that, precisely because its conventions are meant to establish "expertise," confessions of ignorance appear as haughtiness. One is expected to proceed as if the foundations of one's own discipline were set in stone.

My conundrum was not unlike the one faced by Socrates. What after all defines him more than the tension between his own claim to ignorance and the accusations of arrogance that led to his execution? What hope had *I* now of providing even a semiobjective account of Socrates, when it seemed instead that I was hallucinating an inner affinity with the man, as if "understanding from the inside" were an option for one of the iconic figures of Western history? My appropriating the language of the *Imitatio Christi* to define a philosopher's proper relationship to Socrates did not help matters. The fear that the earthquake awakened in me made me aspire to the courage that Socrates had displayed at his execution, as if it were something that could be my own. It seemed to me unimportant that such a profoundly personal quest is deemed incompatible with the prevailing scholarly ethos. My calling, after all, was not to scholarship, but to philosophy. If I was trying to cultivate courage in the face of death, it seemed fitting to begin by displaying as much intellectual courage as I could muster. If respect for academic propriety carries with it the demand that one refrain from thinking and writing in a certain manner, both love of Socrates and love of truth made me want to deliver a defiant *j'accuse* against the various gatekeepers of the scholarly industry who, in the name of scholarly detachment, admonished me to take myself out of the narrative and to quit writing as if language were anything other than a neutral medium for communicating information. But I was *in* my work in large part because I had discovered that language begins with a scream. Philosophers must be poets. Thus, I ignored the demands that I alter my "voice."

Under these circumstances, it is hardly surprising that my post-earthquake book on Socrates, which (in celebration of the *Imitatio*) I had adorned with the rather audacious title of *Becoming Socrates*, was deemed unfit for publication. I saw what I did wrong when, soon after I completed my manuscript, Alexander Nehamas published a similarly themed book, *The Art of Living*.[2] He too celebrated the idea that philosophy should proceed as a conscious imitation of Socrates. But he had the prudence to remove himself from the equation, as evidenced by his subtitle, "Socratic Reflections from Plato to Foucault." Something similar could be said about Pierre Hadot's wonderful book, *Philosophy as a Way of Life*, which also appeared at about that time.[3] Dedicated to a nonacademic understanding of philosophy, the book was meticulous in its scholarship. I had not been as prudent and suffered the consequences. As disappointed as I was that the book met with rejection (it hurts to be silenced), I was heartened by something else, something that often happens to erstwhile scholars who find their way to the higher calling of classroom teaching. Here too Socrates showed the way. He was a teacher; I would be a teacher. He wrote nothing at all; I would write just enough (in an age obsessed with production) not to "perish."

This is what deepened my love for students, people young enough to understand that the search for courage and wisdom was more important than the research imperative to uncover anything that looks like a fact together with whatever might plausibly be argued as constituting its condition. Although students are understandably impressed with the equation of knowledge and power that justifies the compulsive drive to research, they are nonetheless troubled when they glimpse the stark amorality of that collective project. I recall, for instance, the way they respond to the famous "Ring of Gyges" story from Plato's *Republic* (359c–360d),[4] which puts forth the proposition, terrifying in a technological age, that power, far from being a good in itself, damages and corrupts the soul. It is a proposition rendered all the more plausible by the tendency of the powerful to deny the very existence of a soul to be corrupted, as if the decision to deal only with material realities delivers the proof that the material alone is real. I find it admirable that my students are troubled by this kind of thing, just as I find it disturbing that so many of my colleagues have grown numb to the issue.

As tempting as it is to play to the gullibility of young people (as happens when we try to sell them on our particular ideological and disciplinary affiliations), the real reward in teaching comes when we offer them the chance to think for themselves by showing them that reasonable but still questionable assumptions constitute not only the foundations of the various disciplines but the basis of the scholarly ethos itself. If the formation we offer to our students is to make them into young scholars, it needs to be supplanted by the more daring and hopeful project of encouraging their natural love of thought. Students are not dumb. They recognize quickly enough the dubious nature of much that the adult world, in the name of education, places before them as if it were sealed in certainty. If we ourselves were more honest, we would try harder to relieve them of the burden of pretending not to see what they see clearly enough. Heidegger famously observed that science (insofar as it is bound to a predetermined methodology) does not think;[5] students, on the other hand, like to think—and I like to encourage them in the practice.

It was with my students in mind, then, that I decided to resurrect my book on Socrates, packaging it this time around not as a book for scholars but as a book for teachers and for learners. When I speak of "learners," I have in mind anyone who feels alienated not only from the lifelessness of scholarship but, more important, from the lifelessness of the world that the norms of scholarship have helped shape. What makes me think the insights in this book are worth sharing is my classroom discovery that, contrary to well-established opinion, a teacher is not first and foremost a scholar who has information to share. Instead of that, a teacher is that very strange and fragile thing, a human being, one who, hovering on the brink of a known mortality, is able to communicate not merely information but the active *need* to learn. To communicate need, a person has to feel need—and with aching intensity. It is as a teacher in just this sense, not as a scholar, that I offer this book to potential readers, while dedicating it to my students.

At the same time, I do not want to suggest that the book is *not* for scholars. Quite the contrary, if I am correct in my judgment, the accusation I am delivering will have to be taken seriously by two groups of scholars in particular, those at the service of philosophy and those at the service of the humanities, both of whom I accuse of succumbing to a scholarly ethos that, suitable to the sciences, is highly unsuitable for their own disciplines. A case in point concerns the way one cites a source. In providing a textual citation, my goal is not so much to provide evidence for a claim as to acknowledge a piece of writing that has made me think, whereby thinking is the excavation of possibility, not the determination of fact. To apply standards of "correctness" to interpretations is very often to misconceive their purpose, which is to break through to an understanding of truth—even if it comes at the cost of misunderstanding a text. Encounters with philosophical texts, like encounters with works of literature, are living encounters with the inwardness of thought. What one seeks is not secure a new bit of knowledge, but to grow more understanding of oneself and others. I turn to Socrates in search of what an age of technology needs above all else: a clearly articulated philosophy of the humanities, one that, in the vitality of its language, provides evidence of the real and substantial freedom of the human spirit.

If a teacher is made into a teacher by virtue of recognizing the need that makes one search for such understanding in the first place, the best teacher is the one who, like Socrates, begins with an acknowledgment of just how strange it is to be a human being. Although prevailing models of communication focus on the "sharing of information"—that is, the conceptual mediation of all that we know and are coming to know—the premise of this book is that authentic communication is less about shared knowledge than about a shared recognition of the strangeness of existence itself, and of human existence in particular. Scholarship is primarily the concern of knowers, whether the theologians of old who regarded the infinite mind of God as eternal and therefore self-evidently given, or, what so much resembles them, the naturalists of our own day, who take it as obvious that the "universe" (of which our particular universe is but the empirically accessible instance) is eternal and self-evidently given. It takes intellectual courage to recognize that both of these things (mind and matter) have simply been abstracted from the only thing that, in real but difficult truth, is unquestionably given—and that is life itself. There is a reason why it takes courage to recognize this. Whereas big abstractions such as "God" or the "universe" can easily be taken to exist forever, the lived experience of an embodied mind encountering a world is temporal through and through. When, as a knower of the universe, a person goes into his or her death, in a certain real but highly mysterious way the universe dies as well, regardless of how much of it is left behind for other knowers to perceive and attempt to understand. In other words, objective reality is always one-half illusion.

Life is suspended in a void. It is more, not less, life for the fact. Death is real, even if the "nothing" into which it catapults us is neither to be experienced nor conceptually conceived. That which cannot be known invites, as I will now show in my introduction, two responses, one that I associate with Socrates; the other, with Plato. The Socratic response is to acknowledge the unknowable as the very source of our freedom. The Platonic response is to flee the unknowable by positing as "objective" a picture of reality separated from life. The response remains Platonic regardless of whether the picture in question is understood as idea or, in the contemporary manner, as the physical universe. In either event, it serves as the pretext for a scholarly ethos that would have us look at the world as if we ourselves were not a part of it. If Plato is the father of that ethos, Socrates (together with Nietzsche) is its most passionate critic.

To acknowledge that we are part of the story we tell does not preclude the exercise of proper restraint, of what Socrates called "minding one's own business" (*Ap.* 37e).[6] The impulse to write novels—to imagine one's way into the private lives of others—is the source, in the wrong hands, of the kind of gossip and slander that has brought down more good men than just Socrates. But the fact that we should properly mind our own business does not mean that we should slip over into bad faith. Bad faith is hiding what we need to share: the acknowledgment that we can all be better than we are. The veneer of scholarly expertise hides the uncanny strangeness of being human that is the real source of our freedom. True, as strangers we find ourselves standing apart. But it is also true that as strangers (and human beings *are* strange), we meet and touch. By sharing only what is easy to share, a common sense hypnotized into the semblance of the self-evidently given, we end up sharing so little that we see in one another little more than competitors to be surpassed and overcome. Assimilated into the order of the self-evidently given, people are of no importance (why, there are billions of them in this world!). Often, they can be replaced by machines. But people do matter. This is why Socrates was so intent on engaging them in conversation—and why he did whatever he could to "unsettle" them by bringing them into closer contact with the elemental strangeness of being human.

With that, let me try to refine the terms of the *j'accuse* I first delivered when told that academic discourse demands the exclusion of the personal and the poetic. But first a concession: any one of us does not much matter. Death is the proof of that. But what does matter is who we collectively are. We are the only beings we know who can reflect on the meaning of what is intrinsically so very strange: the fact that the world exists, but not as an object exists, for its explanation is finally as malleable as thinking itself. We are free, in other words, with a freedom that, to the degree that it penetrates into the deepest root of reality as such, is not something that has been added to us, something to be found or not found in a laboratory by neuroscientists or anyone else. Freedom is not a function of complexity but of the groundlessness of being, emergent not in the miming of consciousness but in consciousness as such.

We live in denial of such elemental freedom. Out of fear of the death that lies at its bottom, we abuse our freedom by turning the world and everything in it into a lifeless machine. We are so terrified of decision and judgment that, in the name of justice, we seek to objectify the procedures we live by, seeking to deliver them over to the impersonal god Algorithm. That we do this in the name of good scholarship I find deplorable. But what I find even more deplorable is that, in the name of education, we do this to our young people—and do it systematically.[7] *J'accuse. J'accuse.*

Abbreviations

Works by Plato

Alc.	*Alcibiades*
Ap.	*Apology*
Charm.	*Charmides*
Cri.	*Crito*
Euthphr.	*Euthyphro*
Grg.	*Gorgias*
La.	*Laches*
Lys.	*Lysis*
Par.	*Parmenides*
Phd.	*Phaedo*
Phdr.	*Phaedrus*
Prt.	*Protagoras*
Rep.	*Republic*
7th Let.	*Seventh Letter*
Statesm.	*Statesman*
Symp.	*Symposium*
Tht.	*Theaetetus*
Tim.	*Timaeus*

Works by Aristotle

Nic. Eth.	*Nicomachean Ethics*
Post. An.	*Posterior Analytics*

SOCRATES AMONG STRANGERS

Beginning in Silence

Truth demands silence before it will raise its voice.
—Søren Kierkegaard, *The Concept of Irony*

My most vivid memory of the now long-ago earthquake is that, even as it rocked our house and brought the side of a mountain down on our neighborhood, it was for me an eerily silent event, a reminder that silence itself can roar. With the surface of the earth falling like a wave crashing at sea, I too roared silently, but not as the "I" that I always thought I was, but as an "I" unknown and terrifyingly alien. It was as if the mask had been torn off what was really just a screaming body, a body that in its turn clung to the body of the mattress and floor beneath it, all in jerky motion as the walls of the house came down on me and my family. We fear death not with our minds and our beliefs, but with our bodies—and to a depth and degree that we discover only after the fear has been unleashed. If there is an understanding that can set us free, it is not one that is grounded in the self-certainty of a disembodied intellect. Instead, it must be grounded more deeply. A simple lesson, but one I was not to forget. In an instant, the earthquake obliterated my lifelong tendency toward a Platonic intellectualism. If I were to stay true to Socrates, the man who knew how to die, the first thing I needed to do was find a way of disentangling him from Plato.

But why stay true to Socrates? My answer, in a word, is that I take philosophy seriously as the love of wisdom it says it is. But wisdom itself is but an idea, the ever-elusive idea that there might be a way of knowing reality that would reconcile a person fully to it. Given the reality of evil, the idea of wisdom appears either as a fantasy or as something reprehensible, a purported form of knowing that must instead be a forgetting—a forgetting that, again and again, innocent people are made to suffer horrific things by others, by people who should have and could have left them alone. If I am to love wisdom, I have to begin not with the idea of wisdom, which I find objectionable, but with someone who is actually wise—if only with the wisdom that makes no claim to wisdom.

A wisdom that hides itself, a modest wisdom. How strange! How appropriate then that Socrates, who never declared himself wise, did declare himself strange; indeed, he referred to himself as the *most* strange (*Tht.* 149a). And in just that, he was all of us, for life as such is strange. Strangeness does not exclude friendship (*philia*) but first makes it possible. On this issue, Aristotle is wrong when he makes familiarity into the most important condition of friendship (*Nic. Eth.* 1156b7 and again at 1165b17).[1] Socrates was much closer to the truth when he sought to make friends by first disclosing that he himself was a stranger. What, after all, is friendship apart from a mutually exchanged invitation to share that part of ourselves that we generally keep hidden, the part that is most difficult to bear alone. And what is this, apart from our realization of how fragile we are as beings that once were not and later will no longer be? Although it is true that in the public world we are simply people, self-evidently so, alive as everyone is alive, we gain friends only when we dispense with such self-evidence (silencing the impulse to talk about "what is being talked about") and instead give voice to a fragility that links us to the dead we carry in our hearts, those whose only claim to life is that we remember who they were. And who they were is who we all are, mortal beings turned toward the death that, in the strangest act of all, gifts us with life by destroying the illusion that existence has anything obvious about it.

Plato's purpose in writing the dialogues was to create the image of Socrates as the archetypal philosopher. To do philosophy is to imitate Socrates—and thereby to keep him alive.[2] On this assumption, there is no distinction to be made between Socratic dialogues and non-Socratic dialogues or between the philosophy of Socrates and the philosophy of Plato—or the philosophy of anyone else for that matter. Philosophy itself forms a seamless whole and in just this sense: wherever its spirit is brought to life, Socrates is brought to life.

To think of Socrates in this manner is, as Karl Jaspers did, to assimilate him to a list of exemplary human beings.[3] For Jaspers the short list was Socrates, Buddha, Confucius, and Christ. This list reflects an understanding of Socrates similar to the one that motivated Erasmus to proclaim: "*Sancte Socrates, ora pro nobis!*"[4] Such a Socrates is more than a clever man who consistently demands consistency from others. What that "more" is, is, of course, difficult to say. Difficult enough that we might do best to concede at the outset that what we are dealing with is a myth. As Plato wrote in his second letter: "no treatise by Plato exists or will exist, but those which now bear his name belong to a Socrates become fair and young" (*Epistles* 2.314c).[5]

Even so, the fact that a beautified Socrates is mythical does not mean we are dealing with a fiction but rather that Plato imaginatively let the truth of the potentially wise man hidden in Socrates visibly shine forth. If we as human beings are never truly good, we retain the capacity to be so. We owe it to our poets that we can clearly see what capacities, both good and evil, are hidden away in the human soul. Poetry, in other words, is in service of a truth more profound than the merely empirical; instead of showing us simply what we are, it shows us what we can be. The truth that Plato, who loved his teacher, wanted us to see about Socrates was the goodness that motivated his passion for life, a goodness rooted much more deeply than his stated beliefs. Plato's poem of Socrates renews itself ever again by evoking a sense of the man himself, the way he stood before his interlocutors, the always palpable sense of his actual physical presence. Plato's accomplishment was to depict a Socrates who, for all his insistence on clarity, was too mysterious ever really to be understood, too *alive* to be caught. This is why Alexander Nehamas was right to follow up his book on the imitation of Socrates with a book that emphasized the project of authenticity as lying at the very center of the Socratic project.[6] Imitation and authenticity by no means cancel one another out. "Find your own Socrates," Plato effectively told his readers, "so that you may finally find yourself."

What does it mean that the Socrates I have found is a "silent" one?[7] Socrates was, after all, bound to *logos* like no other: talking was his element and destiny. His willingness to engage in conversation with anyone and everyone (both male and female, freeman and slave) is legendary. Although other philosophers might lose themselves in the extremes of arrogance or timidity, Socrates held to the middle way. A friendlier and less pretentious world genius would be hard to imagine.

At the same time, he was continually being called to task for his ironic aloofness. There was a disturbing sense that his show of friendliness was a ruse, that he toyed with people and respected no one. Despite his demand that his interlocutors say exactly what they mean, Socrates often gave the impression of being playful rather than sincere, leaving us to wonder just where he stood. Was he a skeptic or a visionary? Political or apolitical? A democrat or an autocrat? An atheist or a believer? Were his philosophical instincts metaphysical or antimetaphysical? Was he the master of definitions that always cut quickly and decisively to the chase—or was he too sensitive to context for that, a thinker for whom intuitions were finally more important than concepts?

The enigma of Socrates is not simply that we are unsure about where Socrates ends and Plato begins—or about how much credence we should give to what Aristophanes or Xenophon had to say about him. The enigma of Socrates is given with and in Socrates himself. To encounter his true form, one must endeavor to unfold not so much his words as the spirit in which they were spoken. Indeed, to assume that Plato recorded any of his precise words is to demean Plato as a thinker in his own right, making him into a scholar bent on memory work. Spirit has a different life, one that springs forth from words, it is true, but from words that bear traces of what can never be spoken, light that shines forth from a sea of darkness, what Wallace Stevens once called the "muddy centre" that existed even "before we breathed."[8] Always in danger of dying the death of its manifest meaning, the philosophical word is akin to poetry insofar as it commands attention only by virtue of the possibility that it might in fact mean something completely different from what it says. As Gadamer put the issue, "it is enough to say that we understand in a *different* way, *if we understand at all,*"[9] a statement, by the way, that holds not only once but over and over. This is the limit of objective scholarship. Something about it remains Sisyphean work, for it is continuously undone by the unpredictability of the movement that is spirit.

In broaching the "limit to objective scholarship," I run up against one of the key issues of the entire book. Plato, the father of objective scholarship, is at the same time the author of the myth of Socrates, the archetypal philosopher who sustains thought by withdrawing himself even as he shows himself. If Plato defines objective scholarship, Socrates shows its limits. I have already acknowledged that I have no interest in pursuing the historical question of how to distinguish Socrates from the myth of Socrates (it is the mythical Socrates who interests me, not Socrates the man). This does not mean, however, that I am prepared to ignore the question of how to disentangle Plato himself from the myth he created. Indeed, I regard the question as having far more than historical importance. Rightly conceived, it is the question of where we go from here: do we remain bound, as we are, by ideas so inherently public they can be delivered over to Google, or do we recover a sense for the wisdom of Socrates, inhering as it does in the silence of a man who knows something but is unable or unwilling to say just what it is.

An observation about the twentieth-century philosopher Martin Heidegger will help show what I have in mind. Well known for his profound and sustained criticism of Plato and Platonism, Heidegger nonetheless had astonishingly positive things to say about Socrates, whom he celebrated as the "purest" of all thinkers.[10] As far as I am aware, no scholar has stepped forth to investigate this strange anomaly. What makes it significant is Heidegger's claim that the entire edifice of modern science, which he diagnosed as the agent of nihilism, is at bottom Platonism.[11] It is a claim I fully agree with and one, by the way, that has nothing to do with the controversial issue of Heidegger's politics. As for the idea that science is Platonism, one need only think of Alfred North Whitehead to be reminded of how widespread it is. And with regard to the idea that science is nihilism, the name of Heidegger's Jewish contemporary Theodor Adorno should serve as a sufficient reminder that it is not tied to anti-Semitic proclivities. The reason I cite Heidegger, despite the cloud that hangs over him, is simply because of the tenacity with which he defined "thinking" as a radical alternative to the kind of philosophy that ends in nihilism. If Heidegger understood Plato as the father of modern nihilism, he understood Socrates, the purest of thinkers, as the archetype of thinkers who might one day restore the world to life. What so impressed Heidegger (whose collected works contain more than a hundred volumes) about Socrates was the man's refusal to write, his refusal to add to the world's clutter and chatter by sharing an opinion about the nature of the highest Good. Heidegger found Socrates's public statement of his ignorance about what truly matters (*Ap.* 21d) less impressive than the lifelong silence that made him persist in asking others what they thought while refusing to say what he thought. It was as if he lived in such close proximity to the sacred mystery of being that, out of simple respect, he refused to defile it by trying to put it into words. Such a Socrates can serve as the antidote to the garrulousness of an age addicted to "information."

A curious sign of that garrulousness is the speed with which we pass through the sounds of words to attend (if at all) to the meanings that resonate within them. To borrow an example from the previous paragraph, I have dutifully followed the recommendation of the sixteenth edition of the *Chicago Manual of Style* by adding an extra *s* to the possessive *Socrates'*—despite the fact that Chicago concedes that the letter (traditionally not written) is best left unpronounced.[12] The ostensibly Socratic demand for consistency seems to have trumped what I regard as the more authentically Socratic demand that we listen to what we say. The texture of words, the rhythms of language, may have more to do with thinking than we (who have become inundated by a rising sea of words) are any longer able to acknowledge. "Wit" being the greater half of wisdom, the Socrateses among us, masters of irony one and all (Socrates's tease is he likes to tease), need to attend not only to what words say, but to the way they sound. This is an idea that Socrates discusses at great length in the *Cratylus*, a dialogue devoted to words and names and sounds, the conclusion of which Gadamer sums up as follows: "The 'truth' of a word does not depend on its correctness, its correct adequation to the thing. It lies rather in its perfect intellectuality—i.e., the manifestness of the word's meaning in its sound."[13] Against this understanding of language as "natural," we have the contemporary understanding of language as an arbitrary system of signs to which meanings are randomly assigned. It would require a much longer discussion to support my intuition that this structuralist conception of language, which understands itself an alternative to the Platonic (not Socratic) theory of ideas, is in fact the consequence of it. In any event, I regard the Chicago decision to let logic substitute for style as a characteristically Platonic move. Socrates, committed as he was to the spoken word, would have resisted the move of his disciple, delivering meaning to the ear rather than the disembodied mind.

To point in this way to the Platonic roots of our age and to science's role in promoting it is by no means to suggest that modern science is committed to such Platonic notions as the existence of the soul or of a separate world of ideas. Instead, it is simply to recognize that Plato's ideas, which are knowable only through a pure act of the understanding, anchor the mathematical ideas that for science constitute the form of the sensibly perceivable universe. The idea of the purely intelligible One as the idea of all ideas lives on in modern physics in the search for a unified formula that brings together the macro and micro regions of relativity theory and quantum mechanics. In a word, science is Platonic insofar as it understands itself as a theory of the real—that is, as a way of apprehending "objective reality." It is Platonic insofar as it binds past and future together in a unified web of causality, effectively rendering time (and freedom) into an illusion. It is Platonic, moreover, insofar as it puts forth the idea that knowledge as such is to be divorced from opinion. The perspective of the individual is something to be overcome. Although empirical scientists will, of course, resist this characterization (arguing that science is fundamentally about "observation"), in the end they too will have to concede that science is rigorous and attains real predictive force only insofar as the laws it postulates are mathematical in character. Mathematical algorithms finally determine the fate of what now is understood as essentially a "computational" universe. Computers are idea-machines—and in a fully Platonic sense. It is not surprising that they were first conceived by Leibniz, the great seventeenth-century Platonist.[14]

Heidegger renders this characterization of the Platonic foundation of modern science into a critique by suggesting that it systematically occludes access to time, the horizon within which meaning is sought and meaning is disclosed. Because science itself is one of many ways in which meaning is disclosed, it is legitimate to complain that it is insufficiently aware of the historical nature of its own origin. One among many possible ways of understanding the world, science as an ideology presents itself nonetheless as God's own (and eternal) truth. This is why the atheism that tends to cling to the scientific worldview is itself a religion, which just like any other religion offers a comprehensive (and dogmatic) view of the world. It views the universe as so self-evidently *there* that to question why it is there only seems inane. The novel aspect of the scientific version of religion is that salvation is perceived no longer as a gift offered from above but as an accomplishment that will one day be earned by a scientifically schooled humanity. Where once we prayed, now we work. If the mass of humanity is devoted to consumption, their scholar-priests are still ascetics, masters of self-denial who labor selflessly for the good of humanity.[15]

That the scholarly ethos is itself discernibly Platonic can be verified by a reading of Plato's *Phaedo*, a dialogue I will consider in another context in my final chapter. The reason I turn to it in my introduction is that it helps clarify the difference between Plato and Socrates. To begin with, the *Phaedo* is one of two dialogues in which Plato, the great master of restraint who never steps into his work, mentions himself, but in this case only to call attention to his absence. Phaedo, the narrator of the dialogue, says simply, "I believe that Plato was ill" (*Phd.* 59b). It is reasonable to assume, I think, that the "illness" in question is the only one discussed in the dialogue—the illness of not knowing how to face death. Plato so loved Socrates that he could not bear to see him die. Facing death was not Plato's forte. What he recommended instead is that we outwit death by using philosophy as a way to awaken the eternal hidden within as that which alone is capable of cognizing the eternal beyond. Though he called this "practice for death" (64a), it might also have been called (when heard in a Platonic rather than a Socratic register) "learning to avoid death." The way the practice functions (Platonically construed) is that we repeatedly turn our minds away from the sensible world and toward the world of pure ideas. By stripping away the color of life, whatever it is that clings to our mortal bodies and makes us into the concrete individuals we are, we effectively become indifferent to whether we live or die. The discovery we are supposed to make is that our minds, instead of actually dying, come more fully awake as we progressively focus attention on ideas, thereby attaining *tēs alētheias*, "the truth" (65b). Practicing this art is Plato's suggestion for how to cheat death. For one who understands life as constituted by sensibility, as we moderns do, the strategy takes on a very different meaning, quite as if Plato's real assertion is that "only dead men can see the truth."[16] The command that one "disappear" in the face of one's work is the key to the scholarly ethos. It is a command that prevails despite the fact that every important movement for the past 175 years, from Marxism to contemporary feminism and neuroscience, has been aligned against it, leading to the strange paradox that, even while we theoretically proclaim the falsity of any notion that ideas exist independently of the lives of the human beings who fashion them, we nonetheless persist in holding on to the ideal of attaining an objective standpoint that is positioned somewhere outside life itself. The literary critic who regards a work of literature as "only" an expression of class prejudice or gender bias does not add that the same thing can be said of her own work. The scientist who regards thinking as the neurochemistry of the brain does not call a halt to his own search for objective laws of nature that are universal in scope.

As the allure of PowerPoint shows, idea worship survives even as ideas are reductively made banal. Thus, the gesture of the good company man or woman: "Don't worry about me and what I am trying to say, but focus your attention instead on the Idea I am now projecting on the wall." There is, of course, a kind of relief in pretending that one does not have to be the mouthpiece of one's own idea. The obtrusive strangeness of being a human being is dissipated by the cult of universality, which is why we hold on to it (or to its PowerPoint semblance), even after we have convinced ourselves that there is no such thing as universal truth.

But universality has holes in it wide enough for a whole person to fall through. Even if one accepts Plato's argument (as I do) that life as such must belong to soul as such, so that the soul is disclosed as eternal, this by no means implies that this or that person lives forever, but only that the reality of the real is always necessarily a lived reality. Dead universes are only real for the astronomers and physicists who study them. Billions of years may pass by unattended, but they are past only for those who eventually do give attention to them. It is a past that, gone before we arrived on the scene, is yet our own past. It is what we came up out of, real to the degree that we are real.

A person, according to my understanding, is not a disembodied soul but rather an ensouled body. Owing my life to soul as such, I err only by calling it my own. This is what I inferred from my earthquake experience of a screaming body. What makes a person a person is something more than the purity of form with which Plato set out to prove the immortality of the soul. This is why his arguments for the immortality of the soul proceed with no sign of concern for the fate of the embodied individual, who alone, after all, is a *person*. From the point of view of the soul (which in itself could simply be another word for the ungrounded contingency of being as such), the body functions as the principle of individuation. This is the reason that, after marshaling out Platonic proofs for the immortality of the soul, Socrates himself steps into the dialogue by conceding that he has not proven the immortality of anything like his own soul.

And with that concession (*Phd.* 107b), he first begins to speak as

Socrates (and not as a mouthpiece for Plato's views). He starts by observing that life would be better lived if lived as if its consequences were eternal (*Phd.* 107c).[17] In that "as if" one does well to discern the characteristically Socratic refusal to claim anything like final knowledge. Socrates knows, in other words, that he himself might well enough die when he dies. In fact, he stated this explicitly at the end of the *Apology* (40c–d).

The position of Socrates is interesting because of his acceptance that we do not know what death will bring. It is the not knowing that is hard for people and drives them into the pretense of knowledge, as testified equally by the theologically inclined who claim to *know* the immortality of the soul and by the naturalistically inclined who counter with their own claim that they *know* that death is dissolution into nothingness (a rather odd knowledge, given that the same naturalist denies that there is any such thing as a "nothingness" for a life to dissolve into). Not-knowing is the beginning of "thinking," which, with Heidegger, we can distinguish from any merely analytic attempt to use rational argument to shore up one's pet theoretical assumption.

It is in any event the case that Socrates shifts away from the language of rational argument once he acknowledges his own lack of knowledge. He refers instead to old stories we have been told (*Phd.* 107d–108c). He then adds a new story of his own invention (108c–115a), a story that scholars generally refer to as the "myth of the true earth." Socrates introduces the myth with the words *eisin de polloi kai thaumastoi tēs gēs topoi*, "there are many especially strange [or astonishing] places on [and in] the earth" (108c).[18] With the word *thaumastoi* we are reminded, in this last speech of Socrates, of his famous declaration in the *Theaetetus* that the very origin of philosophy is *thaumazein* (155d), which is translated through words ranging from wonder to awe and astonishment. Its trigger is the encounter with what is perceived as strange. The heart of such strangeness, as reported at the end of the *Phaedo*, is constituted once rational consciousness is suspended and everything earthly becomes bigger and more ominous. If for Plato death is a transition to an abstract and "smoothed out" eternity, void of color and sound and any mode of sensibility whatsoever, for Socrates quite the opposite is the case: the earth is bigger, the mountains reach higher, the colors are more vivid, everything is released into the "more" of mythical imagination. In other words, if for Plato only dead men can see the truth, for Socrates the truth is alone for those who *live*, so that, after confessing his lack of knowledge about what lies on the other side of death, he tells us the only thing he can imagine: simply life, more and always more life. If the scholarly ethos is defined by a willingness to ignore the fact that the scholar himself is a person who lives a life, Socratic thought begins with the acknowledgment that all thinking begins with life itself. Contemporary scientists, for instance, who do well to examine the origin of life in nature, would do an even better job if they acknowledged that consciousness, which guides their own work, is the very heart of nature and not simply an "emergent quality" that adheres in an entirely accidental fashion to the "reality" of atomic particles mechanically moving in accord with the laws of nature. Consciousness, after all, is always already part of the reality we perceive; a nature void of consciousness is an abstract idea that could conceivably have no more ontological traction than a hallucination of a beleaguered mind.

The genius of Plato's text is that in it both Plato and Socrates are allowed to speak. The core issue in their disagreement seems to me to be this: whereas the Platonic move extinguishes the place inhabited by the concrete individual, the particular person who calls him- or herself "I," Socrates's countermove is to rehabilitate it as the only place where truth can be disclosed. That such truth is "mythical" is not a deficiency, for the only truth that matters is that which provides guidance for people who face decisions about whether to live life in one way or another. That from a theoretical perspective such freedom can be regarded as an illusion only shows that the theoretical perspective is not adequate to the lives we actually live. This is in fact the justification of the humanities, which are dedicated to looking at the world from the vantage of the human beings who live in it. The dilemma of the humanities in the modern world is that they have been subjugated to a scholarly ethos that is foreign to them. There is, of course, a practical benefit to adopting the theoretical perspective. The more we learn to look at the world itself as a machine, the more machines we are able to build. But this does not mean that the theoretical perspective has thereby been brought into the service of life. Quite the contrary. The theory of the real that views the real as a machine makes life itself over into something mechanical. For one who is uncomfortable with human mortality, this might be regarded, of course, as an advantage. The Platonic view that transcends the viewpoint of the embodied individual promises after all a life without pain. But Socrates has given his answer to that when, removing the chains that had bound him through the night, he observes that the joy of release has pain as its condition (*Phd.* 60a–b). This is the remark of a man who loves life. Whether a Socratic love of life that penetrates all the way down to the strangeness that is life's deepest condition is itself a good thing, is one of the central issues this book intends to explore.

Others, far removed from Greece, have also taken up the task of stripping away the certitudes of what some deem knowledge.

> Nan-in, a Japanese master during the Meiji era (1868–1912), received a
> university professor who came to inquire about Zen.
>   Nan-in served tea. He poured his visitor's cup full, and then kept on
> pouring.
>   The professor watched the overflow until he no longer could re-
> strain himself. "It is overfull. No more will go in!"
>   "Like this cup," Nan-in said, "you are full of your own opinions
> and speculations. How can I show you Zen unless you first empty
> your cup?"[19]

To fully appreciate this story, it might help to recall how consistently
religion has demanded the purity of an empty mind. Even in its archaic
beginnings, sacrifice stood at the center of the religious life. The fiery
transformation of animal flesh into smoke was the revelation of the
ephemeral nature of finite existence, the reminder that there is nothing
we can hold on to. Even Abraham was asked to surrender his Isaac. And
when an Isaiah or an ancient Indian sage stepped forth to lambaste the
idolatry of ritual itself, his call for purification was but the renewal of a
cleansing always already underway. This is what was at stake not only in
the encounter between the Zen master and the scholar but between Jesus
and the scribe, and, yes, between Socrates and the sophist.

Thus, when the apostle Paul (who yearned for humility so pure
that he could become "all things to all people") took on the wise men
of Athens, he was not, as is so often assumed, setting religion apart from
philosophy. He was instead doing exactly what Socrates had done before
him. For Paul, as for Socrates, salvation is only possible if we first confess
our ignorance and "become as little children." This is why the *sophistai*,
the "men of wisdom," were the proclaimed enemies of both Socrates
and Paul. Just as the prophet and sage did battle with priests, and Christ
(whose only written words were traced out "in the sand") wrestled with
the scribes, so philosophy found itself locked in to a confrontation with
sophistry. When Paul renewed that confrontation, he did so, of course,
in the name of religion and not in the name of philosophy. The decisive
point, however, is that philosophy is born in religion's internal struggle
with itself, its perennial realization that dogmatic sedimentation threatens to rob it of its own heart and soul. Philosophy is born, in other words,
out of the internal crisis of religion.[20] Philosophy's struggle to free itself of
ideology is a permutation of religion's struggle to free itself of idolatry—
and fully as difficult.

Because the imperative to resist "ism" goes even as far as skepticism,
philosophy must draw its vitality from what it does not know, though this
may indeed be knowable. As a consequence it does not belong to the

order of disciplines, all of which rest upon a settled (or "foundational") understanding of what constitutes their guiding methodology and their field of research. In contrast, philosophy emerges where this understanding comes undone. A biologist who worries deeply about the nature of his or her own discipline is, by virtue of that worry, more of a philosopher than the philosopher by profession who simply applies a fixed method to a recognized problem. One of the primary reasons for seeking to retrieve the spirit of Socrates is that his battle with the sophist awakens in us, as academics in pursuit of philosophy, the worry that philosophy in an institutional context may be intrinsically self-contradictory.[21] In the mind of Socrates, always intent on defending himself against the charge that he accepted payment for teaching, it was certainly clear that a professional philosopher could never be more than a sophist. Although the foundation of Plato's Academy may have been intended to mollify this worry, one thing remains clear: it lies in the interest of philosophy itself to set the bar high on such issues. Philosophy, to the degree that it freely constitutes (and reconstitutes) its nature, has to continually scrutinize its theoretical presuppositions. This self-scrutiny is what philosophy is insofar as philosophy is the always as yet undetermined science. If a science at all, it is the science that has to start ever anew. Its very freedom is the source of its most binding rigor. To engage philosophy properly demands not simply a theoretical act of self-scrutiny. It demands continual self-scrutiny on the part of its practitioners. "Worrying" about whether one is "truly" a philosopher is quite simply one of the things that philosophers must always do.

And there is much to worry about. What, for instance, if the surfeit of knowledge placed at our collective disposal in an "age of information" were more of a hindrance to philosophy (and hence to the good life) than an asset? Knowing about the world, what all is in it and how it functions, can obscure the Socratic intuition that, not knowing what we are doing here, we do not know what the world is doing here. The issue is not simply one of skepticism. Even Hegel's *Phenomenology of Spirit*, which announces the appearance of Absolute Knowledge, reveals this appearance as the completion of a *via negativa*. There too the scholar is implored to empty his cup, a most difficult thing to do when Google is there to keep filling it up.

A defender of good scholarship will protest that the scholar resists sophistry just as much as the philosopher does. There is humility in the attempt to stick to the facts. There is humility and sacrifice, even an admirable kind of purity, in the self-limitation of the specialist, who, by claiming expertise, may offend against a Socratic sensibility but finds ample opportunity to be offended in turn. When Socratic sorts dismiss actual expert knowing as if it were always necessarily trivial, they exhibit a sophistic arrogance of their own. To live without the lowly knowledge of experts would require the strength of a god. In other words, mere mortals have to make do with science. And it will be left to the schools to decide which science counts for real.

But no school will be able to claim Socrates as an ally. Even Plato lost the master in the moment he founded the Academy, for Socrates is the perennial outsider and vanishes wherever an effort is made to domesticate him. Socrates belongs among strangers. The barefoot Antisthenes, not Plato, became the true heir of Socrates in the very moment that Plato turned from writing dialogues to disseminating a doctrine. And as much as human beings rely on doctrines and do in fact require schools and churches and the complex machinery of the state, in none of this can they appeal to Socrates, for Socrates stands on the outside, somewhere among strangers.

In portraying Socrates as more halting—indeed, more insecure—than he is traditionally viewed ("What, the oracle says there is no one wiser than me? But how can that possibly be?"), it is important to remember the degree to which he was the child of rupture and dislocation. The Peloponnesian War was, for the small world of Athens, as disruptive of tradition as modernity has been for the global world as a whole. The danger of dissolution was the threat that gave weight and direction to the Socratic project and seriousness to his ideal of virtue (*aretē*). Yet at the same time, he was not simply searching for stability. His great insight was that something positive lay hidden in uncertainty itself, for there is virtue already in the act of questioning. If it is a hindrance for a philosopher to take too much pride in the possession of expert knowledge, then insecurity, uncertainty about one's very self, is an asset. For this reason, a disintegrating social consensus about truth is fully compensated by the spirit of questioning it engenders. In our deep ignorance, which comes to light during those painful moments when consensus begins to unravel, we are more intimately united with others than we ever could have been by the consensus itself, for the consensus is something that had been suggested to us, whereas the question is something we ourselves pose. Where a question has not been confronted and the forgotten source of our collective anxiety thus lies concealed, the possibility of heroism is also given: for, even in the face of a consensus that consistently, at times even desperately, wants to maintain itself, the unasked question can be asked. Who indeed are we? What is this strange being we call man?

To ask such questions with any degree of seriousness is reckless, one might say, given that what binds us to society is our eagerness to regard questions as already answered. Socrates called attention to this reckless-ness when, at his trial, he insisted that the real charge against him was the unstated one, the charge that he lacked prudence (*Ap.* 28b). If Socrates claimed to be motivated by his devotion to virtue, what others saw in him was simply a reckless man who defied the social order. His recklessness was apparent, whether he was strutting about the battlefield as if no man could hurt him (*Symp.* 221a), standing up to whatever Callicles or Thra-symachus came his way, or taunting a room full of jurors as he did in the *Apology.* Indeed, he pointed out to the jurors that he was in no small part on trial simply because he lacked the prudence to have prevented charges from being raised in the first place (*Ap.* 28b). He was, in other words, fully aware of that most irrefutable of indictments, "you are guilty because you have been accused," which has as its correlate the always exasperating "your defensiveness shows just how guilty you are." Socrates's first mode of defense, his summary of prejudices that went back as far as the pro-duction of Aristophanes's *Clouds,* raises the obvious question: "If you had been so dramatically and publicly warned, why did you not modify your behavior?" That he then went on to tease and mock his jurors, effectively daring them to convict and execute him, only underscored how wildly imprudent he had become. What a strangely "irrational" way for history's greatest champion of reason to behave!—unless, of course, death were something he had come actively to seek.

This brings me to another of the truly central issues of this book. Given that Socrates, unlike Plato, did not make any claim to know what death might bring, how could he make the extravagant claim that "no evil can come to a good man either in life or after death" (*Ap.* 41d)? To know this is surely to know something of very great importance. It requires, moreover, another seemingly unknowable form of knowledge, the assur-ance that one is in fact a "good man"—a strange assurance indeed for a man who confessed (while flirting with a young boy) that he himself might be a monster (*Phdr.* 230a).

The claim that "no evil can come to a good man" can be quickly destroyed by whatever list the anxious self might want to generate: star-vation, disease, torture, murder, murder by slow torture, etc. There were many good people in Auschwitz. Unspeakable were the horrors inflicted on them. What then is the status of the strange self-assurance that sets Socrates apart? Without the knowledge of what cannot be known, lifting the veil that covers the abyss of death, Socrates must stand condemned, not only for his inappropriate levity during the trial, but for his general failure to give attention to things like making money, securing a comfort-able home, or attaining political power (*Ap.* 36b).

Until his certainty that good people have nothing to fear can be made transparent, it will be impossible to show that the obsession with control does not constitute the highest form of wisdom. If death is something that has to be fought off, the only significant debate that remains is the debate about how best to control our fate. If the Socratic insight cannot somehow be attained, the only truly acceptable projects are technological and political, just as one assumes today. If we are right in our fundamental assumptions, Socrates was wrong. If Socrates was right, we are wrong in everything we think and do. A stranger in Athens, Socrates would be much more a stranger to contemporary America. If introducing the need to question authority was indeed a challenge to traditional society, then asserting the idea that the Good is somehow accessible even as it lies decisively in the beyond constitutes a parallel challenge to modernity, which seeks goods closer to home to the degree that it gives up on the possibility of gaining cognitive access to the Good as such.

The best justification for the Zen master who gave such a hard time to the scholar is that he felt compassion for him. "A lifetime of aping the sutras won't bring you any closer to where you want to go—indeed, where you *have* to go, if you are ever to escape your suffering. So, quick, put your learning aside and tell me what you think."

The same holds true for the rough way Socrates often treats his interlocutors. Behind it, two things are implied. First of all, there exists a knowledge that could set us free, that could make us happy. Second, no one can tell another person what this knowledge is, apart from its having something to do with the mystery of death. More than that we will have to discover on our own. This is presumably the justification for Socrates's commitment to dialogue, his insistence that he had nothing whatsoever to teach, that he could only serve as a philosophical midwife, helping others give birth to their own wisdom. What it boils down to is the realization that an understanding we have been "taught" has value only to the degree that it awakens our own understanding. Philosophy must take place in dialogue, in an act of friendship. The idea of a philosophical knowledge that results from a collective research project and is then packed away in books makes no sense whatsoever. If we are to pursue work on Socrates, let us at least confess at the outset that there is something strange about all the books that have been written about a thinker so pure that he refused to write anything at all.[22]

One may desire to think with the analytic power and comprehensive vision of an Aristotle, to write with the beauty and depth of a Plato. It is Socrates, however, who poses the real challenge, for Socrates (as any beginning student of philosophy can verify) is the philosopher one some-how aspires to *be*. Plato portrayed Socrates as the ideal form of the philos-opher. All others are mere imitators. To become a philosopher is thus to become Socrates. And to become Socrates is, in some strange fashion, to realize one's own true nature. In contrast to traditions constituted from above ("this is the command of God"), there are other traditions consti-tuted by the revelation of what one can be: become a Buddha; become a Christ; become a Socrates. But always this: in the words of Nietzsche, *werde, der du bist,* "become who you are."[23] As a call to authenticity, it is a call to what always must appear as the stranger. Indeed, Socrates refers to the voice that guides him from within as a daemon, quite as if his real self were not himself at all—but the Stranger.

The stranger then is Socrates, but more than Socrates, the stranger is each of us in turn. My purpose in the chapters that follow is, to the degree possible, to get to know this stranger. My first move is, from a scholarly perspective, perhaps my strangest move of all. To shed light on Socrates's strange aloofness, his ironic remove from society, I simply remove him from his world entirely. Instead of following, in an attempt to render familiar what is strange, established historical method by "situ-ating" Socrates in the Athens he lived in, I lift him out of his world and place him in far-away Japan, in the hope that his strangeness might glow brighter when he is viewed side-by-side with strangers.

In a second chapter, I justify what I have done by showing how the scholarly ethos blocks access to the stranger. I do this by examin-ing the work of Gregory Vlastos and Leo Strauss, the leading represen-tatives of the two schools that, in our own country, currently compete over an understanding of Socrates. My aim is to show that conformity to what I keep calling "the scholarly ethos" assures nothing like objectivity: Vlastos, a pacifist, uncovers a Socrates who was also a pacifist. Strauss, a Jew scarred by the Shoah, was anything but a pacifist—just as the Socrates he discloses was anything but a pacifist. And yet both men are truly ex-emplary scholars. They both excel in the capacity to keep track of every-thing that was recorded in Plato's dialogues (and in other works as well). Their ears are keenly attuned to all that has been rendered public. What they miss, though, is the silence of Socrates, the disapproving gaze of the thinker, the one who can never simply be a pacifist or a fighter. Although Strauss would deny this, given his preoccupation with esoteric doctrine, the mere fact that it is doctrine he seeks, supports my contention. In a word, Strauss's fundamental concern, like Vlastos's, is with the political, something inherently public even when it trades deeply in secrets.

Both men ignore what, after the Protestant Reformation, we all have been taught to ignore: the hidden sources of what we have agreed to simply call "faith." This is the real command of the scholarly ethos: "Do not discuss what is properly kept private." There is nothing in this command that guarantees consensus about the things we are permitted to discuss in public. Vlastos is a pacifist; Strauss is not. Unfortunately, however, by neglecting to consider what internally motivates these positions, we find ourselves unable to penetrate to that higher perspective by virtue of which the opposites are no longer opposites. If the pacifist, for instance, refuses to fight the warrior, then in a certain sense he has accepted him. And in like manner, the warrior, determined to uproot evil, may still know well enough (with a knowledge that will always be exceedingly rare) that truly effective fighting requires a spirit that knows not to care. Socrates, properly speaking, may have been just as much a pacifist as he was a warrior. Even saints can be moved to defiance. Even those who are aware that we are all family can fight hard to protect their own particular family. Life itself is fraught with ambiguity, more the stuff of tragedy and comedy than of rationally conceived moral theory.

The direction I am moving in to (which I hope chapter by chapter to deepen) is the profoundly personal nature of what is often called the spiritual. I want to suggest that our discomfort with talking about these matters (especially within a scholarly context) is not the same as the Socratic silence to which I have so often referred. Instead of saying, "Let us keep silent about the Good," Socrates says, "Let us talk about the Good, over and over, so that we can come to understand why it is impossible to say what it is." In anticipating the trajectory I will be following, let it suffice to say that I begin with an account of the education of Socrates in the hope that it can contribute to our own education, so as then to progress to the way he lived out his profound, and hence always unspeakable, understanding. In this movement, two poles constantly come into play: on the one hand, our mortality; on the other, our capacity for friendship. My goal is to show how these two poles of our existence belong together. A love is unconditional only to the degree that it takes its stand in death.

What we need, even more than good politics, is an appreciation for the possibility of *cultural* transformation. I understand culture not as the way people happen to live but instead normatively, as what makes us cultured—and hence better than we are. In alluding to such a possibility, I have in mind how deeply moved I was by the calm with which my Japanese neighbors responded to the Kobe earthquake. To account for that calm, I take seriously what Peter Sloterdijk has recently referred to as the project of the future, the dissemination of "the ancient great practicing powers in East Asia,"[24] by which he was referring to the possibility of transforming entire societies by ritualizing certain aspects of yogic training— that is, training that penetrates into the body itself. Essential to who Socrates was is the regal bearing with which he *stood,* a topic I address in my final two chapters. Pierre Hadot, in *Philosophy as a Way of Life,* discusses something similar with regard to ancient Greek and Roman philosophy. According to him, the ancients subordinated theoretical concerns to spiritual exercise, the true purpose of philosophy. What impressed me in Japan was the thought that such exercise can be sustained even within a whole society and even within the context of secular modernity. I was, of course, quite likely wrong about what I saw there. Where I saw courageous stoics, others saw a people too conventional to tolerate truth and too beaten down to protest mismanagement. I am hardly an expert on Japan. Even so, I was inspired there to entertain the possibility of self-transformation in a cultural context. To exercise the spirit one must first exercise the imagination.

1

Socrates in Japan

When entering a foreign land, one does well to take along a healthy respect for our common humanity. In the language of the contemporary academy, one should not "construct" an image of the other on the basis of a binary opposition, concluding, for example, that Westerners are active and "Orientals" are passive. This does not mean, however, that one should pretend there are no strangers, for one's kin can be strange enough. Indeed, the first stranger, as Socrates reminds us, is the stranger each person already is to him- or herself.[1] The Delphic command "know thyself" is a significant command only to the degree that we are strange to ourselves. Even the great Socrates, who lived his entire life under the obligation of the command, conceded that he still did not know for sure whether he was a complete monster or a mild and good man (*Phdr.* 230a). Strangely enough, both may have been true. To fear the stranger is to fear what is strange within ourselves, the freedom to be both one and the other, a freedom that grows monstrous until bad faith itself appears as duty. "There is much that is strange," chants the chorus in Sophocles's *Antigone*, "but nothing surpasses man in strangeness."[2]

The acknowledgment of the uncanniness of being human is perhaps the explanation for why Socrates, on the day of his execution, advised his disciples to search among the barbarians for a wise man to replace him (*Phd.* 78a). This is a strange thing for any Greek to say, doubly so for Socrates, famous for having left Athens only when he was conscripted into military service. Why would the very Socrates who preferred death to exile outside the city (*Cri.* 50d–51c) advise his disciples to search even in foreign lands for a master? Was it because he himself was so soon to embark on the strangest journey of all by taking up his cup and drinking the poison?

The journey into the foreign was, of course, only half the story. After advising his disciples to go outward into the world, he went on to say that in the end they would have to search among and within themselves (*Phdr.* 230a). Curiously, what lies hidden within is first made manifest outside us. Any person is potentially what other people already are. Indeed, even the natural world outside us is the world that human beings long ago crawled up out of. The extent of the world is the extent of the unconscious self—unless perhaps the unconscious is (as having conjured up the world) yet larger than the world. All knowledge, Socrates says, is recollection (*Meno* 82b–85b).

The world without is the mirror of the world within. It is in this spirit that I place Socrates in Japan. The reason I choose Japan is because Japan chose me—in the very specific context of what I perceived in the face of an earthquake. But as it turns out the passage of the years has only served to heighten the contrast I initially observed. Thus, on the one side, the hysterical response in the United States to the events of September 11, 2001, which resulted in a costly and immoral war. On the other side, the stoic response in Japan not only to the Kobe earthquake of 1995 but also to the even more devastating Tōhoku earthquake and tsunami of 2011. Between the two I place Socrates, famously calm as he drank his poison. I ask myself where he would be most at home—in the United States, the apotheosis of what Nietzsche called the Socratic modernity of the West? Or in a land east of anything he could have imagined as "east"? A strange question, posed by my younger self, immersed in a study of Socrates, now dazed by an earthquake. I had been thrust into an encounter with the uncanny. Could Socrates still be my guide?

A question about Socrates, it was also a question about Japan. I looked at my neighbors and found myself admiring an entire people. I was aware, of course, that I was likely enough romanticizing them, confusing resignation for courage and resolve. *Ganbatte*, often translated as "try harder," was a word I had often heard as a prod to young students. Why, in the aftermath of the earthquake, did it seem to take on such depth and significance? For months I had encountered my neighbors as a rather superficial and unphilosophical people, as proudly pragmatic as most Americans. Why did I now suspect that they had deeper spiritual resources at their disposal than are available to Americans, so many of whom are self-consciously (and even loudly) religious?

The issue had simply been thrown at me when the earthquake struck. Wandering about the ruins of a devastated city, I contrasted my own sense of panic first with the mythical image of Socrates, calm in the face of death, and then with the very real calm I encountered on the faces of my Japanese neighbors. Because there were a number of Christian missionaries in the neighborhood, mostly from the United States and Canada, I had ample opportunity to carry out a simple cross-cultural comparison, made all the more dramatic because we Westerners were the ones who, immersed in philosophy and religion, claimed access to the eternal. I am aware, of course, that these are decidedly impressionistic observations that invite random and subjective reflections about the conflict of "worldviews." Even so, I offer no apology. The philosophical quest begins where we happen to find ourselves, trying to make sense of the world as we ourselves experience it. If philosophy should provide us with glimpses of truth, it should also show us what truth might have to do with life. If we regard ourselves as having grown too sophisticated to search for life-wisdom, we should consider the possibility that we have simply insulated ourselves from the always looming catastrophe of our mortality.

"Calm and courage" are virtues that wisdom would secure. What if there were a culture that could secure them as well? Would the question posed in the *Meno*, whether virtue can be taught (70a), thereby be answered? Or what of the parallel question that is so central to Plato's *Republic*: can desire itself be educated? and, if so, can this education be extended to an entire society? The Japanese history of ritualizing all aspects of life until virtually everything becomes a matter of convention is clearly an attempt to achieve just this. It seems, however, that it would result in a tyranny of normality totally antithetical to the Socratic spirit of inquiry and self-examination. Aristotle, with his notion that the cultivation of good habits is the key to virtue, might be pleased with the Japanese approach. But Socrates? On the face of it, it seems an unlikely match. His mission was to encourage individuals to question both their own decisions and the traditions that informed them. But what if conventionality were the manifest "outside" of a more reflective "within." If conformity to a college binge-drinking "culture" (or simply to the culture of consumption) reduces interiority, wouldn't conformity to a civilized culture enhance it? Idle chatter is little more than noise, but thoughtful speech conveys the gravity of what it keeps silent. This is the moment I was seeking, the moment where Socrates, destroyer of convention, might be viewed as intersecting with the spirit that gave birth to Japanese conventionality. One enters a Zen temple and discovers the highly formalized archetypes of the most everyday customs (such as what to do with one's shoes when entering a Japanese home). And in the zendo, or meditation hall, that constitutes the center of the temple, these archetypal forms are reduced to a bare simplicity, clearing an empty stage for emptying—and thereby freeing—the mind. This is the context in which I found myself wondering whether consistently placing one's shoes "just so" could really provide depth to one's character (an idea that my wife rather liked). More than that, I wondered whether it made sense to regard ritual as the path to freedom. The goal of Zen meditation is spontaneity of spirit. Even so, its practice involves very exacting ritually prescribed ways of sitting and breathing, even to the precise placement of one's fingers and toes. The practice is in fact so difficult and demanding that it requires the supervision of a man who carries a stick, ready to pounce on any slackers. What could such a strict regime have to do with the achievement of spontaneous thought and action? The idea seems profoundly paradoxical, though it is really not that foreign. A pianist, after all, practices by playing scales over and over, in the hope of one day playing music. Repetition and spontaneity are not necessarily opposed. What is foreign is the way the discipline impacts the average Japanese household. How much, one wonders, can a spiritual exercise accomplish its goal in the context of everyday life? Are there really cultural conditions for the achievement of something like courage in the face of death?

One thing that would awaken skepticism is the problem I alluded to before. How does one know that what one sees is really courage? How is one to distinguish it from weary resignation? And as for spontaneity, what if it were just another word for reckless action? I remember a Japanese friend of mine telling the story of an elderly man who survived the Kobe earthquake. Years before, he had survived the atomic bombing of Hiroshima. Leaving the ruins of that city, he moved on to Nagasaki, arriving just in time to survive another atom bomb. It was an amazing story of good and bad fortune. I would have forgotten it, however, if in passing I had not observed that an earthquake is a very different kind of catastrophe from a bombing, for an earthquake leaves us with no one to be angry at. Earthquakes are horrific, but they are not acts of evil—they are not acts that could have been and should have been otherwise. Given that most of my fellow Westerners were indeed angry (someone should have gotten the water and gas back on; the train lines should have been fixed as soon as possible), I think I expected to be applauded for making a good point. As a result, I was a bit taken aback when my friend disagreed, making it clear that, from his point of view, natural and political catastrophes amount to pretty much the same thing. Neither of them should really be called evil.

It touched on something I had already noticed. If for the Westerners in the neighborhood anger seemed an appropriate response to an earthquake (there must be someone to blame), my friend was reminding me that the Japanese do not regard anger as an appropriate response even to acts of war. This shed light on one of the most exasperating things I knew about Japan: the Japanese failure to express guilt about their own atrocities in World War II. Given that they also assigned little blame for the atrocities they themselves endured, I concluded that the Japanese have a very weak conception of evil. Morality, if one can call it morality, will have to be centered on something beyond good and evil. In this context, the achievement of spontaneity could interchangeably constitute the virtue of a Zen saint or of a kamikaze pilot. One meticulously follows social norms in the hope that, by doing so, one will gain enough strength one day to break free of them entirely.

If the Good as Socrates understood it was best represented by the image of the sun (*Rep.* 508b), the only good that makes sense in the Zen context would be a bolt of lightning flashing forth from a storm cloud. Westerners eagerly take up large-scale political projects that require stable and lasting illumination. The Japanese are similarly masters of design, but their best works tend to be small things that mirror the fragility of cherry blossoms. Politics is pursued in the name of enduring ideals and shows itself as the will to govern from above. Culture engenders ideas and insights enough but gathers its strength from below. Meaning unfolds from images long before it attains the sun-clear transparency of concepts and ideas. The question that is raised by placing Socrates among the strangers of Japan is where indeed does he belong. Was he or Plato responsible for the ideal of an overarching Good that has given us the modern state and the attempt to achieve a political solution to the problem of justice? Who is the thinker of the Good thus conceived—the man who was prepared to drink his poison? Or the younger man who called in sick on the day of his death (*Phd.* 59b)?

A country noted for its weak political ethos, Japan is nonetheless a highly disciplined society. Violent crimes are rare. The insulation of its private households from the power of the state does not translate into an epidemic of family violence. Searching for this reason is what forges the connection to Socrates: Japanese discipline derives not from government decree but internally, from its culture.

Culture in the West has suffered encroachments from both the state and the market, becoming so atrophied in the process that it fails to accomplish its task. When "culture wars" erupt and embattled culture has its say, there is usually little to hear beyond nostalgia for the old or self-satisfied affirmation of the latest trend. Yet culture cannot simply be rejected or dismissed as idle distraction. Even the most perfectly organized political and economic systems, while sustaining life, shed no light on its meaning. Quite the contrary, they resolve the question of meaning by making us forget why we have come to ask for it. By the time the deathbed renews the question it is too late. A life secured in bad faith (the pretense that a normal life is a good one) can deliver itself from the need for self-examination, but it will be vulnerable to external manipulation. Only a strong sense of meaning, something we understand from within, opens the arena for free action. Without it, one does what one is told—or, even worse, one does what is done. It is understandable when worried human-ists liken the marginalization of the humanities to the end of civilization. Culture matters.

It would be a mistake then to read a libertarian impulse into Socrates's skepticism about the political life. His goal was not to give free rein to desire, but to educate it. His commitment to this idea trans-formed him into the gadfly of the Athenian democracy. In this role he sometimes appeared as the admirer of Sparta.[3] Against the Athenian lack of order, he found virtue in Sparta's barracks, its stoic simplicity, its rigid discipline, and its strict enforcement of law. The Athenian "luxurious city" of the *Republic* (372e) had to be purged to Spartan levels (416d–417b) before Socrates found it acceptable. He would have appreciated the austerities of the Zen monastery.

Socrates's skepticism about the political applies, however, to Sparta even more emphatically than to Athens. Devoted as he was to the free-dom of thought, he could embrace the Spartan ideal of discipline only in the form of a culturally conditioned self-discipline. One restrains one's desires not for the sake of the state but for the sake of the Good. The same holds for Japan, which has also at times been conflated with Sparta.[4] Once culture has degenerated, discipline that is essentially cultural in nature (and thus fully compatible with freedom) is interpreted as if it were political. Given that Western democracies have traditionally made their appeal to the superiority of Athens over Sparta, and given that those same democracies have largely been stripped of their own inner life by the excesses of the marketplace, it is hardly surprising that the appear-ance of a strong culture awakens suspicion, if not repugnance. When advertisers are given free rein to "lead us into temptation," any talk of discipline beyond the need to work and produce will be greeted with sus-picion. Strange that the Japanese hold on to old customs.

For all that, Japan is a Western-style democracy, closely akin to the constitutional monarchies of Western Europe. Those aspects of its culture that might appear Spartan gray are also recognizable as bound to virtue: stoic resolve, a readiness for self-sacrifice (we do like their work ethic), a capacity to live in harmony even under crowded conditions, and the refusal (so strange for the Westerner) to fully yield to capital's demand for consumers.[5]

If one considers the role of women, perhaps the most typical con-temporary standard for evaluating other societies, what we find in Japan is interestingly ambiguous. A basic point Julia Kristeva noted some years ago in *About Chinese Women* holds for Japan as well.[6] When Western women automatically assume that women in Asia are victims, they do so on the basis of a questionable standard. To the degree that emancipated women in the West have "freed themselves" by entering into the symbolic order of the father, they have entered into a man's world and play at a man's game. Educated women from the upper classes end up perpetuating a patriarchal system that arguably exploits women on a more massive level than ever before. For every woman who "gets" to work, there are scores of women who now suddenly "have" to work. The family that once could manage on forty hours of labor now barely gets by on eighty. In this context, Kristeva idealizes Asian women, suggesting that they may still retain a feminine subjectivity that Western societies long ago destroyed. Her thesis is, of course, not a popular one—and would almost certainly find few supporters among highly educated Chinese or Japanese women today. Nor, for that matter, would the grand patriarchs of politics and business like anything she has to say. Regardless, much of it strikes me as both true and of real importance. She is a Socratic kind of presence.

Specific cases of abuse aside, we have no right simply to assume that a woman's destiny is harder in Asia than in the West. Although this could appear to be the case under the assumption that the value of a human life is best measured by the amount of money it commands in the labor market, Japan is interesting because, to the degree that it has managed to preserve its own traditions, it forces us to question that assumption. The same Japan that, using the criteria of what Max Weber called the Protestant work ethic, appears to be a patriarchy, could still be regarded, by its own standards, as one of the world's largest and most flourishing matriarchies. Japan is first and foremost a nation of households—and households are ruled by women.[7] Salary men march off to work long and hard hours—and are expected to turn their earnings over to their wives, who not only manage the money but keep alive the forms of traditional culture. Only where the sphere of the household has been thoroughly devalued can we assume that the "work world" offers the only opportunity to realize one's humanity. The very notion is the invention of a dark Calvinism that regarded any sign of earthly joy as evidence of one's impending damnation.[8] Even as we give ourselves over to consuming the excess that results from the glorification of work, our guilt holds us away from any true *jouissance*. The idea of a discipline, indeed an ascetic discipline, that aims at orgasmic release is foreign to our entire culture. Believers and atheists both agree on this one thing: only God in the hereafter could ever balance the books.

What I am arguing is that, despite the surface similarities between Japan and the West (the shape of its political system, its industrial organization, the forms of modernity in general), Japan really is a land populated by "strangers." This shows itself below the surface, in its language, its religion, and its culture. As Kristeva pointed out with regard to the

Chinese, it is hard to imagine what the use of a "hieroglyphic" writing system (the thousands of Chinese characters) might mean for the way Japanese think and behave. Kristeva herself discerns in it the priority of the semiotic image (where lack of definition invites an oceanic ebb and flow) to the reified symbolic order in which clearly defined concepts become a possibility. She looks at the Asian system of writing and finds in it the priority of the mother's world (in which the child is still firmly attached to the breast) over the father's world (in which children learn to define themselves and walk away from home).

Be this as it may, the result of the thousands of Chinese characters for a typical Westerner is clear enough: the written language remains hidden. To learn a new Western language, one generally reads before one speaks; to learn Japanese or Chinese, one speaks long before one reads. Writing, for Westerners the doorway to the public order, is rendered virtually inaccessible to anyone but the Chinese or Japanese insider. Unlike a phonetic system, such a welter of signs takes many years to master. Given how much literacy plays into our orientation toward things public, the sudden experience of being illiterate (not being able to read any of the signs) can be highly disorienting. Storm clouds gather in the East. Whether lightning flashes suffice to illuminate one's path through the maze remains to be seen.

I can anticipate the question, what might all this have to do with Socrates? Understood as the one who invented analytic discourse as the proper guide through the ethical dilemmas that make life difficult, Socrates was in fact someone who, over and over, revealed the inadequacy of reason for illuminating the Good. He himself was guided by an inner oracle—one that never revealed the actual content of the Good but could be relied on to warn him away from chasing after false idols.[9] And yet the man was neither a cynic nor a skeptic. It was his joy that won him his disciples. An ascetic for the sake of joy, he gathered storm clouds (by throwing everything into question) for the sake of truth.

But what is the strange world I want him to enter? To help with the contrast I have been drawing between East and West, I offer some lines of Dogen, the thirteenth-century Japanese Zen teacher: "Acting on and witnessing myriad things with the burden of oneself is 'delusion.' Acting on and witnessing oneself in the advent of myriad things is enlightenment."[10] To the degree that there is a general Western bias (and, yes, things are more complicated than that), it yields an activist stance ("acting on and witnessing myriad things with the burden of oneself"), a stance that may ultimately reflect a grammatically constituted predisposition. Granted that our shared humanity places on each of us, regardless of cultural formation, the "burden of self," it strikes me as a burden that is intensified by the subject-object structure of Indo-European grammar. Although this is not the place to go into the intricacies of substance metaphysics and its relation to grammar, I think it is easy enough to see that an ethics of responsibility (and guilt) is reinforced when every sentence is provided with a subject and a predicate, that is, an actor and what it does, what it acts upon. Japanese grammar is different. Its verb denotes less an action than a situation, which is why an adjective can constitute a perfectly acceptable verb. Although one might imagine saying in English "is tasty" (*suki desu*) or even just "tasty" (*suki*), we are still grammatically predisposed to say "I like it" or "it is tasty."

In Japanese (I am referring to the grammar of the language, not what a person "burdened with oneself" understands by it), there are not so much actors as people or things that stand in different degrees of proximity to a situation or even to a property (why should "yellow" be any less substantial than "banana"?).[11] Love, for instance, is not something one person does to another; instead it is a state of being in which (incidentally almost) two people become entangled. Thus, the Japanese declaration of love (*aishiteru*) does not read "I love you" but rather "doing love," with the I and you left out of it. It is a declaration, moreover, that presumably should not be made at all. Just as the I and you can be left to the understanding, the fact that we are in love goes equally without saying.

Another example of a sentence with a missing subject would be "I understand Japanese," which as *Nihongo ga wakarimasu* is a sentence not only without an "I" to do whatever is being done but without an object as well. True, the word for Japanese (*Nihongo*) is in the sentence. But it is grammatically marked with the weak subject marker *ga* rather than the object-marker *o*, leaving us with something to the effect of "Japanese and an I that doesn't need to be named stand together in proximity to an 'understanding' way of being."

But what is this suspension of a subject if not denial of responsibility? Consider how the same grammatical observation plays itself out on the stage of world history. Westerners regard modernity as something Europeans made (first they made science, then they made representative forms of government, and finally they made the industrial revolution). As surely as a subject has a predicate, Europeans made the modern world. But in Japan, a very different story unfolded, one that reflects another grammatically conditioned sense of reality. Arriving fully fledged from the outside, modernity had the look of something that just happened. With the arrival of Europeans, the form of the world had simply undergone a sudden alteration, creating a new situation from which the Japanese spent more than two centuries trying to hide. But because, in renouncing European modernity, Japan had also renounced guns, the country grew weak enough that the new situation eventually swept over its borders. Like people transformed by love, Japan was transformed by modernity. But in the transformation there appeared to be nothing for which Japan could assume responsibility. The refrain "whatever we have done wrong, we have learned from you" was used even to justify the imperialism of World War II, an imperialism that from the Japanese point of view had its roots less in its own history than in the history of the West. The need to secure "markets" for economic overproduction was a lesson learned from Britain and France and the United States, whereas the totalitarian and nationalistic manipulation of the nation's "resolve" was a more recent import from Germany and Italy. Letting the "myriad things" determine the shape of the self may represent the standpoint of wisdom, but from a Western point of view it looks like an abnegation of responsibility. What gets dismissed as "Oriental" passivity, the inability of Japan to accept its responsibility for the deeds of the past, the stoical resignation to crowded subways (the resignation to everything), the silencing of anger and resentment (or more likely its transference into the inscrutable realm of the inner self)—it is all part of the same gestalt, a deeply and mysteriously foreign one, which has to be understood before it can ever be judged. That this may be tantamount to not judging at all is a possibility that, even as it grates against the live nerve of the Western soul, brings us nonetheless closer to the daemonic spirit who first fashioned that soul: the inscrutable spirit of Socrates, whom I now invoke as my guide through the inscrutability of Japan. Although Socrates is often evoked as if he were the embodiment of the very spirit of judgment and engaged subjectivity, one has to remember that it was much rather his interlocutors, people such as Euthyphro and Callicles, who were the judgmental ones. Socrates only engaged in the persistent attempt to wipe the self-certainties away, to establish in others the silence that was his.

Socratic dialogue unfolds within a dynamic tension. On the one hand, attention must be focused on what it is we are trying to understand. On the other hand, we must never forget the concrete individuality of the person with whom we are talking. Socrates, the master of such dialogue, never assumed that all cognitive subjects are interchangeable. To do so would be to assume the very understanding and agreement that require so much work and effort to achieve.

Mathematical rationality is, in theory, fully public. Its understanding requires no special experiences or background but is open to all who are patient enough to endure the explanation. Yet that same rationality is hermetically sealed from the uninitiated. Despite its insistence on public scrutiny, science is esoteric, the more so the more complete it is. An essay in advanced logic is accessible only to the initiated. The tension between the universality of the concept and the particularity of the embodied speaker thus holds even where one would least expect it. The concept can, of course, be explained. It can be discursively demarcated. But it can only be appropriated by an individual human being in a private moment of insight.

Insight is something each of us has to achieve alone. When we are trying simply to bring something into view, we have no choice but to rely on our own resources, adding the prayer, perhaps, that we may be strengthened by whatever power renders things visible in the first place. In the Socratic understanding, that power belongs to Apollo. Philosophy for Socrates stands under Apollo's aegis in the same way that the discursive as such assumes the intelligibility of the things we are talking about. We do not carry out scientific investigations in the dark.

Thus, Socrates's entry into Japan, the strange land far to the east. What illumination does Apollo throw his way? Out of what dark cloud will lightning flash forth? It could be as simple as a ramen chef evoking mountains and earth and sea, forests and fields, when trying to explain how one makes a proper soup. The Japanese are enamored with analogical relationships. As a result, Japan appears first and foremost as a land of reverberating echoes, a kind of gigantic hall of mirrors. The great virgin forests of the Northwest are reflected in the few towering cedars that surround each shrine and temple, which in turn are reflected in rug-sized gardens that can be found on even the most cramped balconies in the city. The whole nation is built on ritual, everyone meticulously following everyone else, seemingly in desperate need of that critical interrogation that, according to Socrates, is the philosopher's service to Apollo (*Phd.* 23b). For in Japan the moment of insight, "this is what I see, what I understand," tends to retreat behind the need for repetition that underlies all ritual. Socrates in Japan would be, as always, a gadfly. It is highly unlikely that he would be welcomed with the same open arms that greeted Derrida in 1984. In a nation where filial piety and ancestor worship still count for something, it is not only possible but likely that the Japanese would react to Socrates with that same sense of horror that presumably greeted the audience of Aristophanes's *Clouds* after Pheidippides threatened to beat not only his father but his mother as well. We owe it only to luck that Aristophanes's play did not incite a mob.[12] In a society governed by tradition, the accusation of parricide is not to be taken lightly.

It seems inevitable that the philosopher's encounter with a land and culture as bound to tradition as Japan would be a violent one. A purely discursive encounter hardly seems likely. Japan is not Greece, and rationality—even of the sophistic kind—is not its strongest feature. Socrates would presumably have trouble getting his interrogations off the ground. "Is what you are saying consistent with everything else you say you believe?" would awaken laughter in the Zen adept. Still, Japan is much more than the Zen denial of the discursive. A highly modernized society, it has become so thoroughly determined by Western rationality that contemporary Japan could even be called a Greek colony. Although this is to some extent true of the entire world, the case of Japan is a special one because the process occurred so rapidly and was carried out so completely. It is curious that Japanese schoolchildren seem to know more about the culture of ancient Greece than any other children in the world (with the possible exception of the Greeks themselves).

If we find the two thus joined, then let us peer more closely at this strange pairing of Japan and Greece.[13] We can begin by evoking some similarities. Both countries lie on the same latitude, endure similar summer heat, and are constituted by the same striking mixture of mountains and sea. Yet what a difference between those seas! The Mediterranean has only a narrow opening to the Atlantic. With storms and tides thus modified, it is easily navigable and makes neighbors of all the lands that border it. The Greeks were seafarers and established colonies throughout the Mediterranean world. Although it took Rome to transform wanderlust to empire, the mediating connection to the world outside was already Greek: Odysseus, its characteristic hero; globalization (at least within the spheres of travel, communication, and commerce), its ultimate consequence.[14] In Japan the sea is the ocean itself, capable of a degree of violence unknown in the Mediterranean. As a result, it separates more than it mediates. The Japanese tendency to insularity and isolationism is geographically determined. Even more, the very irrationalities associated with Zen "spontaneity" are consistent with the character of the place itself. Typhoon and earthquake determine the Japanese experience of nature to a degree unknown in Europe. Although the mask of "Oriental" calm is impressive, the suddenness with which violent emotion can tear through it is a standard preoccupation of Japanese literature.

One may want to reject these observations out of hand as instances of cultural "stereotyping" (lazy Southerners who lie in the sun; industrious Northerners whose work is never done). They conflict with the contemporary presupposition that people everywhere are at bottom "the same," so that cultural differences are to be regarded as fully arbitrary (and thus alterable) conventions rather than as necessary adaptations to differences inscribed in nature.[15] The encroachment of the political on the cultural can nowhere be more clearly seen than in this severance of the cultural from its root in nature.

There is reason to assume, however, that this conventionality thesis (the privileging of culture over nature) has been exaggerated in recent times. There is simply too much at stake behind it: Power wants a world that it can bend and shape. The market requires mobility; technology and politics require utter manipulability. The extension of human power over the world is not promoted through the acknowledgment that there are "givens" that one has to accept and even respect. To argue that a "place" leaves its imprint on a "culture" is thus deemed suspect, but not necessarily with good reason. The Cartesian-Newtonian conception of a homogeneous space-time continuum that can be "captured" by the coordinate systems of analytical geometry represents a powerful presupposition for the natural sciences, but it does nothing to destroy our fundamental experience that places are, after all, irreducibly unique—particularly insofar as they have withstood the leveling effect of the marketplace.

Greece, the piece of earth out of which Western culture (well on its way to becoming world culture) began its growth, is pastoral, given to both commerce and conversation. Its gift to the world is the agora. In contrast, Japanese culture formed itself through a more violent struggle with sea and soil. Its sense of nature retains always a glimmer of the untamed, traces of otherness at times rooted in the explosively volcanic.[16] Its own gift to the world could be the possibility of preserving a sense of place, even in the face of the market's steady self-expansion.

Confronted with such contrasts, it is appropriate to return to the field of similarity. Both Greece and Japan are defined by a nature that is filled with life. Both tend, as it were, to a kind of natural paganism (though not one as ornate as the jungle-conditioned cultures of Africa and India). What this means is that both the Greeks and the Japanese share a predisposition to accord fate and the gods their priority over the will of man.

But Greece is drier than Japan. In the summer, Greece is almost completely dry; Japan, soggy and wet. The mountains show the difference. In Greece they are stark, dominated by crag, cliff, and boulder. Any tree that stands juts forth as a particular tree, visible in its clearing.[17] Outline and definition are themselves features of this remarkable place. Blue sky, vivid clouds—and everywhere such clarity! Add the light of Apollo, the gleaming splendor of midday sun, and everything might be revealed. Socrates, demanding definition upon definition, is a child of Greece, servant of Apollo, completing what the god himself had begun.

In Japan, however, humidity and heat combine to render everything murky: boundaries blur and vine, bush, and tree fall together to hide whole mountains in a diffuse ocean of green, all encompassed, but half lost, in the opacity of earthen sky. Or, pursuing nature's cultural reflection: Japanese cities, with high-rises, small roof-dominated houses, sporadic clumps of trees gathered together in a chaotic mix, form the antithesis of Greek towns with their whitewashed, flat-roofed homes, like so many beaded pearls, planted in rows against the hills. A Japanese shrine is made of wood and surrounded by great towering cedars; the Parthenon is made of stone and stands naked on top of a hill. The contrasts have again overwhelmed the similarity: kimonos versus the nude. Greece exchanged its paganism for the severely modified paganism of Christianity (where gods became demons or angels), whereas Japan adopted Buddhism only on the condition that its pagan cults might be preserved in their entirety. When a mountain in Greece is shorn of its trees, it remains bare for millennia to come; in Japan the trees keep returning, regardless of how relentlessly they are logged. Its forests have so far withstood even the ravages of industrialization.

The question raised by such contrasts should be clear: how are we to locate *Socrates*, son of Apollo, in the midst of such opaque and impenetrable density? Heraclitus, with his dark and obscure sayings, his nature that "loves to hide," might well fit into such an environment, but Socrates is another matter. According to Aristotle (*Meta.* 1078b17–32), Socrates's real contribution was to initiate "syllogistic reasoning," laying the foundations of science by his unification of induction and "definition by universals"—and doing so without ending with the metaphysical monstrosity of "separate forms" that was subsequently perpetuated by Plato. The "clear-headed" Socrates belongs in a world of light. In fact, this is so emphatically the case that the most compelling modern portrait of him, the one painted by Nietzsche in *The Birth of Tragedy*, depicts him as a crusader against everything dark and "untamed" that still clung to the underbelly of the Mediterranean crystal world of light and order.[18] The friend of Apollo was the foe of Dionysus. Indeed, he was the very hinge on which the door of history swung open to the light of Western rationality. With Socrates, we are assured, Dionysian intoxication was left far behind—a forgotten memory of someone else's forgotten dream. "Banish the flute-makers and flute-players," advised Socrates, for we prefer "Apollo and the instruments of Apollo to Marsyas and his instruments" (*Rep.* 399d).

This is the Socrates of the agora speaking, the one who, according to Phaedrus, acted as if he "were a stranger being shown the country by a guide" (*Phdr.* 230c–d). It was a remark to which Socrates consented, adding that "trees and open country won't teach me anything, whereas men in the town do." This is an exchange that has been so often quoted, so often taken to reveal the very soul of Socrates, that few have considered its heavy irony: the men of Athens have taught Socrates nothing, for his interrogations have always disclosed the same empty shell of ignorance

cloaked in verbal pomposity. And had Phaedrus himself not been ham-
pered by the same pride, he might have noticed that it was not he, but
Socrates, who displayed a knowledge of the land, locating the "altar of
Boreas" "about a quarter of a mile lower down" from where Phaedrus had
guessed it was (229c).

Socrates's secret knowledge of the land is filled with significance.
It indicates that he was more at home "outside the town walls" than he
pretended to be. Open to the voices of the cicadas (262d), he concludes
the dialogue by referring to teachings gleaned from an oak tree (275b)!
Socrates seems in fact to have made it his custom to visit not only the
great temples of Athens with their Olympian deities but altars hewn from
river crags as well, altars where wind, stream, and lowly wood nymphs, the
spirits of this place and that, all received their due. Socrates in Japan can
be pictured trudging up into the hills, behind the great temples of Buddha, to pray like a Shintoist, before phallic stones scattered in the woods.
Socrates's Thracian witch doctor (*Charm.* 156d) has never received the
attention he deserves. As Meno knows, he taught his apprentice only too
well (*Meno* 80a).

The Socratic refusal to write is, in one respect, consistent with the way
Greek is written. Greek was the first language to be written in a fully
phonetic system.[19] Its articulation is contained immediately in the letters
themselves. Where writing and speech are seen thus to merge, writing
appears dispensable, as if it is no more than a vehicle for a spoken word
still bound to intentional consciousness. What results is the prioritizing
of the spoken word, fully transparent to the consciousness that delivers it,
that so worried Jacques Derrida, who saw in it a kind of epochal departure
from the mystery of a writing that writes itself.[20]

Eric Havelock and Walter Ong have written wonderful books in
which they detail the significance of the sudden shift of Greek culture
from speech to writing.[21] The written word that abides on the page serves
as the model for the Platonic theory of ideas and the more general hope
that rationality can reveal an abiding presence (e.g., the laws of nature)
behind the flux and flow of experience. According to their accounts,
Socrates represents an interesting intermediate figure, who, though still
committed to the oral, is nonetheless caught up in the search for ideas
that have been inscribed into the eternal pages of truth. Although the
transformation from speech to writing is every bit as significant as these
authors make it out to be, another observation needs to be added: precisely because of Greece's rich oral tradition, the transition to writing was
postponed until the arrival of the phonetic alphabet.

The history of writing in Japan is, of course, a different one entirely. Phonetic syllabaries were a relatively late innovation. And instead of replacing, they were grafted onto an older, hieroglyphic system of Chinese characters. The syllabaries (given in two systems: hiragana and katakana) are used to record either foreign words or the grammatical endings and short particles that denote logical and grammatical relations. They have a limited number of characters and are easy to learn. Indeed, they are as clear and transparent as the Greek alphabet.

Yet the Japanese never seized on the advantage of such clarity. The syllabaries are used sparingly. The logical transparency they denote is used only to set language on its tracks. It is the intuitable itself—concrete sensual reality—that first gives rise to words that breathe with any fullness. Whether nouns, verbs, or adjectives, these words are written with Chinese characters (kanji), which are in turn as sensually intuitable as the things they denote, a feature that makes them multiply into the thousands. Each kanji is unique (as a place is unique). One can recognize them with consistency only after years of practice, aided at times by visible similarities between the form of the sign and the form of that which the sign denotes. The character for "east," for example, is the pictograph of the sun rising above a tree. Each character is thus, in a certain sense, a separate work of art, retaining a particularity that makes it resist easy appropriation.

But this feature of the Chinese character, its refusal to dissolve back into the clarity of the universal, sets it apart. Indeed, because Japanese contains so many homonyms, the Chinese character becomes an indispensable device for avoiding ambiguity. When a word is uttered that also bears an entirely different meaning, native speakers sometimes resort to the device of etching the written character into the air.[22] Sound can be dispensed with entirely—as is demonstrated when Japanese, Chinese, and Korean scholars nod their heads in agreement once the right Chinese character has been put before them—even though within their minds three entirely different phonetic utterances reverberate. The mysterious "inner word," the elusive intelligible structure that is supposed to conform to the word that is silently thought just as the thought conforms to the spoken word, is rendered concrete and visible. At the same time, it is mute and inarticulate.[23]

The great tangle of kanji is not only a mirror for the tangle of trees on a Japanese hillside or the tangle of buildings in a city, it also illuminates the Japanese soul itself. Ritualized actions frame an elusive personality. Such elusiveness reflects (and is reflected by) the obscurity of the Chinese character. Remarkably enough, such mute icons also assert a kind of universality: it is that "same thing" that the Japanese, Korean, and Chinese all seem to understand, despite their using different words to describe it. The Chinese character is thus strangely akin to the "concept," despite the fact that the concept can never be drawn in the air. The period at the end of this sentence is not a point, for a point has no extension. The circle I draw is more a polygon than a circle (any tangent will pass through more than a single point); in actual fact, the circle I draw is not even a polygon, because a polygon is made of lines, lines are made of points, and points have no extension. Once our intellectual intuition is sufficiently awakened to intuit the real circle, it would seem that we have left the clutter of the Japanese kanji world completely behind. Yet in another respect, we have taken a step closer. The mathematically intuited, insofar as it is *only* intuited intellectually, shares something with those sensually intuited forms that refuse to dissolve into abstractions. Both reduce the soul to silence. Both mark the border of the discursive. And for this very reason the "inscrutable" Socrates is an appropriate guide to the inscrutability of Japan, for within his puzzling persona lies a recognizably Japanese characteristic. The master of irony (as best portrayed by Kierkegaard), Socrates communicates only from a distance.[24] Rather than saying what he himself thinks, he asks questions—and thus folds his conversation into a silence that is rendered all the more enigmatic by his constant readiness to talk.

The Japanese describe themselves in a similar manner, through the duality between *tatemae* and *honne*, the face one presents versus the true self, what one really is.[25] It is a duality that differs from simple hypocrisy, insofar as the false self is not masquerading as the true one. When the mask is quite simply a mask, conventionally understood as such by all, it ceases to be duplicitous and becomes another word for honesty. An example of this most Japanese of attributes can be found in Alcibiades's description of how Socrates "lived a lie." The duplicity he has in mind is the opposite of the hypocritical lie, where ugliness is hidden behind a beautiful appearance. According to Alcibiades, Socrates was ugly not on the inside but on the outside, while within he was beautiful—even "godlike" (*Symp.* 216d–217a).

Or at least Alcibiades strongly suspects that what is hidden within Socrates might be godlike. Beauty that does not make its way into appearance is not reliably beauty, remaining mysterious enough that Alcibiades claims only once to have caught a glimpse of it (217a). When, in his attempt to seduce the master, he tried to make an issue of it, he was confronted with a warning: "My dear fellow, you really must be careful. Suppose you're making a mistake, and I'm not worth anything at all. The mind's eye begins to see clearly when the outer eyes grow dim—and I fancy yours are still pretty keen" (218e–219a). We might want to decide for ourselves the issue of Socrates's beauty by referring to the beauty of his actions, for instance, his courage in the face of death or the enormous moral strength he displays in resisting Alcibiades's advances. Even so, we will never be able to dissolve the duplicity altogether. Socrates himself suggests the possibility that even his courage may not have been as pure as it appears. By asking Crito whether life is "worth living with a body which is worn out and ruined in health?" (*Cri.* 47e), Socrates plants at least the suspicion that his actions may have been determined by a cowardly fear of disease and old age.[26] Death by a paralysis-inducing poison is, after all, a relatively easy way to go. It is far more compatible with philosophical calm than torture and a crucifix—or even intense nausea—would have been.

As with the stereotype of the "inscrutable Oriental," Socratic sensibility is determined by the refusal to be determined. Whereas the dialectic of hypocrisy permits the utilitarian insertion of a "felicity calculus" to dissolve outer into inner ("it's all just an act"), this is not the case with the Japanese variation of duplicity. By the open acknowledgment that it is a mask, the mask is fixed—and remains the same mask, whether worn by a Zen master or a shopkeeper. What lies on the inside is kept indiscernible (it is not a matter of what simply happens to be unconscious). As for the "outside," instead of being overtly and noisily obsequious, it is calmly and reservedly *polite*, tending even toward frigidity. Socrates embodies a similar coolness in the way he brings together politeness and irony. When he is about to raise his catastrophic "what-is-it" question, he pauses long enough to make a demure disclaimer: "Only I find one slight difficulty, which Protagoras will of course easily explain away" (*Prot.* 328e–329c). In Japan there is an entire level of speech, with its own set of grammatical endings and even a degree of independent vocabulary, that serves the function not of politely elevating the status of the person with whom one is speaking (as is still common in any European language except English), but of politely *lowering* the level of oneself as speaker. Socrates achieves something similar through the almost dreary plainness of his speech: "his talk is of pack-asses, smiths, cobblers, and tanners, and he seems always to be using the same terms for the same things" (*Symp.* 221e). The true master of humility understands that deflation is the key to elevation. Aristophanes's portrayal of Socrates hovering in the air in a basket may have been more appropriate than it first seems (*Clouds* 218–238).[27] The ironist is hard to love, not because he is obnoxious, but because (as Alcibiades learned) he is hard to catch. Kierkegaard's intuition that Socrates was not simply an intellectual skeptic but an essentially aloof persona, whose very substance was permeated by negativity, is accurate, if not exhaustive. Although he could often be seen talking with others in the agora, he was engaged in criticism and rebuke, not in the communication of his own essence. Whether or not he was with others, Socrates stood alone (*Symp.* 221c).

Japanese society is characterized on all levels by this same inner duality. The often discussed alliance between politicians, bureaucrats, and big business is to some extent a Western construction: the Japanese mode of thinking doesn't support such coordinated alliances—as is made manifest in the bewildering disarray of a Japanese city. A consciousness that is unable to plan a city is certainly not able to plan the life of a nation. The talent for organization that Germany has displayed (in ways both positive and catastrophically negative) is rooted in a very specific tradition. Where metaphysics and Christianity come together to constitute the ideal of a God's-eye perspective, "central planning" is a thinkable option. Where the idea of a separable deity (one God under whom everyone stands together) has never taken root, society experiences a kind of entropic diffusion. Emperor worship is a possibility only insofar as the shrine of the nation is a reflection of the shrine in every household; it is a form of familial piety, and although it can be usurped by government (as the Pacific escapade proved), it stands distinctly apart from it. Japan is a nation of multifarious communal associations. Some are as large as Mitsubishi, but most are simply households. Because households in Japan are multigenerational, they are not to be confused with Western-style "nuclear families." This is the reason, for instance, that the Japanese save money. An individual is mortal. A household lives forever. The multiplicity not only of households but of associations of every sort reproduces the tangled web of Japanese nature: it is the kanji world of human habitation.

In itself, there is little in any of this that is entirely unique to Japan. One could simply say that Japan is a traditional society, reflecting structures that were common throughout the world and that still remain intact for much of the world's population. The remarkable and unique feature of Japan is simply the tenacity with which it has held on to its traditional configuration in the midst of its transformation into a major economic power. It combines a mastery of market modes of exchange with a refusal to surrender its entire social substance to the mechanical structures of the economic system. Attuned to the concerns of the market, Japan nonetheless lives large portions of its life outside it.

Within this "outside" lies the real answer to the charge that Japan is the contemporary Sparta. The communal associations that retain their independence, both from the state and from the market, provide protection from the self-universalizing drive of the public order. This public dimension dissolves human existence into the transparency of the barracks, where thoughts and actions can always be scrutinized, examined in terms of the purity of their attention to "politics" and "career." Although the Japanese home does not separate its individual members (rooms are connected by sliding doors rather than doors with locks), it does separate the family as such from the world outside. Before entering a house, one passes through the entryway (or *genkan*) where shoes are removed and slippers put on. In truly traditional homes, suit and tie are removed and exchanged for a traditional Japanese robe. Ideally, the transformation is qualitative and complete. When the work ethic is so overwhelming that it interferes with the intimacy of the private sphere (a major problem in contemporary Japan), one hears talk not of self-fulfillment but of self-sacrifice. The familial sphere thus exerts its priority even when its members expend their energies elsewhere.

The centrality of the notion of self-sacrifice is what gives the Japanese world its Platonic atmosphere (*Rep.* 419e–420b). Not only is education accorded an importance that goes far beyond that of other societies, but its structure is evocative of the *Republic*: it starts with an emphasis on gymnastics and music that is slowly shifted to mathematics. Pedagogical concerns are subordinated to the goal of building character. Stripped to their shorts and T-shirts, children march in unison through schoolyards covered with snow. The image of Sparta the Bad looms closer here than in any other facet of Japanese life. Who would make children walk barefoot on ice? The "noble lie" of national unity (414c–417b) plays its role as well. Were the regimental aspects of the educational system not counterbalanced by the liberty (and pampering) accorded children in the home, the issue of totalitarianism might again have to be broached. As it is, the disciplinary dimension of education, the stress on self-sacrifice, is geared toward the service of one's family and immediate community, not the state. The sidewalks in front of private homes are kept meticulously clean; public areas are trashed (something familiar to an American, but shocking to North Europeans).

The totalitarian potential is actually easier to discern in Plato than in Japan. Whereas self-sacrifice in Japanese culture represents the subordination of the individual to the life of the family, in the *Republic* it is aimed at subordinating both the individual and the family to the life of the polis. Plato has Socrates suggest what could never occur to a Japanese leader: the dissolution of the family and the communal rearing of children (424a). The usual way of defending Socrates from the charge of totalitarianism that closely follows is to assert that the *Republic* is Plato's book alone. It was he, not Socrates, who was engaged in proto-Nazi reflections about breeding men like animals and surrendering sexual life itself to the control of the state.[28] Socrates, however, was a gadfly and free spirit. He would have suffocated under such conditions.

There is another way of defending Socrates. He can be taken seriously when he says he is merely groping and may in fact be completely wrong (450d–451a). In addition, one can appeal to Socratic irony. One does not (really) establish a state by first expelling "all inhabitants above the age of ten" (541a). Nor does one send men and women off to exercise together in the nude while insisting that their mating be directed solely by the state in accordance with the "necessities of geometry" (458c–e). The joke is, after all, a fairly simple and obvious one: finite beings cannot achieve perfect justice. The intensity—and irrationality—of human desire assures that the just order will either be overly repressive or overly susceptible to change and corruption. There is no political solution to the problem of justice.

An ironical reading of the *Republic* has the advantage of eliminating the abyss that otherwise seems to separate the work from the *Apology* and other early dialogues. The apolitical Socrates (who is nonetheless intensely concerned with the well-being of the polis) is the one that we have to live with. To appreciate him at all we have to modify the prevailing conception of goodness, according to which it involves a fully public service to the community—either through one's job or one's political engagement. That moral virtue comes before civic virtue is a truth that we have nearly forgotten: private existence does not have to exhaust itself in the pursuit of wealth and pleasure. Socrates may have turned his back on both career and politics, but he did not do so to egotistically gratify his own private wishes. To assert that there is no political solution to the problem of justice is not to assert that there is no solution at all: justice, to flourish, must first be rooted in the heart. One who is apolitical is not therefore an anarchist.

Kierkegaard's assessment of Socratic irony as "infinite absolute negativity" goes too far. Not only did Socrates remain a virtuous man, but he did so from another standpoint than the fully arbitrary one of "subjectivity." In the *Phaedo*, when he was asked why philosophers, if they truly look forward to death, do not simply kill themselves, he answered by saying that we humans belong fundamentally not to ourselves but to the gods (62b). Because we did not bring ourselves into the world (the "self-made man" is the great fiction of modernity), we have no right to take ourselves out of it. In other words, Socrates was well aware that existence conceals within itself an irreducibly positive moment that takes precedence over the negativity of critical reflection and abstract thinking. In the *Crito*, this positivity is named: one comes into the world through the agency of one's parents, in an act that must be sanctioned by the laws of the state (50d). Irony is pitiless in its mockery of the certainties people put forward, but it knows where to draw the line and yield to reverence. The Sophists wander from city to city; Socrates stays in Athens. He is the child of a specific place—and the child of his parents.

Although Plato himself carried the theme of devotion to parents almost to the point of ancestor worship (*Laws* 717b–e), it may seem strange to associate such a notion with Socrates. Family life was never regarded as his strength. On the contrary, we have always been presented with the caricature of a Socrates who, hounded by Xanthippe the shrew, repeatedly runs off to be with the boys. The caricature seems to be substantiated in the *Phaedo* insofar as the dialogue opens with Socrates sending away Xanthippe and his little boy (60a). The relative shortness of the ensuing philosophical conversation is apt to go unnoticed. It does not reach half the length of either the *Sophist* or the *Statesman*, conversations that were supposed to have unfolded in the same period of time. The reason is that, by early afternoon, Socrates took leave of his disciples, bathed himself, and spent the rest of the day with "the women and children of his household." Only Crito, his most intimate friend, joined him inside (*Phd.* 116a–b). He did not return to the company of his followers until almost sunset. Although he once again said goodbye to his family, he did so to spare them the scene of his execution. What Socrates had to say during those last hours with them is not reported—nor should it have been. What transpires beyond the *genkan* is private.

The kind of moral training I have alluded to is usually associated more with Aristotle than with Socrates.[29] Aristotle was aware that "knowing" what is right does not necessarily lead to right action. It is for this reason that he emphasized that ethical inquiry must not be aimed at "knowing what virtue is," but at "becoming good" ourselves (*Nic. Eth.* 1103a15–1103b27). In other words, Aristotle rejected Socrates's famous identification of knowledge and virtue. If one's emotions and desires have not been properly trained, one will often find oneself permitting them to veto and overrule one's knowledge. The need for moral training reflects the divergence of will and knowledge ("the spirit is willing, but the flesh is weak").

Socrates's own "position" is well known. A person is able to will one thing alone: what he thinks is good. If he does wrong, he does so only because he is ignorant. This is the basis for the contention in the *Apology* that wrong should be righted through education rather than punishment (26a). The theoretical justification is worked out at great length in the *Protagoras* (351b–358d), in which Socrates is almost shockingly utilitarian: "Everyone acts in accord with a felicity calculus," he seems to say, "so the important thing is to bring into the calculation as much knowledge as possible." The problem, however, with assuming that this constitutes a coherent position is the sheer impossibility of knowing what one needs to know. No one knows how long he will live (and thus whether he should live for short-term pleasure or long-term happiness)—and no one knows whether this life is all there is. Socrates is aware of the bold "as if" that he will have to insert (*Phd.* 107c). He is aware of what Aristotle seems to have missed: that his position is a rhetorical ploy.

If Socrates sincerely believed that an intellectual knowledge of virtue (something on the order of a "definition") is enough to make one virtuous, a number of things follow. First of all, he would have lacked passion to the degree that he conducted his life in accord with rules. But his emotion was apparent each time he grew impatient with his interlocutors (especially in the *Protagoras* and the *Gorgias*). It takes self-control to maintain a quiet conversation with a Sophist. Self-control is a virtue only where one's patience threatens to wear thin. That Socrates was a man of passion shows itself in other ways as well. He fathered children, even as an old man. He flirted openly with beautiful boys, whether their beauty was primarily physical or spiritual.

Socrates was, moreover, no anarchist. If his intellectualism had been as pronounced as legend has it, he would have regarded the state, with its laws and punishments, as superfluous. A philosophical determination of the nature of virtue would have sufficed to permit the complete dissolution not only of the state but of all other social institutions as well. Socrates would have been a radical libertarian, at home in no society at all, but certainly preferring an Athens to any of the alternatives.

His modified praise of Sparta only makes sense in the context of a deep insight into the complexity of human nature. Each of us is "both Typhon and a gentler spirit" (*Phdr.* 230a), each of us requires more than a rational guidebook: we require discipline. If we are to preserve the thesis that virtue is knowledge, it will have to be modified in two directions. First of all, Socratic ignorance will have to receive its due: desire will never be led by anything stronger than an opinion, hopefully a right one. Second, knowledge—insofar as it is attainable—will have to be more deeply situated than "in definitions."

The simplest proof that Aristotle was wrong about Socrates's moral intellectualism is that Aristotle was right about the need to ground virtue in practical wisdom and the morality of sheer habit.[30] If virtue has to be situated in the flesh itself, and if Socrates was a virtuous man, then his virtue has to be understood as extending into the innermost folds not simply of his mind, but of his body. In considering Aristotle's and Nietzsche's critique of Socratic intellectualism, it is helpful to call to mind Alcibiades's recollection of Socrates in the *Symposium*: "There was one time when the frost was harder than ever, and all the rest of us stayed inside, or if we did go out we wrapped ourselves up to the eyes and tied bits of felt and sheepskins over our shoes, but Socrates went out in the same old coat he's always worn, and made less fuss about walking on the ice in his bare feet than we did in our shoes" (220b). The portrait Alcibiades paints is of a man with remarkably good health and physical strength. The Socratic thesis that it is the soul that is important and not the body still holds (otherwise we would not find him walking barefoot on ice), but it holds in a way that grants the body its full weight and integrity. A rigorous gymnastics may hold the key to a rigorous education of the mind. In the same way, the thesis that virtue is knowledge will still hold, but it will require a major transformation of what we mean by knowledge.

Japan, a nation weak in civic virtue, is strong in moral virtue. It is not a litigious society. This is an important observation because Socrates's confrontation with the Sophists was primarily a confrontation with "lawyers"—and with the kind of society that enables lawyers to flourish (*Rep.* 405a, 464d).[31]

Racial and cultural homogeneity is the usual explanation for the harmony of Japanese society, a harmony that, given the extreme density of its population, remains impressive despite its occasional disruptions. This kind of explanation is, however, in a certain sense circular, for were a lack of harmony to prevail, implicit differences would become explicit, so that racial and cultural heterogeneity could be evoked to account for the disharmony (as is the case when discord prevails among the common "race" of human beings as such). The Hatfields and the McCoys would have seemed indistinguishable to an outsider, but for themselves the difference in clan was as ominous and complete as any difference in race.

One has to concede, of course, that a common language helps. Where people are able to communicate effectively with one another, cohesion is the ideal result. But the cohesiveness of Japan also has prelinguistic roots. The ritualistic determination of the "right way" to place one's slippers, the right way to hold chopsticks, the right way to fold a *furoshiki*, does not amount to an assault on individual liberty. Instead, it represents the slow embodiment of form that constitutes the condition of form's spontaneous actualization. Thus, the laborious attempt to internalize the multifarious forms of one's own culture may have more to do with freedom than simply being allowed to do whatever one wants to do. And if those forms carry with them an intrinsic and comprehensible

justification—whether on moral or aesthetic grounds—the case for freedom becomes undeniable. Within the Western tradition itself, the warning has surfaced over and over that the liberation of desire—without its
prior education—is the formula for enslavement rather than freedom.
The dialectic of addiction is evinced in the transformation of liberty into
crude consumerism.

As Plato himself taught, Eros is bridled not through a pious litany
of "shalt nots" but only through a thoroughgoing reorientation toward
the Good.[32] This reorientation is not achieved through the power of argument. Socrates saved no one by merely dangling before them the tautology "good is good." This is the justification for his insistence that education must begin with music and gymnastics. The reorientation must
be situated within the flesh. In Japan, this is accomplished through an
elaborate system of ritualistic actions. That a Japanese woman commonly
takes courses in "flower arrangement" and calligraphy does not constitute
proof that she has no real work to do. Culture retains more power than
Money. Mastery of form is mastery of the soul.

True mastery shows itself in action. According to the premises of
Zen Buddhism, it is only to be achieved through a "wordless" transmission. One enters the meditation hall without being told anything about
what one does there. One simply looks around and does what the others
are already doing. All have the same slippers. One finds where the slippers are kept. All hold their hands thus. One does the same. All remove
their slippers in the same discernible way. With an arching movement of
the leg, they climb up onto the meditation platform and assume the same
Lotus posture, sitting for hours in meditation. One also sits. If the body
begins to slouch, the master straightens it with ritualistically placed blows
of his staff. Because the platforms face one another, one sees before one
an arrangement of robed figures as evenly formed as the right arrangement of flowers. But because the eyes are cast down, parallel with the
nose, one sees only the slippers on the floor. If they have been placed
even slightly askew, the master adjusts them with his staff. Only where they
are evenly placed is form constituted. To turn a slipper in any direction
is to fill emptiness and thus destroy form. Thoughts too are to be evenly
placed. Form grows as emptiness grows.

In the *genkan* of every Japanese house, the shoes are deposited in
the same way. If they are left askew, then the mistake is wordlessly cor-
rected. The form of the One is thus reflected throughout the whole.

Form, as Plato tells us, is the nature of what is; it is not something
produced. It is to be discovered, not made. The presupposition of modernity, that nature itself (because it is fundamentally determined by en-
tropy) must be regulated by an input of energy (work), was anticipated by

neither Plato nor Socrates. For them, form is nature; nature is form. This is, in fact, the key to the characteristically Socratic method of elenchus, in which an argument is moved forward by systematically interrogating assumptions. After all, the removal of confused ideas can lead to wisdom only if the order of the Good is already established within us. The self-consistency of the perfect ideologue can hardly have been what Socrates was looking for! Viewed in this way, elenchus corresponds with anamnesis, the idea that knowledge can be achieved only through recollection of what we already know. Although elenchus is a negative and critical procedure, whereas anamnesis assumes that we possess real insight, the two in my view go hand in hand.[33] The right order of the soul is established by nature itself. It is corrupted only by the illusion that we ourselves can improve on it, bending nature to satisfy will and desire. The affinity is not a fictional one. The main work of Japan's most significant philosopher, Kitaro Nishida, goes by the Platonic title *Zen no kenkyū* (*A Study of Good*).[34] It is a conscious attempt to mediate Zen Buddhism with the tradition of the West. Nishida's conception of the Good as the self-realization (through rigorous and prolonged discipline) of the self can be read as the real goal of anamnesis. The way to such self-realization is through a method that resembles the negative procedure of elenchus. The master accords his disciple a koan, a paradoxical assertion that the student is commanded to solve. The solution is attained only where thought itself is broken apart on the horns of the paradox. The need to reflectively mediate everything through words must finally be turned on itself. The communicative obsession itself must be silenced. A right "answer" lacerates the unstated presuppositions of the question and, as an action, sets itself free from words.

Socratic wisdom is identical with Socratic ignorance: "I am conscious that I am not wise either much or little" (*Ap.* 21b). The wisdom to renounce "claims" is not a purely negative entity, for it is the actual knowledge that one doesn't know (21d). Such knowledge can be more positively described as the realization that reality is, despite all the appearances to the contrary, ultimately good, so that it has no need of our conceptual limitations and determinations (nor of the technological assault facilitated by such determinations). Our own need vanishes with the realization that reality itself has no need: we are thus freed from the maze of propositional affirmations and beliefs that we use to shore up our vulnerable existences. The open mind of Socrates is the mind free of attachments, the mind that has grown secure enough to withstand the full mystery of being. It is the mind whose wild imaginings have been tamed by proximity not with an eternally frozen midday sun, but with a beauty as ephemeral as cherry blossoms caught in a breeze.

Clarity is achieved by definition, the analytic and conceptual separation of what does not belong together. The opaque is constituted by the mad blending of what is full not only of itself but also of its other. Silence announces itself in the opacity of forms that collapse back into the void of generic universality. It completes itself, however, where the forms thus gathered, following the eternal law that forbids the unification of opposites, are released into the different places they come to inhabit. In the beauty of an ordered separation out of the same, the mind is torn open and awakened into full life. Socrates in Japan is a difference released from the obscurity of an inarticulate identity: in silence, the opposites touch, then scatter.

2

Socrates beyond the Academy

They say that I am *atopōtatos* ["very strange"; lit., "most out of place"] and that all I create is *aporia* ["trouble" or "perplexity"].
—Plato, *Theaetetus*

Plato hides himself in the dialogues. If he has something to say, Socrates (who was dead by the time Plato began writing) is his mouthpiece. In my introduction, I have therefore associated Plato in particular with the implicit claim in the *Phaedo* that "only dead men can see the truth"—a claim that I regard as constitutive of the prevailing scholarly ethos to this very day. A good scholar takes pains not to make a personal appearance in his or her work. Students know this as the first command of writing: do not ever say "I." It is a command that I myself do not take seriously to the degree that I follow Socrates rather than Plato on the issue. And Socrates not only always says what he thinks, but he demands the same thing of others.

In the same passage of the introduction, I referred to the "myth of the true earth," the last speech that Plato placed in the mouth of Socrates before he drank his poison. In the mouth of Socrates—the mouth, that is, with its repulsive donkeylike lips, half-hidden by an unkempt beard, and sheltered by the famously flattened nose and large flaring nostrils. The strangeness of Socrates begins with his notoriously ugly physical appearance, whereby each feature is described as protruding in such a way as to refuse to blend in—to harmonize, to disappear, to do, in other words, what beauty does by inclining toward the spiritual. It is fitting that the final words of the man with the donkey lips are dedicated so emphatically to the earth—and to the bodies that the earth shelters. It is the embodied person who steps forth and speaks the forbidden "I."

What I want to show in the present chapter is that the divide between Socratic obtrusiveness and the Platonic invitation to disappear by joining a school is even more significant than the often discussed division between "analytic" and "continental" philosophy. Ultimately, it reflects the abyss that separates the first school, those who regard Being as self-evidently grounded in the self-evidence of its own luminosity (how could Being possibly not be?), and the second, those who regard rationality itself as obtrusive, as strange and inexplicable in its emergence as the astonishing jutting forth of all that is from the abyss of nonbeing. If the members of the first school are inclined to establish common ground, those of the second (Slavoj Žižek is a contemporary example of what I mean) would rather celebrate the freedom that derives from the groundless abyss.[1]

To make my case for saying this, I discuss the work of two "school" philosophers, one analytic, the other continental. I first discuss the work of Gregory Vlastos, the father of the analytic school of Plato scholarship. After that, I take up the writings of Leo Strauss, who inspired a school of interpretation all his own that draws heavily from the continental tradition.[2] By referring to "schools," I want to draw attention to the conventions scholars are asked to respect as a condition for having their work published and read. On the one side, the demand for analytic clarity. On the other side, the call for caution: no claim without a footnote!

By placing Socrates himself "beyond the academy," I am suggesting the inappropriateness of developing *any* "school" interpretation of him, whether based on analytic rationality or on philological rigor. I do this while conceding that, educated in Germany, I work out of a tradition of my own. But, even so, when taking, for instance, Gadamer's side in his debate with Strauss,[3] I operate with the understanding that some traditions are better than others at keeping alive the imaginative spirit that should always pulse through the humanities, a spirit that, by virtue of its very flexibility, best accommodates the individual as the final site of truth, even as he or she is held up and sustained by community with others. In other words, traditions need always to be revitalized in silence—and silence can be a lonely place.

> If you were going down the Agora and saw a crowd around Socrates you could take three to one on a bet that Socrates would not be saying anything about the improvement of the soul, nor acting as though he cared a straw for the improvement of the interlocutor's soul, but would be simply arguing with him, forcing him into one corner after another, until it became plain to all the bystanders, if not the man himself, that his initial claim to know this or that was ridiculously false.
>
> —Gregory Vlastos, *The Philosophy of Socrates*

Vlastos's portrait of Socrates, not silent at all, standing in the agora and constantly arguing with others, seeking always the refutation (if not humiliation) of his opponent, is drawn from a very limited number of Platonic dialogues.[4] They are, not surprisingly, the ones that Vlastos calls "Socratic," on the (questionable) assumption that they were written in Plato's youth, before he had views of his own to place into Socrates's mouth.

Vlastos is only the most prominent of the contemporary analytic thinkers who, despite analytic philosophy's traditional scorn for historical investigations, have made their appeal to the historical Socrates.[5] Their goal, it would seem, is to secure the authority of the archetypal philosopher for the analytic project of constructing a coherent web of belief. Socrates is appealing both for having insisted on the principle of coherence and for realizing the importance of scrutinizing everything (leave no stone unturned!). But, in turning to Socrates, they look too quickly to his arguments, ignoring Plato's warning that he hid both himself and his master in the dialogues. As I have already pointed out, a Socrates "fair and young" is more a myth than a man. As I understand it, neither the historical Socrates nor the historical Plato will ever be found—nor is it important to look for them. Plato has hidden himself behind a mythical representation of a Socrates who, by virtue of his poetic reconstitution, both was and was not the very Socrates whom Plato once knew and loved. And if Plato hides, he does so for good reason: he wrote not for himself but for us. The proper response to a Platonic dialogue is a deeply personal response. One finds who one is by discovering what one thinks.

It is only fair to point out that in many ways Gregory Vlastos is an exception. His engagement with Socrates is at times strikingly personal. Despite his careful attention to argument, Vlastos is clearly taken by the figure of Socrates himself, whom he paints as relentlessly cheerful. His is a Socrates who, having revealed the secret of our shared rationality, is at home among others, secure in the knowledge that no one is *really* a stranger. Yes, Socrates was ugly to look at, but how reassuringly beautiful were his words! For Vlastos, Socrates's famed ugliness was just one more opportunity to be exploited. Far from alienating the man, it became part of his brand. Together with his assumption of a rough-hewn and plainspoken demeanor, Socrates's ugliness became part of a comic mask that ultimately had the effect of magnifying the serene beauty of what lay disguised underneath.[6] Vlastos's conception is profound and elegantly stated, but by focusing so fully on Socrates's achievement, it does not allow us to consider what Socrates may have suffered—what may have compelled him to become Socrates in the first place: the difficulty of being so odd.

Vlastos's Socrates is the quintessential philosopher of the agora. He is visible only in Plato's "early" dialogues. The problem, however, is that because so few of Plato's dialogues contain cross-references, any fixed chronology ultimately has to rest on circular reason. We know which dialogues are early only after we have convinced ourselves that we know just when it is Socrates who is doing the speaking—as the man who, loving to argue, belongs in the marketplace, engaging in an exchange of ideas in the same way that others deal in an exchange of money and commodities. Such a Socrates makes no pretense to higher wisdom. He is simply on the lookout for moral beliefs that can survive the critical interrogation called elenchus—beliefs that he then collects and uses whenever he has to make a moral choice. This, at any rate, is Vlastos's picture of Socrates.

Among analytic philosophers Vlastos stands out by making it clear that his concern for argument is subordinate to his concern for morality. A vocal opponent, in his day, of the Vietnam War, he was not afraid to play the role of Socratic gadfly.[7] He presents Socrates, in other words, as a proper hero, a man to be emulated. Reason, in Vlastos's world, is something that matters, something that makes us better than we are. Because of this concern for morality, he emphasizes Socrates's belief that an argument must be seriously intended. Even so, given that his project is to specify the precise status of elenchus as a philosophical method, he never does full justice to the crucial issue of authenticity that this entails.

This is a deficiency remedied by Alexander Nehamas, whose books I have already cited with enthusiasm. As a student of Vlastos, Nehamas gives us a fuller sense of just how seriously Vlastos took the actual person of Socrates. At the same time, he helps us see where his teacher came up short. In *The Art of Living* Nehamas argues that Montaigne, Nietzsche, and Foucault remained true to Socrates not by imitating his method but by embracing his spirit, with the result that they finally left him behind entirely, becoming profound and strikingly original thinkers in their own right. But Nehamas takes the concern with authenticity much further than Vlastos could have taken it. That Nietzsche might have learned literally everything from Socrates even while completely rejecting both Socratic method and doctrine makes complete sense in the account that Nehamas gives, but no sense at all with what we find in Vlastos, for whom method and doctrine are themselves the crucial issues. I would go so far as to say that Nehamas, in contrast to Vlastos, has followed Socrates beyond analytic philosophy—and beyond the naïve hope analytic philosophy places in theory. Nehamas's encounter with Socrates has, in other words, transformed him in much the same way as the authors he discusses were transformed by the same encounter. But even with Nehamas, the scholarly ethos prevails. As I observed already in my preface, Nehamas fails to include himself in his discussion. He writes as a detached scholar, as someone who just happens to know a lot about how Montaigne, Nietzsche, and Foucault were transformed by their own readings of Socrates.

To what degree his scholarly pose represents an ironic mask is left to the reader to decide.

Vlastos, however, cannot even be suspected of wearing a mask. His goal is clearly put forth: to present the Socratic method of interrogation (the elenchus) as an antidote to analytic philosophy's emphasis on deduction.[8] He rightly believes that, just as science is always open for revision, philosophy should be open for revision. And given that he further believes that philosophy's primary task is the search for moral knowledge, it is appropriate that he puts forth elenchus as an alternative to mathematical reasoning. The advantage of elenchus, as he sees it, is that it is intrinsically open-ended, insofar as one's beliefs are constantly subject to revision.[9] Philosophical elenchus is important more for the inconsistent beliefs it strips away than for whatever beliefs happen to remain standing. Beliefs we retain might always turn out to clash with other beliefs we have not yet considered. For this reason they are never more than provisional.

But for that very reason I am suspicious of Vlastos's suggestion that Socrates maintains "a clear map, on which he constantly relies to figure out, many moves in advance, the direction in which he would like to press an argument."[10] The idea of a web of belief that always needs to be woven and rewoven[11] is a coherent idea, to be sure. And it makes sense to say that Socrates was virtuous to the degree that he utilized whatever the most recent version of his ever-progressing moral theory happened to be. The problem, however, is that he never once referred to such a thing. My own assumption is simpler: what made Socrates effective in cross-examining others was that he combined a questioning spirit with clarity and flexibility of mind, this and little else.

What facilitated his virtue, however, was that he saw something that he could not put into words (or at least not into words that his listeners were able to hear), something that again and again accomplished the task of revealing both the vanity of worldly goals and aspirations and the insufficiency of whatever plan one might have for how to make the world better. When later in this book I come to speak of the transcendence (and even supertranscendence) of the Good, my goal will not be to undermine the virtuous actions with which we seek (as best we can) to embody that Good. Instead, I want simply to show that the root of such actions lies in something other than a rule or law we hold before us and dutifully follow. When it comes to what Socrates saw, it helps to assume that he saw both with his mind and with his heart.

The figure of Socrates is remarkable because, in addition to representing the courage and wisdom to which we aspire, he also represents the fragility of one who knows the limits of reason. To read Plato's account closely is to discover a Socrates who is as insecure with himself as we are with ourselves. Carrying out the imitation of Socrates would be a hopeless task if this were not the case, if it were not true that already within our simple humanity (within that which makes us question our very existence) we are the ones we seek. The oracle of Delphi was right to command that we seek self-knowledge, whereas Vlastos's Socrates is so protected by his theoretical knowledge that he is elevated above the sphere of the human. I understand the aloneness of Socrates as an aloneness that he *suffered* (an aloneness that in some sense we all suffer, thus an aloneness that paradoxically brings him closer to us). In contrast, Vlastos interprets it as an elevation, the source of his aloofness, something that protects him by making him supremely happy. From this point of view, the purpose of engaging oneself with Socrates is to know what he knows, for "if you believe what Socrates does, you hold the secret of happiness in your own hands. Nothing the world can do can make you unhappy."[12] Vlastos so thoroughly believes in this possibility that, in a chapter on the "sovereignty of virtue," he criticizes the Neoptolemus of Sophocles's *Philoctetes* for struggling to be good, suggesting that for Socrates virtue always comes easily because, well, Socrates *knows*.[13]

Socrates as I understand him struggles. "The unexamined life is not worth living" (*Ap.* 38a) is a proclamation we have all repeated so often that it is hard to hear just how strange and paradoxical the statement is. The imperative to reflect on our lives reminds us that even the most common life is not as self-evidently structured (not as common) as we pretend. What characterizes our common humanity, once we are honest with ourselves, is an insecurity bleeding into anxiety and depression—an insecurity that, as Socrates understood it, is the greatest treasure we have. To examine one's life is to encounter one's life as a question. And in this lies the paradox: the insecurity that society always endeavors to educate us *out of* is presented as something we need to be cast *into*—quite as if it were a good thing to feel lost and to suffer the strangeness of being human. Philosophy may have happiness as its goal, but it originates in melancholy, the mood of self-examination.[14] Philosophers must brood. We are as likely to find a philosopher in a homeless shelter (see *Symp.* 203d) as in a university, perhaps more likely.

By ignoring context and making consistency a purely internal matter, analytic philosophers are little likely to get the real point of elenchus. Consider briefly, for instance, Peter Singer's popular arguments for vegetarianism,[15] which "work" only to the degree that they sever themselves from the real world of nature, a world in which, when vegetables are grown, mice are plowed under and birds are robbed of their habitat. By pretending that we can simply turn away from the "whole" that is reality itself, analytic philosophy not only makes thinking into piecemeal labor but generates thereby the false impression that philosophical problems are capable of resolution. We enter into discussions about morality already assuming that we could live without guilt. The "right argument" becomes the proof of our own moral purity, thus undermining the sense of compassion that flows from the tragic recognition that there will always be suffering to share. Nor is this problem limited to analytic philosophy. The same paradox we confront in Singer underlies the Kantian position as well, which would have us adhere to a categorical imperative (never lie! never kill!) that in fact presupposes a world in which everyone is guided by the same imperative. That, in a world dominated by irrationality, I may have to lie to prevent a murder is glossed over. In the process, a fiction is made to substitute for the world as it is.

My point is not that realism should supplant morality, but that it should temper it—make it wiser, which is to say more understanding and, just possibly, more forgiving. The sense of righteousness that too often accompanies a Kantian kind of moral Puritanism is dangerously poised to morph into a self-righteousness that, knowing its own purity, seeks to punish those who are not as good. This, the will to punish, is in turn the source of most of the evil we find in the world. There is wisdom in Socrates's entreaty that those who err should be instructed rather than punished (*Ap.* 26a). From this entreaty Vlastos derives the principle that we should harm no one—not even our enemies, recognizing in it Socrates in his most "Christian" guise. But just how to apply this principle in a complex world is a difficult matter. For that reason it is helpful to examine Vlastos's interpretation of Socrates in the light of his principled opposition to the Vietnam War.[16]

The obligation not to harm is interesting because it appears to be contaminated by the same kind of incoherence that one associates with the doctrine of universal tolerance—is intolerance to be tolerated or not? Are those who cause harm to be punished or not? Leo Strauss, that other great icon of American Plato scholarship, is well known for using this apparent incoherence as a wedge for shattering the principle of not causing harm altogether: Strauss would say that Socrates knew that punishment is the "best thing" for those who deserve it, just as he knew that wars are often necessary. Socrates was, after all, too wise to be a utopian. Just as the vegetarian should understand that life always feeds off life, the pacifist should understand that people have a right to defend themselves. Even Socrates was prudent enough to avoid going into politics and patriotic enough to go to war.[17] From Strauss's perspective, Vlastos is simply naïve: because a world at peace represents an analytic possibility, he thinks that it represents a real possibility. What he fails to comprehend is human nature—and the way that nature is embedded within nature as a whole.

Vlastos is in fact vulnerable to this kind of critique. Even so, we have to be wary of any cynical elevation of politics over morality. Socrates presumably would have us defend morality in open-eyed acknowledgment that the world is—and will presumably always remain—a deeply flawed place. In other words, against the Straussian contention that refusing to harm one's enemies is too dangerously utopian ever to be taken seriously, what one has to show is that it is compatible with realism. The attempt to overcome evil by fighting it is, after all, demonstrably self-defeating. When we set out to cause harm to our enemies we only reinforce their hatred and anger. And when we set out to destroy them entirely (every man, woman, and child), we may successfully defeat an enemy, but we will hardly have defeated evil; instead, we will simply have become the evil we set out to abolish. Those who defend the justice of warfare have an unfortunate history of emphasizing the causes that provoke war over the way in which war is conducted. Many are those who have fought with just cause but in ways that can hardly be called just: firebombing cities is not the way to rectify the bloody excesses of a tyrant. Vlastos seems to me to be closer to the truth than Strauss.

But still, to be realistic: those who turn the other cheek can end up nailed to a cross. Vlastos is aware of this—and accepts the consequences. He is a pacifist because he is the kind of Christian (rare indeed!) who is able to descry what lies behind Christ's injunction "resist not evil."[18] But what one has to see is that at precisely this point he ceases to be an analytic philosopher. The principle of doing no harm is ultimately a religious principle, one that requires faith in God. To refuse to do evil, even when evil seems to represent the best strategy for achieving something good, is to entrust the consequences of our actions to God. And given that the immediate consequences of the best-intentioned actions can prove disastrous, one has no choice but to conclude that self-preservation is not the highest good. The good one seeks is a good in eternity and not in this world. For Vlastos, when he argues as a secular practitioner of analytic method, it makes sense that he, like Strauss, applauds Cicero's notion that Socrates was "the first to call philosophy down from the heavens."[19] But when he argues as a pacifist, it makes no sense at all. Although a purely political philosophy may need no connection to the beyond, a moral philosophy cannot do without it.

At the same time, we have to stay focused on the world that lies before us. Vlastos loses his focus when he creates the portrait of Socrates as the perfectly virtuous man, in possession of a knowledge of the Good so clear and reliable that it consistently points to the Good as the only option. But in this case, what are we to do with the Socrates who not only participated in a war, but in a war of choice, one of Athens's imperialistic adventures?[20] And what do we do with his participation in the siege of a city, which involved the systematic starvation of innocent children? If Socrates was virtuous, it was not because he was always kind and compassionate (even as an old man he struck an arrogant and belligerent posture). Socrates's virtue was his courage and his singular devotion to truth. Before he stood in lonely defiance, staring down his accusers, he stood on a battlefield, like so many Greeks before him.

But, again, the ambiguity: he took his stand not only for his city, but against it as well. What made that possible is what made him content with a life of poverty, what made him always ready and willing to die. This is where Socrates's virtue was secured, not in a web of beliefs he carried in his head. If we still find it helpful to say that his virtue was secured in *knowledge*, we have to qualify the remark by pointing out that it was an incommunicable knowledge directed toward the eternal, not the kind of sharable knowledge that binds a person to the men and women of the marketplace—or the kind of knowledge that can serve as the foundation for an academy.

Vlastos came closer to recognizing the real Socrates when, early in his career, he distinguished Socrates from Christ: "Jesus wept for Jerusalem. Socrates warns Athens, scolds, exhorts it, condemns it. But he has no tears for it."[21] But in the end, motivated by his love for the man, he let the "Socrates without tears" become the compassionate Socrates who held himself back only because he had broken through to the higher understanding that one has no choice but to let people be, for the simple reason that whatever goodness they achieve, they have to achieve on their own.[22] It is a wonderful idea. It explains why Socrates did not do more to correct the misunderstandings of people like Euthyphro. But does it explain why he remained indifferent to the fate of children in a besieged city?

From an analytic perspective, such indifference cannot be explained. One will simply have to conclude that he was not as good as Vlastos thought he was. There is, however, a perspective that renders his indifference understandable—if sadly so. If the highest good conceivable is the goodness of God himself, we might well enough anticipate that the goodness of a saint would have to reflect the indifference with which God looks onto a humanity engaged in mutual slaughter. The problem though is that what makes God's indifference tantamount to wisdom and compatible with compassion is something hidden from us, just as God is hidden from us. It is senseless to speak, for instance, of "tough love," given that such love is supposed to help people grow, not to turn away as carcasses are scattered on the killing fields. If God's wisdom is accessible at all, it is accessible only to an intuition that, rooted in time, penetrates yet above and beyond the world of experience. Philosophy may endeavor to reach so far—but analysis of our common assumptions and certitudes will obviously not take us even one step of the way. In other words, if the wisdom we need is a wisdom that enables us to endure the vision of a decimated city (whether decimated by siege or by bombs or by an earthquake), we shall have to find some other way of finding it than by turning to analytic philosophy.

If wisdom is a knowing applicable to life, it obviously has nothing to do with that self-evident truth of analyticity that assumes first and foremost that what we know is that $A = A$ and that $A \neq$ not-A. If this is what we know, then our understanding of life remains impoverished, for there is nowhere in the world, nowhere in time and space and in life itself, as much as a single A that remains A. Time, the movement of A into not-A, passes by in even the briefest of instants, so that the idea of a frozen instant in which A is simply A is itself an abstraction, a fiction. To rationally account for any A is to seek its deduction from not-A. Reason has non-reason at its very ground. This is the context in which elenchus serves as a better method than deduction. Logic is accurate but empty of content, good for making machines, perhaps, but no good for life (any machine that can be used for good purposes can be used as well for bad ones).

But elenchus too comes up short. Truly core beliefs are insulated from elenctic scrutiny. Vlastos, for instance, does not hide the fact that his own deepest convictions are religious in nature. But he understands the world of contemporary scholarship well enough to refrain from saying any more than that he has such beliefs and that Socrates too must have been a man of faith. None of this is subjected to philosophical analysis. Open to scrutiny are political beliefs alone, which, as political, are public and thus fair game for analysis. This limitation to what is public is a feature of philosophy as it unfolds within the academy. But what are we to do with the Socrates who was "a man of faith"?

Not only did Socrates like to engage (as in the *Euthyphro*) in rather heavy theologizing, but we find him thinking constantly about death—and not just in the context of his trial and execution. In dialogues ranging from the *Gorgias* to the *Republic*, we are continually being reminded that the philosopher—in opposition to the sophist—has looked into death and discovered that it contains nothing to fear. Although others attempt to overcome the fear of death by looking away from it, they fail to do so. Instead, like Callicles, they go on to invest their entire energy in the project of securing their lives and escaping death. So, regardless of whether the fear is acknowledged as a fear, it ends up determining the shape of life itself, replacing virtue with prudence. This is the life that Socrates subjected to constant criticism.

What I am suggesting is that the relationship to death constituted the whole of his philosophical being. One who lives in poverty lives close to death: to have chosen that poverty is to have chosen the proximity. To go to war as a simple foot soldier is to take death upon oneself; Socrates did this as well. He also sat, as a relatively young man, in the audience when Aristophanes's play *The Clouds* was performed, a play that placed before the entire city the idea that Socrates eats away at everything we hold sacred—not only our respect for the gods but our veneration for our elders. In this context, the staged burning of Socrates's school— presumably his home—could easily have been understood as an incitement to mob violence.[23] But Socrates remained sitting, even laughing. In a certain respect, he spent not only the last weeks of his life but his entire career philosophizing under a death sentence. The threat of a violent death always loomed before him. If Athens flourished, he would be tolerated. If ever things went poorly for Athens, he was always already the one marked for death. And still he lived as he lived. This is the enormous fact one must bear in mind.

If Socrates was out of place, the perpetual stranger, it is not because he was fundamentally different from others, but because he had the courage to unveil the mortality that we all have in common, the source of the strangeness that lies at the very heart of our humanity. Reason is the veil that hides mortality. It is under the shelter of that veil that we live out our social being. This is why the single-minded commitment to truth, the determination to tear all veils asunder, always appears as the greatest danger. Reason offers security: A = A. But the truth is that no A remains A. Entire cities can be brought down in an instant. One who harps on this danger is considered a menace. For the sake of truth the mind has to be released from the confines of A = A assurances. Elenchus is the systematic cleansing of the soul. It is not the game of "working toward" irrefutable arguments. The most irrefutable argument of all, the A = A itself, is decisively refuted by whatever steps into existence, for not only is birth a disruption of identity but it comes with the promise of extinction. The self-certainties have to be surrendered for the sake of living in the truth.

With regard to such "living in the truth," Vlastos calls attention to the way Socrates was most distraught *not* when he found people contradicting themselves (as they always do) but when he heard them conceding ideas "for the sake of the argument."[24] More important than what follows logically from an idea is whether one commits oneself, heart and soul, to what one has to say. It is life itself that matters. Socrates, not Rousseau, was the inventor of the language of authenticity—and that language has no analytic measure.[25] Socratic discourse seeks to educate the soul first by eliciting its most genuine commitments and then by disclosing their inadequacy. What gives Socrates his allure is the sense that possessing the self-knowledge that results (living in uncertainty) can make a person better and stronger than finding oneself armed in platitudinous self-certainty. It is better to live without the armor of conviction.

When Socrates listened to others, he responded with the knowledge that anything said rests on presuppositions that extend farther than one realizes. What he understood is that the contingency of his existence—and the contingency of any existence—engulfs whatever web of belief results from spelling out presuppositions and their implications. The final horizon is constituted by the indeterminacy of death itself. In other words, Socrates was not aiming at anything like a new principle or idea capable of making the world an easier place to understand or reshape. If he had been looking to the ideas themselves, he would have told us what he had in mind. If he asked others to tell us what *they* had in mind, it was only because they had not yet encountered the limit to speech that he knew so well. One's plan to save the world should be worked out to its final implication. Only thereby does one discover the folly of the plan and just how important it is to trust the secret operation of nature herself, wise with a wisdom always hidden.

Elenchus is an art, not a method—and its presupposition is an enormous amount of insight into who we human beings really are. Vlastos suggests something similar by stressing the difference between debate, the noisy clash of propositions, and discussion, the laborious examination of beliefs.[26] In a discussion, the bearer of the proposition has to be fully present. To assure this presence Socrates always shapes his arguments to fit the specific needs of his listener. But this takes psychological insight, something that Vlastos leaves out of his account.

Reason unfolds in a person-to-person encounter and is thus necessarily ad hominem—elenchus being a rational strategy that is right for some, but not for others. If the problem is one of knowing "how to live," and if that problem has its roots in a corruption of the soul that causes it to desire what is bad for it (so that a simple increase of scientific knowledge will not only be irrelevant but dangerous), then the proper mode of reasoning is one that can reach in and transform the soul rather than simply add to the number of correct propositions at its disposal. Socrates orients himself in such a procedure not only by a vision of what the soul should finally come to resemble, but by recognition of what the specific soul before him actually is—and will be capable of "hearing."[27] "Aporetic" dialogues are not the logical, "Socratic" dialogues that Plato composed before composing his own "literary" dialogues. The rhetorical (person-to-person) dimension is just as pronounced in one kind of dialogue as in the other. Socrates adjusts his manner of speaking depending on whom he is addressing.

In dialogues such as the *Protagoras, Gorgias, Hippias* (*Major* and *Minor*), and *Euthyphro*, he uses his arguments like heavy artillery. Those dialogues depict the kind of conversation that, according to the *Apology*, earned him so many enemies. These dialogues are negative not because they faithfully portray the agnosticism of the true, historical Socrates, but because they were written to demonstrate the messy work with which philosophy must begin: one first has to debunk pretensions, deflate ideological certainties, and expose the cynicism that underlies it all.[28] To read such dialogues and then want to show, with the assurance of a master scholar, how they establish the belief that virtue is (or is not) teachable, that courage is (or is not) separable from knowledge, or that the soul is (or is not) immortal, is to demonstrate one's own need of elenctic cleansing. Socrates's faith in the *logos* was not a faith in the power of propositions to "capture" the truth but instead a faith in the power of speech to inspire in others the courage to think (*Phdr.* 277a).

Socrates recognizes, of course, the legitimacy of certain propositions. He affirms in particular the legitimacy of mathematical propositions (e.g., *Euthphr.* 7b, 12d; *Charm.* 168e), of propositions about what is empirically observable (*Alc.* 1:111c), and of whatever propositions guide the craftsman and enable him to teach his craft to others (Socrates's most frequent example). The problem, however, is essentially what Wittgenstein talked about at the end of the *Tractatus*: what is truly important for human beings to know, the nature of the Good, withdraws itself from this kind of propositional articulation. There can be no "science" of the Good—if by science we mean a propositionally communicable "theory" (*Charm.* 165b–175d). Socrates goes as far as to speak of a "dream" he has had about a future world governed by science, a kind of technological utopia in which tremendous progress would occur in general health and physical well-being (173b–d). But he concludes that such progress would be worthless without what is essential, the knowledge of "good and evil" (174c), which knowledge, however, is impossible to attain as long as it is sought in the form of propositional knowledge. The aporetic structure of the early dialogues is supposed to lead one out of the propositional fetish. It can do so, however, only if it is combined with a deep desire to understand the Good. Where this desire is absent, one could easily adopt the position of the "responsible man of science," letting the illusory knowledge of the Good vanish into skepticism, while resting content with the things one can indeed know. And if the result is a more effective killing machine or a new strategy for pillaging the planet, so be it. One is just doing one's job.

What unifies the aporetic dialogues is not the fact that they were the first ones Plato wrote (who could possibly ascertain that?) or that they faithfully reflect the position not of Plato but of Socrates, but instead that their arguments are directed against a specific kind of "person," the potential tyrant, the one who claims to know "perfectly well" what is right not only for himself but for all of us. When Socrates attacks such pretensions, he is under no obligation to provide his interlocutor with an account of his own beliefs. In fact, to do so would be wildly imprudent. One does not disarm the know-it-all only to turn around and provide him with new and better weapons (*7th Let.* 341e–342a). These observations enable us to better understand the shift from the so-called early dialogues to the middle ones. Instead of regarding it as a shift from Socratic agnosticism to Platonic dogmatism (the position of Vlastos and so many others), it is better to see it as a turn away from the question of how Socrates made so many enemies to the question of how he won such devoted friends.[29] What we have come to know as the middle and the late dialogues are records of Socratic conversations with a truly rare kind of interlocutor: the one who both knows his own mind and knows how to listen.

This is clearest in the *Republic.* Its opening book, despite its belonging organically to everything that follows, is often cut apart from all the rest. Indeed, Vlastos contends that Plato was making use of a dialogue written much earlier, one still steeped in the heavy influence of his teacher.[30] It seems more reasonable, however, to acknowledge that Socrates speaks in a different way to Glaucon and Adeimantus (Plato's older brothers) than to Polemarchus and Thrasymachus (exactly the kind of men of power that Socrates always addresses in the "aporetic" dialogues). To those who are well aware of their ignorance and sincere in their devotion to truth, philosophy paints, in loving detail, the portrait of visions to come. But to those who pride themselves on everything they know and make repeated use of their "wisdom" to further their own power, philosophy must withhold what it knows. One does not feed the vanity of those already vain by offering them "answers" and "doctrines" that they can add to their stock of standard ploys. For those who don't know how to wonder, philosophy is at its best when it concludes its arguments with the case for perplexity. For those who are already perplexed enough, philosophy offers the palliative of the illuminative power of bold speculation.

As discussed in the *Phaedrus,* the true contrast is not between rhetoric and logic but between good rhetoric and bad, whereby "good" does not mean "effective" but instead what is truly good, that is, what helps make a person virtuous and wise.[31] The key to the good rhetoric that is philosophy is not only dialectic, attention to the truth of what is being discussed, but also psychology, concern for the soul that is being addressed (*Phdr.* 271d). One speaks in one way to the soul that (judging from what a person has to say) appears to be governed by the appetites (to a Thrasymachus or Callicles). The nature of the conversation changes when one addresses someone who is governed by the passions (a Glaucon or Phaedrus). The dialogue with those who are governed by intelligence (a Theaetetus or Philebus) is entirely different. In battle with the Sophists and the politicians, Socrates is ironic to the point of being mean, and the words he uses are in fact ugly. "Take the case of horses" is the plainspoken hold of the grimy wrestler in words; it is not a philosophical invitation to the sublime. But this hardly exhausts the figure of Socrates. The revelation of dazzling inner beauty (*Symp.* 216d–217a) and the whole mythical account of the soul's upward journey take place in a very different setting. The change in tone signals not a shift from Socrates to Plato but within Socrates himself. Something happens to him when he is in the presence of one who is beautiful.[32] To maintain that Socrates is only the intractable critic is to content oneself with the ugly version of the philosopher. It might result in a Socrates that is closer to the one Xenophon knew, but it will not result in the Socrates Plato knew, the Socrates we ourselves need to know.[33]

Socrates as critic might have been a sterling humanist, but so are we all. He may have been admirable in his devotion to ethical questions, but who today isn't? And although he may have been a master of consistency and argumentation, he hardly bested his contemporary Protagoras (*Prt.* 350c–d), nor does he stand up well under the scrutiny of the logicians who critique him today.[34] The identification of Socrates's philosophy with his ability to argue fails to take note of his single most important lesson: the distinction between philosophy and sophistry. It is a distinction that has nothing to do with technical finesse and everything to do with character.[35]

If it is Socrates we stand in need of, it is the Socrates who captured Plato's imagination: the one who, intent on saving the soul of all of Athens, could take on Protagoras and Gorgias, stare down a Thrasymachus (*Rep.* 336d), bring tears to the eyes of a Glaucon or Phaedrus, follow the arguments of the Eleatic Stranger, and drink his poison "without trembling or changing color or expression" (*Phd.* 117b). To limit Socrates to the "aporetic" dialogues is to ignore those very works, the *Phaedo* and the *Symposium*, in which the portrait of Socrates is most vividly painted.[36] They are, indeed, the only dialogues in which Plato's entire intent seems to have been to tell us who Socrates really was. His answer is not "the smartest man who ever lived" but instead "the most noble, the most just."

But it is a nobility compatible with what Socrates says of himself in the *Phaedrus* when he confesses that he has never gotten to the bottom of the command to "know myself," the command "to discover whether I really am a more complex creature and more puffed up with pride than Typhon, or a simpler, gentler being whom heaven has blessed with a quiet, un-Typhonic nature" (230a). Caught up in the divide between Typhon, the beastly serpent, and a possible spirit divine, Socrates has no choice but to continue working toward his own salvation. It is the condition of philosophy that we always remain strangers to ourselves. It is this intrinsic strangeness that thrusts us into the need to seek wisdom from strangers other than ourselves. Virtue lies in the way we negotiate the dialogue between strangers. Because there is no rule that can govern the interaction of those who, strange to one another, are always capable of taking one another fully by surprise, virtue itself remains elusive. In the end, virtue reveals itself as little more than the quest for virtue, which begins, of course, with the confession of sin.

The notion that Socrates may bear within himself a beast should be taken seriously despite everything we think we know about the incompatibility of evil with the Platonic understanding of reality. The place of evil is always first and foremost within ourselves—even if that self is the self of a Socrates. He, the consummate examiner of others, must begin, as we have seen, by examining himself. His ability to "read" the souls of his interlocutors suggests that they are somehow what he is. And what both he and they are is at bottom so monstrous that Socrates seriously considers the possibility that some souls might prove irredeemable (*Phd.* 113e; *Rep.* 615e). This represents a point within us so horrific, the possibility of an estrangement deep enough to be regarded as eternal, that it justifies the use of the portentous word "beyond." If friendship is a relationship between strangers, it is a relationship that has to contend with the possibility of unbridgeable separation. Some things, after all, are quite simply beyond fathoming and cannot but tear the web of reason apart. A city destroyed by an earthquake can be understood geologically. But a city destroyed by systematic bombing puts us up against something that challenges any conceivable mode of understanding. Behind the veneer of good strategy lurks a lust for blood revenge that is only enhanced by the vision of slaughtered children. Freedom may be a favorite trope of a specifically modern philosophy. But Socrates clearly knew something of the abyss it opens up—an abyss that Vlastos's philosophical method keeps him from peering into.

With this answer to Vlastos, I reveal my proximity to authors like Leo Strauss. By emphasizing the relentlessly ad hominem character of Socratic discourse, I ally myself with those who insist on a literary reading of the dialogues. And by acknowledging that the principle of individuation, which makes each of us the person he or she is, is bound to something intrinsically irrational, I reveal a certain affinity to Strauss's Hobbesian fascination with the dark side of humanity. Even so, I would like to distinguish my approach from that of Strauss just as emphatically as I distinguished it from that of Vlastos—and for a similar reason. I believe that he too succumbs to a scholarly ethos that closes off access to the living spirit of Socrates. He too is blinded by the allure of "pure objectivity," the desire to sink his anchor into something that is just clearly right.[37] For Strauss it comes in the form of political (not moral) philosophy, and, more specifically, in the form of the political philosophy of the ancient Greeks. This, at any rate, is the claim he lets lie on the surface. Unlike Vlastos, Strauss is a man who likes secrets just as much as he likes that which is "clearly right." In important respects he resembles the portrait of the enigmatic Socrates that I have painted.

Where he differs from Socrates, however, is in his affect. Socrates depicted the moving spirit of philosophy in the guise of the daemonic form of the god Eros, a god impetuous to the point of recklessness (*Symp.* 203d),[38] who retains the power to drive people to frenzy and madness (207b–208b). When I read these passages, I am reminded of similar passages in the *Phaedrus* and assume that Socrates is talking about the philosopher's search for wisdom and truth. But when Strauss, in his commentary on the *Symposium*, turns to the extended passage on frenzy, for example, he emphasizes that it is not love of the Beautiful or the Good that underlies all this frenzy but instead love of one's offspring.[39] The only frenzy he affirms is the one that makes men and women fight for their children—or a nation fight to protect itself. Passion in the search for truth is not something he praises. As a result, he finds himself rewriting the life of Socrates until he ends up not with the erotic hero of Plato's dialogues, but with the more subdued Socrates favored by Xenophon, who wrote as a retired general. For *this* Socrates the virtue of virtues was prudence—despite Socrates's clear explanation that the real reason he was placed on trial is that, dedicated to courage, he lived his life in an imprudent manner (*Ap.* 28b).

One can get a good feel for Strauss's method by considering how, in his commentary on the *Apology*, he responds to this passage. He begins with the assertion that Socrates was more prudent than he pretends to be.[40] With regard to his military exploits, for instance, Strauss points out that two of the three battles mentioned in the *Apology* were defeats, and "in the case of the defeats, courage consisted less in remaining or staying than in honorably withdrawing or fleeing."[41] The point is so simultaneously subtle and stunning that one might be inclined to agree that Plato surely intended us to notice this. The problem, though, is that by reading the passage in that light, one will have to forget other things that Plato wrote. Why, for instance, does Plato have Socrates insist in the *Republic* that courage rests on our capacity to intuit the eternal (486a–b)? Strauss, by deriving courage from prudence, has provided a completely different explanation. People are courageous because they want to protect their lives and the lives of those they love. But this creates more problems than it solves. If Strauss's reading is correct, what are we to make then of the explicit statement in the *Phaedo* that the philosopher's courage, guided as it is by wisdom, stands in sharp opposition to the courage that stems from prudence (68c–d)?

For Strauss wisdom and prudence are identical. Out of Socrates's declaration that his *daimonion* protected him by vetoing any move toward a political life, Strauss infers that a "digression which begins with voicing utter contempt for concern with self-preservation culminates in a vindication of self-preservation."[42] At this point it would be easy to forget that Pericles had warned that any refusal to engage in political life could not be tolerated in Athens. Against Strauss's conclusion, one can say that the philosopher's dedicating himself to a private life takes courage. Indeed, it doesn't take a Pericles to remind us that human societies can be greatly offended by the mere image of the barefoot outsider. There is obvious irony in Socrates's suggestion that it was prudence that led him to thumb his nose at the group. Yes, it kept him out of politics, but in the end he was killed for it.

The problem then is that Strauss often places us so close to the text that he draws us away from what we encounter in other texts. His general strategy in reading Plato is to ignore the more metaphysical dimensions of the dialogues in order to highlight the "everyday" features of the general setting. This allows him to use Plato to confirm a reading that makes Aristophanes and Xenophon the true authorities on Socrates. I find it significant that, at a later stage of his career, Strauss came to devote far more attention to Aristophanes and Xenophon than to Plato. Indeed, his last word on Socrates came in the form of a commentary on Xenophon's *Oeconomicus*, quite as if what he had been looking for all along was a Socrates who was interested in things practical, such as the prudent management of a household.[43]

As legitimate as it is for Strauss to want us to see what he finds important in the text, the procedure becomes problematic at the point that he claims a kind of superobjectivity, as when he suggests that he reads closely enough to understand Plato just as Plato understood himself. This is what Gadamer objected to in *Truth and Method*. In his defense, Strauss said that he always understands interpretation as having an "occasional" character.[44] Although this is presumably true, the ferocity of his attack on historicism seems to have led many of his followers in a different direction. I think, for instance, of Allan Bloom's sustained tirade against the evils of "relativism," curable, he suggests, by the rather simple device of going back to the classics.[45]

Strauss's own position was considerably more sophisticated. The real point of political philosophy is not (contra Bloom) to determine all the values that a community should embrace but instead to show that the very impossibility of doing this discloses one value that must always be respected: societies must assure that the quest for wisdom can go on unimpeded. Strauss refers to this as a Socratic principle.[46] He derives from it the natural right to liberty. At the same time, he sees liberty as deeply endangered by two things. First, the desire of traditional religious societies to regard the question of wisdom as a question that has already been settled. Second, the desire of modern societies, based as they are on science, to regard the question of wisdom as superfluous, belonging not to the hard bedrock of fact but to the always shifting horizon of the way particular societies understand themselves (as if it were just one value like any other). At the heart of the matter there exists an antinomy of sorts: only revealed religions offer a comprehensive view of reality, but at the cost of slamming the door on reason; science, however, gives reason full reign but refuses to acknowledge its own inherent limit: the impossibility of providing a rational account for the very existence of a rationally comprehensible world. Reason and revelation constitute a twofold antinomy that can never really be resolved. This is indeed a "Socratic" situation—and Strauss is to be admired for having placed himself fully in it. He experienced it as the problem of his own Jewishness: how does a secular intellectual express solidarity with his people, and this precisely in the time of their greatest need, when it is religious faith that constitutes them as a people?[47]

Such questions constitute a profound existential dilemma for one who is actually caught in the divide between revelation and reason and between the ancient and the modern. The problem, however, is that Strauss, caught by the scholarly ethos, seldom allows us to catch a glimpse of who he is and what he is struggling with. As scholars so often do, he feigns his own death, assuming a posture that suggests that what he himself happens to believe is of no real importance. One must be dead to see the truth. Or is it that one must play dead in order not to be killed? Or, still again, play dead in order to give one's own beliefs the authority of the great names who have been taken into the pantheon? I discern a kind of dishonesty at the heart of the scholar's posture of objectivity.

Strauss himself defends just this kind of dishonesty under the banner of prudence. In this regard, perhaps his most characteristic work is

Persecution and the Art of Writing (1952), in which he describes how Maimonides hid his most esoteric insight (that the true God is the impersonal God of Plotinus) within a craftily constructed labyrinth that was rendered all the more inaccessible by the fact that he had also written an exoteric and conventionally pious treatise for the masses.[48] If people need to be assured of God's presence, it would be imprudent to be explicit about his absence.

The scholarly posture turns out to be a political tactic. Strauss is more passionately engaged than he lets on. To be convinced of this, it helps to remember the full details of what made him struggle so hard with the question of Jewish identity. What I have in mind, of course, is the Nazi attempt to solve the "Jewish problem" by systematically destroying the Jewish people. This was a catastrophe that makes a mere earthquake appear trivial. Earthquakes are random acts of nature, for which no one is to blame. In contrast, the Shoah was carefully planned and systematically executed. It was evil on the greatest possible scale, the responsibility of the people who willed it and carried it out. How can one not join Strauss in saying that politics matters? Someone should have stepped in and put a stop to what happened. This is what accounts for the political part of Strauss's concern. A deeply religious people, having placed its trust not in arms but in God, was abandoned and left to fend for itself. God did not act. Without arms, there was no way to ward off the disaster. The conclusion is obvious. Jews should have been gathered together and protected by a powerful state. If Strauss has no interest in the philosophical pursuit of the Good, he has good reasons for that. The Good did not save his people. At the same time, he is too sophisticated a thinker to believe that this solves the theological-political problem.[49] Theology and faith constituted the Jewish people as a people. Politics is called to protect the life of that people, using instruments that betray the loss of faith. In my mind, this tension gets overshadowed by another narrative, one that too cleanly pits reason against faith. The result is that Strauss's discussion of religion too often appears to be motivated by purely political concerns.

As for metaphysics, Strauss seems to like it for not being religion. We can see this in his commentary on the *Apology*. Although most of us fall prey to Socrates's rhetoric and end up convinced that he was right to defend himself against the charge of impiety, Strauss takes the charge seriously and applauds him for having stood up to religion. At the same time, he applauds Aristophanes for having understood all along what Socrates was up to. According to his understanding, the dilemma of Maimonides is simply the dilemma of philosophy as such: any metaphysical rendition of the Good must end by taking the person out of God. Socrates, guilty as accused, is his hero. The Socrates who pretends to speak spontaneously (as if possessed by a god)—or pretends to be doing the bidding of Apollo—is to be applauded for his artful deceptions: of course his speech is strategy through and through; of course he knows that Apollo is a fiction. A remark Strauss makes about Heidegger in his *Studies in Platonic Political Philosophy* clarifies his own position: "There is no room for political philosophy in Heidegger's work, and this may well be due to the fact that the room in question is occupied by gods or the gods" (30). Socrates's positive accomplishment was not to have articulated the correct political philosophy but simply to have opened up room for the political as such by turning talk about the gods into talk about the Good. Political philosophy begins with an act of impiety: we human beings can start to order our lives only after we quit looking at life as if it were prey to divine whim.

This cannot mean, however, that Strauss (who after all was always struggling with his own Jewish identity) is simply dismissive of religion. In a powerful passage from his essay "Jerusalem and Athens," Strauss seeks to reveal the moral superiority of the irrational man of faith over the impious man of reason. He by no means intends thereby to reject the position of philosophy. After all, it always easier for him to identify with the impious philosopher than with the religious man. Even so, he believes that a religious man is better—in a moral sense—because he is armed with a delusion that makes him more courageous. Quoting from 2 Sam. 12:1–7, he recounts the story of how the prophet Nathan told King David of a grotesque act of injustice. When David responded in anger that the man who so acted must die, Nathan said to his face: "Thou art the man." Against this, Strauss quotes Xenophon's *Memorabilia* 1:2.32–33, which describes Socrates's parallel reproof of his former companion, the tyrant Critias. But the comparison does Socrates little honor, for it highlights just how careful and prudent he was. Yes, he criticized Critias "*somewhere,*" but hardly to his face. His remark, Xenophon tells us, "was *reported* to Critias."[50] The philosopher, of course, is to be honored for seeking the truth. But if speaking that truth to power is the measure of courage, then Socrates himself, the very archetype of the philosopher, can be deemed only marginally better than a coward. The passage is illuminating, but why should we judge from this example alone?

After all, the conclusion he now wants us to draw, that Socrates is a very careful man, is incompatible with Socrates's alleged impiety. In a conventional society, it is dangerous to question convention. Aristophanes's *Clouds* makes that abundantly clear. Strauss wants to turn Aristophanes into a teacher of Socrates,[51] indicating that Socrates learned prudence from him—and thereby became a better man. But, having restored prudence to its rank as the central virtue, it will now appear that the "cowardly" philosopher is superior to the morally righteous prophet.

By indicating that Aristophanes's reprimand hit home, Strauss seeks to understand Socrates by revealing how he was educated by Aristophanes's critique, which enabled him to come down from the clouds enough to become a good and prudent judge of character. According to Strauss, one can see this in Plato's *Republic*. Only after the old man Cephalus has left the room to say his prayers does Socrates dare to throw the conventional order into question by leading a group of young men into a discussion of whether justice has ever been rightly conceived.[52] He was, in other words, as impious as ever, but only in the company of youth. But if this now is goodness, what of the goodness of the prophet? Strauss's turns are not always easy to follow.

Unfortunately that matters. After Strauss's death in 1973, many of his students made their way into government, where they distinguished themselves by their eagerness to use the language of prudence to endorse the principle of preemptive warfare. Although Strauss himself affirms the virtue of a martial spirit, he does so always in the context of a nation's response to invasion from the outside. Had he lived long enough to see his followers assuming positions of power, he surely would have cautioned them not to make such an imprudent use of the language of prudence. Little Israel is in real danger of attack. Mighty America just pretends to be in danger, making a terrorist attack, for instance, look like an invasion by a world power. This is folly: wars of choice not only needlessly shatter lives, they can also shatter entire national economies. Although it is true that Strauss is not entirely to blame for the folly of his students, it is also true that he is not entirely innocent. Impressed that Socrates was actually killed for speaking the truth, he is the one who spun out a narrative in which all philosophers thereafter became prudent, hiding in obscurity what they really had to say. But hiding what he himself had to say was, it turns out, not at all wise. Too many of his followers wreaked havoc by thinking that Strauss had taught them how to govern.

A more sophisticated sense of history would have made it clear to Strauss that he had no reason to hide. After all, there was a time when entire societies viewed governance as a device for forming souls and inculcating virtue. In other words, there was a time when philosophy was taken seriously enough that philosophers had to watch what they had to say. But as Strauss is the first to remind us, modernity construes governance as simply a means for maintaining security (Hobbes) and economic well-being (Locke).[53] The time for obscurity has passed. Philosophers need to come right out and say just what they think.

The Shoah was not directed against philosophers who too clearly spoke the truth. It was directed against an entire people by Nazi thugs who were inebriated with a sense that truth was whatever lie they wanted to tell. Politics untethered from truth and goodness only leads to a war of all against all. If the principle of realpolitik is to fight evil with a lesser evil (one thinks of Machiavelli's ploy of defending Cesare Borgia by summoning the image of Oliverotto of Fermo),[54] then philosophers must endeavor to set limits to the principle by reminding us that our responsibility to "our own" is always already a responsibility to the stranger. Emmanuel Levinas, who witnessed the Shoah up close, is a better authority on these matters than is Strauss.

Although agreeing that the catastrophe proves that the Good is utterly beyond Being, Levinas did not draw the conclusion that we are therefore best advised to forget about it. Instead, we are to understand that the very transcendence of the Good places responsibility for our fellow human beings squarely on our own shoulders. Recognizing that the reality of history is war does not mean that we must accommodate ourselves to that reality.[55] The messianic possibility is never given to us in history but only from outside it. It is the eschatological event that comes in the form of the impossible event: the discovery of the Messiah in the face of the complete stranger.[56] To bring the point home with force, let me choose the most radical possible formulation: the Messiah must appear in the face of the suicide bomber who is even now headed our way. Whereas Strauss says, "do what you have to in order to protect yourself," Levinas says something remarkably like, "love thy enemy." If asked why my responsibility extends beyond my kin to those who are fully and completely there without me, the only reply he gives is that there is no logical answer, only an eschatological one.[57]

The Good, in other words, has a claim on us, even in a transcendence so radical that it cannot be said to exist. Nor will it ever exist. Even so, we cannot give up on it.

It is of crucial importance to us as human beings that we recognize that the Good towers above anything we ourselves can know as good. Why this is the case can be inferred from an extraordinarily troubling sentence that Strauss wrote in the midst of the Cold War. "We are now brought face to face with a tyranny which holds out the threat of becoming, thanks to 'the conquest of nature' and in particular of human nature, what no earlier tyranny ever became: perpetual and universal."[58] The fight against Hitler had given way to the fight against worldwide communism, a threat so ominous that it seemed to justify stockpiling enough nuclear weapons to destroy all humanity. In the context of the arms race, Strauss's statement seems imprudent to say the least. To enter into the risk of total destruction would seem justifiable only under the assumption that it would be better to destroy the world entirely than to let it fall into the hands of a power that, thanks to the progress of modern science, has become capable of establishing everlasting tyranny.[59] I am not suggesting that Strauss's statement should be understood in this fashion. But I am suggesting that it *could* be so understood.

What is needful, it seems, is the Platonic assurance (so necessary, as Augustine showed, for any coherent response to Manichaeism) that the Good alone can be eternal, for the simple and very rational reason that it affirms rather than denies. Whether we are talking about a lover's capacity to tolerate serious difference in his or her partner or about the theological idea that God, incapable of suffering harm, has no enemy to fight, the upshot is the same: the Good cannot be envisioned as needing to defend itself. Instead of recognizing that evil, the principle of destruction, is always doomed to destroy itself (i.e., the Soviet Union would quickly enough face the consequences of its own excesses), there were those in the time Strauss was writing who clearly thought that we were the ones who had to destroy it and by any means available. What this reminds me of is the peculiar dialectic whereby, because evil is self-destructive, it is able to survive and perpetuate itself only to the degree that it awakens anger and hatred in the heart of good people. The good city, caught up in the division between "ours" and "yours,"[60] is located far from the Good. Confronting an evil that it misconstrues as absolute, the city responds by trying to make itself absolute. The empire of good arises to combat the empire of evil, oblivious that the empire of evil arose out of the same impulse, out of the same conviction, out of the same need to control and harness a nature conceived as entropic. This is the nightmare vision: Zeus and Kronos locked into endless battle.

In this context, it might have helped if Strauss had stated clearly that "there can be no empire of good." After being invited to do so in an exchange with Eric Voegelin,[61] he instead said something much closer to "I only pretend to oppose empire as such," opening the door to his errant disciples. Here is the quotation:

> To stress the fact that it is just to replace constitutional rule by absolute rule, if the common good requires that change, means to cast a doubt on the absolute sanctity of the established constitutional order. It means encouraging dangerous men to confuse the issue by bringing about a state of affairs in which the common good requires the establishment of their absolute rule. The true doctrine of the legitimacy of Caesarism is a dangerous doctrine. . . . It is better for the people to remain ignorant of that distinction [between Caesarism and tyranny] and to regard the potential Caesar as a potential tyrant. No harm can come from this

theoretical error which becomes a practical truth if the people have the mettle to act upon it.[62]

Unfortunately, the greatest harm can come from saying such things as "the world is such a dark place that the truth is something we need to hide" or "while we know that Caesarism may be necessary, we will always tell the people that ours is the fight against tyranny." The danger is particularly great if, after making or even implying such statements, one immediately adds something to the effect of "I will entrust the truth only to my trusted disciples, for they alone have the mettle to rule."

Strauss, the warrior-philosopher-scholar, who claims to "understand Plato as Plato understood himself," in the end gets both Plato and Socrates wrong. The *Republic* makes clear, for instance, that the member of the good city will be a philhellene (470e), will not wage war with other Greeks, and will establish strict rules for the conduct of war. The good city will not target entire populations and will not lay land to waste and burn houses (471a–c). Glaucon asks Socrates "not to go on in this fashion" because the entire discussion seems too utopian (471c). He seems worried that Socrates may take the next step and say not only that one must be a philhellene but, as he says in the *Euthyphro*, a *philanthrōpia* (3d).[63] Socrates, after all, is the man who said that a seeker of wisdom searches "even among the barbarians" (*Phd.* 78a). Or, as I have put it, Socrates took his position "among strangers." He did not assume (with Vlastos) that there are no real strangers. Nor did he assume (with Strauss) that there are strangers, but one must be wary of them. Instead, he looks to the stranger as the one who could bear the gift of wisdom we all so desperately need. Philanthropic goodwill toward humanity must be bound together with the realization that there is no humanity "as such." Against the globalization that threatens to level all differences, Socrates would have us respect (not fear) the strangeness that generates difference ever anew.

3

The Education of Socrates

If philosophy is the imitation of Socrates, one will have to ask what made Socrates into Socrates. What was the nature of the education he himself underwent? What kind of education facilitates authenticity instead of obliterating it? What serves as its ground such that the very source of authenticity appears as a *daimonion*, an inner oracle to be sure, but like all oracles one that carries the appearance of a daemonic other? What enables one to live one's life in the open field where all of us are strangers? What does one have to see and understand, if not just this, that nature itself endows everything that is born out of it with the mark of a strange excess? That nature itself *is* this strange excess, so much so that true naturalism is filled with all that contemporary naturalism denies: life as essential rather than accidental; freedom and consciousness at the heart of reality rather than at its periphery; and, yes, God, the impossible being, nowhere to be found in a world marked through and through by his absence, and yet real, to the degree that what is natural gives birth always to its own daemonic double.

When it comes to the education of Socrates, Plato's dialogues point us in widely different directions. In the *Crito*, the personified Laws of Athens say they have educated Socrates (50d). But at the same time, they emphasize that they have done this through the agency of Socrates's father (50e), a rather strange assertion given that they are now prepared to keep Socrates from educating his own sons. Presumably what the Laws are saying is something like what I discussed in the opening chapter on "Socrates in Japan." Laws align us in the direction of the Good, providing the discipline that is the first step to virtue. They turn a self-centered soul into one "unfettered by the burden of self"—or in more recognizably Socratic terms, one that is public-spirited. But, as the reflection on Japan also tries to show, laws alone are incapable of effecting such a transformation. Although the threat of punishment, the dark side of a legal command, can provide a selfish incentive for acting on other selfish impulses, it can hardly render one selfless by doing so. Laws can mandate the worship of divinity, a good higher than the good of the self, but the Divine has to show itself as divine if worship is to be anything but a fearful mumbling or a counterfeit going-through-the-motions.

Perhaps the most plausible way of rescuing the claim that the Laws were responsible for the education of Socrates is to point out that, by law, Athens was a democracy: instead of dictating what people were to do, they left them alone to decide for themselves. The Laws educated, in other words, by not educating but instead by adopting a merely negative role, akin to that of Socrates's *daimonion*. "This is what you cannot do; decide for yourself what you can do." Indeed, the Laws actually had less to say than did the *daimonion*. What law would intervene and tell someone, on a given occasion, not to exit the lyceum (*Euthphr.* 272e)—or not to plead for mercy at a trial (*Ap.* 40b)? By thus restricting themselves, by removing themselves as much as possible from the sphere of actual everyday existence, the Laws accomplished something important: they let Socrates achieve his self-education.

In contrast, the state depicted in Plato's *Republic* is supposed to deliver a positive education, tending to the actual formation of souls. And yet, because it was a schoolhouse for producing philosophers, it could never have produced a *Socrates*, who can only have emerged spontaneously, fully outside the constitution (520b). But how are we to understand the possibility of a spontaneous formation? How can the free play of impulse do anything but (as the great libertarian experiment of capitalism shows so well) enhance our enslavement to desire, thus strengthening the hold that nature has on us? So dangerous is the possibility of this enslavement that the laws of Sparta and Crete, which aim at sculpting good citizens and freeing them from the tyranny of desire, have to be defended. Athenian law never accomplished so much. Yet precisely in its failure, Socrates can still discern its strength. The best citizens are the ones who, instead of being "sculpted," sculpt themselves. The highest form of governance is self-governance, which sets us free of the law altogether.

But because self-governance is so rare, Socrates remains positively predisposed to Spartan discipline. If one does not stand under a self-imposed law, one must be made to stand under the law of society. Book 5 of the *Republic* makes it clear that Socrates knew the tyrannical potential that was the shadow side of Athenian libertarianism. If freedom is a great boon to a good man, it may still be a bane for society as such. Regardless of their degree of entrepreneurial ingenuity, pirates—the offspring of states that fail to govern—are to be feared rather than praised. At the same time, if laws are thus rendered necessary, they should never be elevated to a tyrannical extreme. Socrates clearly believed that a Spartan citizen, schooled to self-sacrifice, was morally superior to an Athenian citizen, accustomed to self-indulgence. At the same time, he knew that a hypothetical Spartan philosopher, systematically schooled to wisdom, would in every way be inferior to his Athenian counterpart, whose only school is the open *scholē*, leisure itself, still for Aristotle the indispensable condition of any philosophy worthy of the name. Only in the double recognition that our needs require minimal attention and that our truest desire is the desire for knowledge can we turn our attention—playfully— toward that which evokes wonder, opening ourselves thereby to the claim that philosophy has over us.

But what kind of formation arises in the spirit of idle play? What discipline is implicit in such play? What good—what order—emerges in and through nature instead of being set against it? A city that has given nature free rein may give birth simultaneously to monsters and to saints. Is this tension not related to Socrates's strange vacillation, whereby he ridiculed Meletus for suggesting that the people themselves are the best teachers (*Ap.* 25a–c), even after spending a lifetime interrogating others—men and women, freemen and slaves—in the hope of learning from them?

The hope is interesting for being improbable. What after all do people really have to offer? In the *Phaedo* Socrates links the danger of misology (the distrust of reason) to the danger of misanthropy, which he described with the compelling sense of one who had himself been much disappointed by people (89d–e). Not only had he experienced treachery from avowed friends such as Aristophanes, but he was soon to be executed by the city he loved. Even so, he cautioned his disciples to maintain both their faith in reason and their faith in humanity. A lifetime of elenctic inquiry had made him acutely aware of how consistently people go astray. They entangle themselves in beliefs that are filled with contradictions and easily mistake good for evil and evil for good. Blinded by pain and simple ignorance, they convince themselves that friends are enemies and seek systematically (and often with unspeakable cruelty) to destroy what once they loved. Socrates was as aware of human cruelty and stupidity as anyone—and yet at the very end of his life he affirmed the life of the city, cautioning his followers against the danger of misanthropy. His defense of reason and humanity at the hour of his death is wrought with the kind of paradox that one can discern in the words uttered a few centuries later by the crucified Christ: "Father forgive them, they know not what they do." To forgive is to recognize the appalling state of human ignorance, but the banal brutality of what results from that ignorance makes one wonder how anyone is worth forgiving. To love the city is to see more than the extent of human folly; instead, it is to respect the degree to which folly serves to corrupt a will that in itself is only good. How has Socrates come by such a conviction?

To resist misanthropy fully one must first and foremost have discovered something about oneself. If humanity is disclosed as redeemable, where else can this take place but in the heart of the good man? Skepticism constitutes only one side of elenctic inquiry; the other side is characterized by a hopeful intuition into the harmony of reason with itself—or even the harmony of the human spirit with the universe. Annoyance with human error is already a celebration of lost truth. It is within this celebration that compassionate acceptance of humanity is rooted. Those who place their trust in the law alone are hardly in a position to forgive the inevitable transgression of law. Reason in this form can only compound one's misanthropy: positive forgiveness implies the active play of a reason that has questioned itself sufficiently to permit transgression in the name of a good that itself remains unnamed. In the *Phaedo*, Socrates calls this "faith" (or "trust") in reason.[1]

This point is crucial for everything I want to argue in the present chapter. A relentless critic, to be sure, Socrates was emphatically not a misanthrope. One of the things that makes him appealing is that he clearly liked people, just as they are. He was the rare Greek who reached out to women, not only by referring to himself as a "midwife" but by naming two of them (Diotima and Aspasia) as his teachers. He was comfortable with all the social classes. He often received visitors from outside of Athens. And as we have seen, he thought it was important to carry the search for wisdom beyond the Greek-speaking world. His critical challenges, moreover, were never reactive, never forged in anger. Instead of being outraged at the extent of human folly, he seems above all else to have been amused by it—as if he were impervious to even its most catastrophic consequences ("no harm can come to a good man"). Ever the provocateur, Socrates was nonetheless insulated from the society he passes judgment on, so thoroughly so that his judgments remain relatively mild, quite as if he were convinced that a communal search for wisdom and virtue were still within the range of possibility. Socrates, the lover of reason, was a lover of people as well, as mired as they are in unreason. If one reads a dialogue such as the *Euthyphro* under the assumption that Socrates saw in his interlocutor nothing more than a pompous fool, the dialogue will make him appear sadistic, as if his only intent were to force Euthyphro into experiencing the full extent of a confusion he never knew he had. But if one believes Socrates when he says that he seeks instruction from Euthyphro, a different picture emerges. It is significant, for instance, that, in the attempt to define piety, it is Euthyphro who first hits on a definition that, while fallacious, at least has the structure of a real definition, containing as it does both genus and differentia (12e). Although it is true that Socrates has led him to this insight, the fact that he achieved it still teaches something of value. If a fool is considerably more confused than he realizes, he is also a good deal wiser. Truth and error belong together. Socrates, who never agrees with anyone, nonetheless finds himself in harmony with everyone. But given that the harmony remains always a hidden harmony (no one sees it except Socrates), we are justified in asking how Socrates was led into it. Who bears primary responsibility for opening his eyes?

The Laws of Athens did not stop at suggesting that Socrates had been somehow educated by "everyone." They called his attention to one educator in particular: his father (*Cri.* 50e). But this too makes no sense. From his father, Socrates learned only the craft of sculpture and stonemasonry, a craft he so consistently ignored that he could only have earned the kind of rejection that fathers are notorious for giving. Hegel depicts this almost as an Oedipal situation.[2] But we hardly need Hegel's word, given that Socrates himself makes it clear that if his education derived from his parents, it came not from his father but from his mother. He nowhere calls himself a sculptor, but he often calls himself a midwife and says explicitly that it was an art he acquired from her (*Tht.* 149a). And because midwifery is the opposite of sculpture in the sense that, instead of fabricating a new being, one simply lets it emerge of itself, we can say that Socrates derived from his mother less a calculus for how to make something of himself than the courage to give birth to what he already was. Remembering his mother confirms our sense that the Laws of Athens, as Socrates envisioned them, were simply wrong—but wrong as laws must be wrong, oblivious as they are to all that a mother's love is able to sanction. To the degree that Socrates was self-educated, he owed a debt neither to Athens nor to his father (*Rep.* 520a–b).

It is true that when Socrates refers to someone as his teacher, he generally does so ironically. This holds not only in the obvious cases of Euthydemus and Euthyphro but also when he more plausibly mentions Anaxagoras or Prodicus. These were not, in a positive sense, true teachers. But are we really to conclude that the philosopher, self-educated as he must be, simply had no teacher? If this were the case, what are we to make of the lineage that leads from Socrates to Plato to Aristotle—or the lineage that leads from Socrates through the entire Western tradition? If a Socratic education enables its recipients to think for themselves, how and from whom did Socrates himself receive that education?

To answer the question, I will devote the following three chapters to two encounters that are not accompanied by disclaimers. Despite Plato's stated intention to present us with a Socrates "made young and beautiful," the dialogues provide us with only occasional glimpses of Socrates's youth. In the *Parmenides*, we find a very young Socrates in conversation with a very old Parmenides—who both tears apart his "theory of forms" and offers to teach him the art of philosophical thinking. The other example is from the *Symposium*, in which Socrates describes the education he received from a mysterious priestess, a woman named Diotima, who serves as a kind of archetype of the "stranger." The two dialogues, one "logical" and the other "erotic," are usually read in complete isolation from one another. Yet they belong together. They are, for instance, the only dialogues in which a contemporary narrator tells us a story that he heard from a narrator who had heard it from one who had actually been there. Set thrice-removed and in a distant past, they assume a kind of mythic quality (could Socrates truly have had an encounter with Parmenides? Was Diotima a real person or a fictional character?). If we are indeed dealing with fiction, we are left with the question, if Socrates never had an educator, how did he receive an education? The question of how he came by philosophy is as mysterious as the question of how humanity came by language. We find ourselves standing, in other words, at the threshold of meaning's first emergence.

Parmenides was everything that Socrates's own father was not. Instead of producing idols with chisel and stone, he used reason to destroy all idols—even at the risk of reducing the entire field of everyday experience to the shadow play of mere appearance. If, as a Greek, Socrates's first love was Homer (*Rep.* 595b), Parmenides was the great and utterly lone anti-Homerian (*Tht.* 152e), the man who defied tradition by announcing that reason rules with such force that space and time collapse into the empty singularity of a point severed from all relation: A = A, that realm in which all instances of "not" (both the not there but here of space and the not then but now of time) are eradicated. Whereas Socrates's father was sometimes called on to render gods visible by making sculptures of them, Parmenides's "Way of Truth" marks the breakthrough to an understanding of divinity so absolute that it can never be conceived as appearing in space and time. The truth put forth in Parmenides's poem is a truth not of the heavens that shine upon the earth but of a heaven beyond the heavens, the true abode of divinity, what alone remains after death has torn the veil of transience asunder. From the perspective of this truth, there are no gods apart from the one God, unborn and undying, that is Being itself. Indeed, it will hardly be surprising that a tradition will emerge that regards eternal being as so pure that it itself must be regarded as somehow standing "beyond being." If this is what Socrates learned from Father Parmenides, then we can understand his break from his own father—and even deem him guilty of a kind of patricide.[3]

In contrast, Diotima represents not Parmenidean negation of the world of becoming but its affirmation. Instead of regarding being and not-being as contradictory principles that exclude any middle, she reminds Socrates that they are in fact contraries, capable of flowing into one another. Being and not-being are mediated in becoming; by virtue of the irrevocable tension between them, they posit a between realm so filled with life and passion and desire that reason appears as a moment of forgetfulness. Nor does this mean that the eternal One of Parmenides is simply rejected. Irrevocable tension creates the desire for at least momentary glimpses of the great Absolute beyond, the place of rest beyond all tension. But such glimpses, instead of constituting severance from the world of appearance, constitute instead the source of its most thoroughgoing revitalization. Culture lives out of a vision of the beyond. If Parmenides, slayer of tradition, would have represented the possibility of rejecting the father altogether, there is no compelling reason for distinguishing Diotima in any way from Socrates's mother, for she too teaches the art of self-education, insisting that any truth worth knowing has to come up from the depths of one's own need and desire. By uncovering all that is contained in those depths, she reveals the power of love, the intensity of that passionate enthusiasm that gave birth to human culture even as cultures have backed away from it in fear of its intensity and power. In so doing, she simultaneously vindicated the truth of mythology, underscoring the majesty of whatever deity prompted the destructive fury that erupted when Achilles discovered the death of his friend Patroclus—or whatever other deity was responsible for the reckless imprudence of Antigone, who defied the laws of her city in order to remain true to a divine command that even her sister could not hear. Perhaps Socrates was right when he displayed his own act of reckless imprudence in mythological terms, defying his city for the sake of fulfilling a command of Apollo that was similarly inaudible to those around him. Martyrdom is an act of passion. Socrates lived out his entire philosophical life in accord with an erotic doctrine, a gift of the mother.

But in introducing both Parmenides and Diotima as educators of Socrates, we are left with two very significant questions. First, how can exactly these two ever be brought together with one another? Second, how can we reconcile the idea that either—or both of them—is Socrates's teacher with the observation that he was self-educated or had somehow emerged "spontaneously" from nature? In attempting to answer these questions, I want to begin by taking up the claim of the German poet Hölderlin that the Greeks received their most fundamental education directly from nature.[4] The idea is doubly paradoxical. What, after all, is the purpose of education if not to free us from the savagery of nature? And what is the one thing tradition has agreed on, if not that Socrates turned his back on nature?

Be this as it may, Socrates himself recounts in the *Phaedo* (in yet a third rare glimpse into his youth) that his early investigation of nature gave him his first insight into what we have come to know as "Socratic" wisdom. Something lying at the heart of nature (Hölderlin calls it beauty) taught him quickly to "unlearn" the mechanical assumptions that he first carried into his observations of nature (96c). Whereas one assumes at the outset that natural processes can be explained by resorting to material and efficient causes (e.g., a body "grows" by assimilating food), one who has been caught by nature's beauty will realize that understanding is really only given through forms (e.g., growth is growth into largeness). In other words, whereas mechanical causes force us to look away from what we would like to understand ("he grows because he eats"), formal causes invite us to peer directly into the phenomenon itself. Nature's allure constitutes the very birthplace of form.

Such a direct gaze is, however, dangerous. Just as Zen teachers have been known for warning their students not to let their gaze be caught by cherry blossoms (not because they represent distractions but because their beauty might constitute an abyss too deep to climb back out of), Socrates speaks of the dangers posed by dazzling displays of natural beauty. "It occurred to me that I must guard against the same sort of risk which people run when they watch and study an eclipse of the sun; they really do sometimes injure their eyes, unless they study its reflection in water or some other medium" (99d–e). To see nature as standing "in the good, which must embrace and hold together all things" (99c), what I assimilate to the experience of beauty might prove literally to be "too much."[5] Better then to separate the forms out of nature (which is possible to the degree that forms make language possible):[6] thinking from form to form, Socrates is given by nature (by the natural difficulty of standing in the light of truth) that second-best way of proceeding, which involves a movement through arguments. The point is not that nature has forced him to flee into "metaphysical thinking," for the intelligibility in question does not constitute a supersensible place of refuge or even an imaginative positing of the supersensible. Instead, it is an intelligibility that already lies at the heart of nature, although in a disguised (or eclipsed) fashion.

The issue emerges more clearly if we contrast it with a similar reflection that Hegel places at the beginning of his *Phenomenology*: we start as empiricists, assuming that open ears and eyes are all we need to learn directly from the book of nature.[7] But as we try to speak about the particularity we intuit as truth, we discover that we are thrust into the most abstract universality conceivable. Just as Socrates recounts, nature pushes us into language. But in Hegel's dialectical reversal, sense certainty is left behind. From here on out, it is the self-reflective subject that speaks. This is not the case in that parallel movement that Socrates famously refers to as a "second sailing." When the wind fails to blow, sailors have to take out their oars. When the muses grow still, philosophers have to resort to arguments. Although the adoption of a more reflective standpoint does indeed imply a departure from a certain kind of "natural science" (one so impervious to the siren song of beauty that it remains naïvely empirical), it by no means entails anything like what the tradition has made of it: an abandonment of nature for either politics or ethics. The intelligibility unfolded in reason is an intelligibility born out of nature: the Good for man lies not in the "conquest" of human nature but in its realization and liberation.

As Socrates makes clear throughout the entire discussion in the *Phaedo,* he seeks an account for why the things of nature are as they are. If he rejects purely mechanical explanations, it is because they fail to do justice to a blinding excess that lies at the heart of nature itself: "the strange,"[8] perhaps even the monstrous. Indeed, the very move to the forms, the final result of the "second sailing," is presented as a move demanded by this excess. One looks away in order to preserve one's eyesight. And although it is true that the stream of words into which Socrates submerges himself bears little resemblance to the physical body of nature, it may yet belong to what is *innermost* in nature—the principles of its seemingly ungrounded emergence. Again, spirit is not the antithesis of nature but the disclosure of its hidden essence.

The degree to which nature was Socrates's true concern becomes fully apparent at the end of the dialogue. As I mentioned in the introduction and will describe in some detail in my last chapter, the last words of Socrates are devoted to the story of the "true earth"—an earth far more vast and real than what we generally allow ourselves to see. It manifests itself in an excess so dazzling that it ultimately blinds us, which is the reason that Socrates awaits the approach of death before removing his own blinders and throwing himself to the wind. The discursive proofs of the immortality of the soul that constitute the *Phaedo*'s version of a second sailing are now unceremoniously cast aside as Socrates acknowledges that they have demonstrated no more than a kind of plausibility (107c).[9] Now that death awaits and blindness is no longer a thing to be feared, Socrates can simply deliver himself over to the truth of what is. As made manifest by his final and perhaps most alluring speech, Socrates ends his life by delivering it over into the deep abyss of the very nature from which it first emerged. The beauty of a swan song (84e–85b) lies in the affirmation of a life as it has actually been lived.

At the same time, the reference to something overpowering, even horrific, at the heart of nature helps us overcome an obvious objection that can be made to the notion that nature is the ultimate teacher. If Socrates sprang forth from nature, then why was he so unnaturally "out of place"? Why is he a stranger even in this strange world that is filled with strangers? Why, in other words, do the rest of us not follow? Why do we invest so much energy into the denial of a strangeness that Socrates so strangely affirms, seemingly oblivious to the fact that all dogs bark at strangers? How does one so uncannily enter into sync with a nature so uncannily out of sync with itself? The *Apology* provides our hint by making it a crime to be a thinker "who has theories about the heavens and has investigated everything below the earth" (18b). If Athenians opposed the disclosure of the truth about nature, they must have regarded their myths as lies, less disclosures of reality than substitutes for the harshness of what is. If they feared the one who peers into nature, they must have had a presentiment that the truth of nature was incompatible with the beliefs they pretended to hold. In other words, they, not Socrates, were the ones who no longer believed in the gods, as evinced by their refusal to submit their beliefs to examination.[10] Socrates may have been one of the few who remained who actually believed that nature is filled with divinity. And indeed, the story of the true earth makes clear that, like Heraclitus, he saw gods everywhere. The citizens of the true earth "have sanctuaries and temples which are truly inhabited by gods" (*Phd.* 111b). As for the long-standing prejudice that has circulated through the writings of Aristotle, Cicero, Diogenes Laertius, and Hegel, all the way up to Vlastos and Strauss, according to which the *Apology* somehow proves that Socrates had no interest in investigating nature, they ignore the fact that the only knowledge of nature he disavows in that address is the one depicted by Aristophanes, the one that would give him the capacity for "walking on air" (19c). And with regard specifically to the investigation of nature, all he says is that most Athenians believe that it is incompatible with belief in the gods. Why one would assume that Socrates believes what most Athenians believe is a puzzle.

But what is it about the vision of nature filled with divinity that should be described as "horrific"? And how does this observation help us understand why learning from nature, instead of constituting humanity's natural condition, is instead a most rare and seemingly unnatural occurrence? This is where the reference to Hölderlin proves helpful. In

Hyperion, the youthful friend of Hegel and Schelling attributed the entire splendor of Athens to the bounty of Greek nature—and then wondered not only why the blossom had faded and died but why over a period of 2,000 years it had proven so impossible to renew.[11] The Greek sun, after all, is still the Greek sun. If culture is the gift of nature, it is a gift that is seldom realized as such. From this point of view, the historicity of history derives directly from humanity's oscillation before the eclipse of nature's fecundity. The flight from the blinding light of truth throws us ever again into the blindness of simple ignorance.[12]

In his novel, Hölderlin assigned the task of poetic renewal to a fictional Greek contemporary, whom he calls Hyperion—avatar of the great Titan, born of the wedding of earth and sky, who first gave birth to the god of the sun. In conceiving a poet worthy of such a name, Hölderlin took his bearings from the great sun-worshiper Socrates (*Symp.* 220d), who famously placed philosophy as such under the aegis of Apollo (*Ap.* 21b). To make the parallel with Socrates unmistakable, Hölderlin gave his Hyperion over to the tutelage of a woman named Diotima, who, like Socrates's Diotima, reveals that the most authentic education is the one that springs out of love. The Delphic injunction, "know thyself," has its correlate: "follow thy heart." What prevents it from being an empty platitude is that, as often as the idea is evoked, it is never followed. Nature, cursed even as man is cursed (Gen. 3:17), is not trusted, for seen through a deadened spirit, it too appears deadened. Thus, we toil for a living. Education is turned into hard discipline. Talk as we will about love, work is the only thing that commands our respect. As much as we idealize Athens (city of leisure), Sparta is our reality.

It can hardly be my purpose in a brief aside to show how the poet Hölderlin interwove these themes. I have to concede as well that precisely because alienation from nature is the condition of modernity, much of what he says must simply sound absurd, as when he answers the question of how Athens became Athens by replying in effect, "it was a city open to the light of the sun"—or when he explains its fall from splendor by pointing out that the Macedonians marched in from the north, bearing with them an inclination to empire building that reflects the insecurity of northerners, accustomed as they are to building shelters from the winter cold. Or when he suggests that, lacking the natural protection afforded to Athens, Sparta was thrust too soon into war and lost the benefit of a collective childhood, so that "discipline began for them too early,"[13] whereas Athens enjoyed a thousand-year incubation, allowing both its political institutions and its traditions of art, religion, and philosophy slowly to ripen in idle play.[14]

Still, although the idea that nature forms culture (which I also emphasized when contrasting Greece and Japan) is difficult to hear in the modern context, it must be heard, if only as a needful corrective. Nature should be understood as the principle of birth and transformation—and not as a barrier to spirit or as the rigid straitjacket of an "essence." Hölderlin's belief that culture has its roots in nature renders visible the degree to which spontaneity and enthusiasm constitute its formative principles. The beauty of nature awakens love and love in turn gives birth to the beautiful display that is the highest form of human culture: this is of course the romantic vision. That I am appealing specifically to Hölderlin, however, has to do with something that is harsher and harder and truer than this romantic vision. Given that modernity has closed the door to the beauties of nature (even if only in the very literal sense with which we have made a collective retreat indoors), it would appear that nature can no longer serve the role of educator. Thus, after Diotima implores Hyperion to retreat to Italy in order to allow his own poetic powers long years of playful gestation, he instead opts for the modern response, marching off to war, determined to overthrow Turkish rule. He will put this world aright, displaying the hubristic excess that leads to Diotima's death and his own emotional undoing. Within the novel, of course, this only intensifies the romantic vision. In the last pages, hope returns when Hyperion has a vision of Diotima resurrected in the beauty of nature. Harmony is restored in the end: "The dissonances of the world are like lovers' strife. In the midst of the quarrel is reconciliation, and all that is separated comes together again."[15]

But this very Hegelian kind of resolution is not truly the final word. The real dissonance lies elsewhere. Hölderlin knew the severity of the Socratic *atopōtatos* (of being "most out of place")—and could not endure it. We sense this already when he describes the modern poet who lives in the stifling world of German industry: "They live in the world like strangers in their own house. . . . Full of love and spirit and hope, the children of the Muses grow up among the German people; one sees them seven years later and they wander like shades, silent and cold . . . and when they speak, woe to him who understands them."[16]

Seven years after writing these words, Hölderlin had completed his own descent into madness. The harmony of nature concealed within it a hell yet to be harrowed. If this is the nature that serves as the truest educator, it is understandable that one steps back, reluctant to receive the lesson. The task faced by Parmenides and Diotima was the task of preparing Socrates for the deepest initiation. The reference to Hölderlin is meant to highlight what is most uncanny of all about Socrates: his startling and seemingly incomprehensible sanity, the calm dispassion and sobriety that

still offended Nietzsche centuries later. How dare he live in the truth—
and not die of it! Perhaps for this very reason he had to die *for* it.

Diotima teaches Socrates "the ways of love" (*Symp.* 201d). She says that
Eros, the spirit of nature, is a daemon, not a god. Ever-again dying, he
is ever-again renewed. He seeks, with impassioned ardor, not beauty but
conception and giving birth in beauty (*tēs gennēseōs kai tou tokou en to kalo*,
206e). Giving birth is what he is really all about. He is fully active even
in nonhuman nature, driving animals into frenzy as they seek to mate.
At the same time, he is responsible for the creative energy that produces
art and religion. Philosophy is his highest achievement; erotic passion,
its indispensable condition. That Diotima's doctrine of Eros turns Socrates forcefully toward nature can hardly be questioned. She advises him
to engage the passions by starting at the most immediate level of erotic
encounter: lust after the body of a beautiful young boy (210a).

But how can one possibly assert that Parmenides is Diotima's partner in turning the young Socrates toward nature?[17] To answer that question, it is necessary first of all to understand that Plato's *Parmenides* represents, while scarcely alluding to it, a bold interpretation of Parmenides's
poem on Being (which often appears under the somewhat misleading
title "On Nature"). Because the "Way of Truth," which constitutes the
heart of the various fragments that remain of the poem, emphasizes the
unity of Being in a way that separates it completely from space and time,
one very important consequence of Plato's reading is that it challenges
us to reconcile this "Way of Truth" with the remaining "Way of Opinion."
As a result, the One that is Being can be understood as the unity of life
that mediates all oppositions. The eternal One, beyond birth and death,
beyond space and time, is not only separate from the many, it also gives
birth to the many—even entering into it in the guise of the discrete singularities that are woven into its fabric. The very inexhaustibility with
which the singularities come and go bespeaks a being that is eternal. The
never-to-be-traversed infinity of time without beginning and end (or of
space without boundary) is the only adequate manifestation of the eternal One that is so full and complete that it has nowhere to go and suffers
no rift in its abiding. Indeed, the two are quite simply one, all antinomies
resolved in an eternal life that manifests itself through the infinite-finite
of lives that come and go.

Although this seems consistent enough with the doctrine of Diotima, the terms of discourse could not be more different. If the terse
A = A of the original poem on Being has been replaced by a complex
dialectic of opposites, the *Parmenides* still remains a highly abstract exer-

cise in logic, without passion to the degree that its determinations are (or would seem to be) predetermined. Given over to its constructions, which, while they can be varied infinitely, unfold strictly according to method, the dialogue cannot accommodate anything remotely resembling the daemonic face of nature. As we enter into the sanctuary of pure thought, nature appears to have turned her back to us: animal frenzy no longer appears even as a speculative possibility. If the movement of concepts is to be comprehended as a "life," it is a life purely of the mind. How then does Parmenides open Socrates's eyes to nature?

In proposing this question, let me begin by drawing a hint from the *Meno*. Against the assumption that it is easy to define—and therefore to teach—virtue, Socrates above all else tries to communicate to Meno the understanding that virtue is difficult and perhaps impossible to define—and thereby seemingly unteachable, whence would presumably follow that one should simply accept what one is by nature, giving up on the prospect of transforming one's life and making it better. Although Meno himself is not constituted by nature to be overly concerned with this conclusion (momentarily "stunned," he is hardly silenced), others will be. Those who struggle hard to be virtuous—that is, the virtuous themselves—are hardly likely to accept the idea that virtue is given "by nature." It is a characteristic of virtue that it seeks to promulgate itself by taking up the project of the education of desire. This does not mean, however, that virtue constitutes itself *against* nature, but that it is the refinement of nature's own art of doubling in on itself.[18] *Transformation* is what nature does best. What this means is twofold: because virtue must accord to naturally emergent form, its accomplishment is play, not work; but because nature stands in the way of its own production, the play in question is a laborious one.

Nowhere can we see the laborious nature of such play more clearly than in the complex mental gymnastics that stands as the centerpiece of Plato's *Parmenides*, a gymnastics that Parmenides enters with the good-natured resignation of an aging horse throwing himself into one last race—or of an aging man who, the victim of a necessity (*anankē*) beyond his control, finds himself falling in love yet one more time (137a). In this instance, one has to recognize in part what one confronts throughout the dialogues: the strange urgency of a play so serious that it can lead a man to neglect both his own affairs (*Ap.* 31b) and the affairs of the city (31c). Socrates, the man of leisure who always has time for a conversation, has no time whatsoever for earning money or engaging in politics. The paradox is similar to what is at stake when a Zen master implores his disciples quickly to dispatch their soup so that they can get back to the urgent task of sitting meditation,[19] the leisurely "doing nothing" that leaves no leisure for even the most pressing engagement (*Phdr.* 227b). Although the need for salvation does indeed account for the strange urgency of "idle talk" (*Par.* 135d), this does not mean that what will be talked about will always circle around the Good and the Beautiful. Parmenides makes this clear by imploring the young Socrates to deliver himself, in earnest play, to a perspective from which the forms of "mud, hair, and dirt" are fully as important as the form of justice (130c). Socrates, the thinker who is often said to have invented ethics, is to school himself in a theoretical metaphysics that, rightly understood, represents the logical extension of physics.

Part of the education that Parmenides delivered to the young Socrates can thus be understood in terms of a series of corrections to the Socratic theory of forms: (1) although a form serves the classification of particular things, it should not be regarded in turn as itself a particular; (2) although a form unites particulars into a whole, it should not in its turn be regarded as if it were a whole consisting of parts; (3) although elusive forms (e.g., the Good) are thought to be discoverable only to the degree they exhibit their own nature, forms as such are meant to exhibit not so much themselves as things visible in the world; (4) although a form is an object of thought, it is wrong to think of a form as if it itself were a thought; (5) although a form might be approachable through an analogy, we are not to conclude that a form is a pattern inscribed into nature; (6) although forms are not things, they are knowable through the properties of things they bring together; and (7) forms are therefore just as dependent on things as things are dependent on forms: the metaphysical is the physical comprehended.[20] In a word, Socrates has to learn that a form has no self-subsistence. As the Buddhists say, it is empty of self-standing existence—and for that very reason is as dependent on things as things are on it. Buddhists call this "co-dependent origination." This is what is then enacted in Parmenides's long and detailed "gymnastics" that follows upon the critique of the theory of forms. He tells Socrates explicitly that he will not be able to salvage the theory of forms unless he is thoroughly at home with these interdependencies.

Even though Parmenides regards that theory not only as worth salvaging but as indispensable to dialectics (*Par.* 135c), I believe it is wrong to read the mental gymnastics merely as an attempt to open up to Socrates a promising avenue of reflection. As important for thinking as it is to legitimate the objects of thought and discourse, something else turns out to be even more important. Just as Meno must be stunned for a passing moment ("what we are looking for can never be found!" *Meno* 80a), Socrates must be stunned for the rest of his life. He must be made to realize that forms can be brought into serviceable union with nature only by virtue of a separation or purification that is absolute.

The premise of the entire dialogue is given in the initial way Socrates responds to Zeno, who has just attempted to show that the possibility of multiplicity rests on the impossible condition of things being both like and unlike: "If someone showed that the likes themselves come to be unlike or the unlikes like—that, I think, would be a marvel; but if he shows that things that partake of both of these have both properties, there seems to me to be nothing strange about that" (*Par.* 129b). In other words, a form is frozen into self-identity while a thing is left free to participate, from one moment to the next, in contrary attributes, a separation that, as we have seen, has the unfortunate result of making forms quite simply irrelevant to an understanding of things. Parmenides's version of the purity principle is much more radical: not only are forms not things but, strictly speaking, they are not—period. Their not-being way of being is not only the source of life and movement through time, it is also the source of intelligibility. An articulated whole cannot derive from a being that is but only from a being that is not. To demonstrate this, discourse itself will have to be reduced, again and again, to absurdity.[21] The entire exercise is attended to by a Socrates who listens in silence, perhaps amazed that forms can move—or perhaps stunned that reasonable assumptions can lead so quickly and relentlessly to apparent absurdity. In either event, the future master of elenchus is being given an education.

To show how far the reduction to absurdity might go, let me offer what is self-consciously a plausible rather than a definitive interpretation. What draws me toward the merely plausible is the observation that the young Socrates's unfortunate reification of the forms resulted primarily from an insistence on the definitive that left him vulnerable to Parmenides's objections—and open to his teacher's subsequent demonstration that the marvel of forms flowing into forms is demanded by logic. In other words, "likes themselves do become unlikes and unlikes like." Only by thus breaking the bounds of identity can Parmenides show that forms are supple enough to infuse things with intelligibility. In this way, he serves the goal of discursive reason, rescuing the theory of forms. I want to argue in addition, however, that the erasure of boundaries may have accomplished another task entirely, one that to my knowledge has never been commented on.

Famously and significantly, the entire dialogue is presented as a memorization of a memorization of a memorization of a conversation that once took place between Parmenides and Socrates. Cephalus relates what he heard from Antiphon, who related to him what he heard from Pythodorus, who related to him what he heard at the actual conversation, which occurred some fifty years in the past. In this entire transmission, the most amazing feat of memorization was accomplished by Plato's half-brother, Antiphon, who not only carried the words inside himself for a considerable portion of the time that had passed but did so while growing progressively more indifferent to philosophy. A man devoted utterly to horses, he seems an improbable narrator for the long and highly abstract dialogue that follows.

The usual way of reading this is to assume that Antiphon has been chosen as proof that even the constant repetition that enabled him to memorize the dialogue (*Par.* 126c) failed to teach him anything. After all, why else would he spend all his time with horses and blacksmiths? Against this reading, the plausible interpretation that I would like to advance is that Antiphon has been chosen for another reason entirely. Living in the sea of words, he experienced the insight that comes when discourse has been ruptured entirely. Parmenides's admonition that "mud, hair, and dirt" have their place speaks more to Antiphon than it ever spoke to Socrates. Instead of devoting himself to the project of rescuing discourse by refining the theory of forms, Antiphon bespeaks the possibility that Parmenides's real goal was to stun his listener entirely, so thoroughly reducing him to silence that he realizes the One in the direct and unmediated play of life itself.

To back up such a reading, plausible if not clearly definitive, there are any number of junctures I could choose in Parmenides's strenuous mental gymnastics where reason will appear strained to the limit. Although an exhaustive analytic inventory of the separate arguments (ninety-two in all) discloses almost all of them to be valid,[22] there are strange clusters of absurd arguments that disrupt the flow, as if something has suddenly been broken. Even more disturbing, the gymnastics itself breaks with Parmenides's straightforward proposal to examine all the possible responses to the hypothesis that A is or A is not. The first four exercises are responses to the following questions: (1) If A is, what are the consequences for A taken in itself? (2) If A is, what are the consequences for A taken in relationship to what is not A? (3) If A is, what are the consequences for what is not A taken in relation to itself? (4) If A is, what are the consequences for what is not A taken in relationship to A? The final four exercises consider the same variations of the hypothesis "if A is not." The hypothesis to be examined starts with Parmenides's own famous contention that "the One is."

As readers of the *Parmenides* know, the pattern is disrupted from the beginning. Instead of simply asking "if the One is," he asks first "if the One is *one*" and only in the second movement "if the One *is*": in other words, a tonal shift is interposed over what was supposed to be a simple shift from self-relation to a relation with others. Even so, the consequences are still straightforward: if the One is *one* and stands only in relation to itself, then the One is revealed first as not being in space and time—and by the end of the sequence of arguments as not being in any sense whatsoever (if simple self-relation turns out to be impossible under the presupposition of naked unity). If the One is *one*, the One is not. More precisely, it is the neither/nor of whatever set of contraries one tries to impose on it. In other words, perfect unity is not given in the form of a One that is one of many but simply in the utter lack of distinctions that is nothing whatsoever. It is difficult to read through this first movement without conceiving it as a rigorous negative theology: beyond multiplicity, beyond all space and time, we are pointed toward the eternal itself, so "in itself" and "out of" relation to anything else that it lies beyond even the naming of the eternal. In contrast, the second movement, which places the One in relationship to the not-One that is multiplicity, discloses that the One is in every manner thinkable. Consistently both one thing and its contrary, it moves freely through space and time, now here, now there, now this, now that: all the unique individuals that in fact make up the world we experience.

What is surprising is that the complex dialectic prepares the way for a major disruption in the flow of arguments. After revealing first the empty neither/nor of a One considered purely in relation to itself (which presages the death of any form whatsoever that is construed solely in itself) and then the utterly filled both/and of a One brought into relationship to its other (suggesting that forms live only out of their relationship to the other that is nature), Parmenides launches a third movement that is not at all anticipated in the eight proposed exercises. Generally, this is referred to as an appendix to movement two, but more properly it has to be regarded as a transformation of the first two movements taken together. If the first movement marks the place of the utterly transcendent and the second movement marks the place of all that is stretched out into time and space, the third movement transforms everything by proposing that the utterly transcendent is radically immanent in time—indeed, it constitutes the moving heart of time and first makes time possible. If time unfolds in the parsing of a "both/and" into now this, now that, then it does so—and this is Parmenides's most serious contention—only on the basis of the neither/nor that is the naked instant before either this or that has manifested itself. Given that what is at rest is at rest and what is in motion is in motion, it must be the case that both that which, while resting, comes to be in motion and that which, while moving, comes to be at rest will undergo their change not in time (where what is at rest is at rest and what is in motion is in motion) but only in a

timeless instant that stands at the threshold of time. The eternal neither/
nor gives birth (eternally) to a both/and that, because it is logically impossible, has to be distributed through time, which is itself then the eternal working out of that ineradicable and utterly unthinkable contradiction that is the union of the neither/nor and the both/and, each "now"
being the rupture of eternity into time. The very reduction to absurdity
is revealed as the simplest and most direct saying of what is.

We now come to the heart of Parmenides's exercises, which shows itself
with even greater clarity once one varies the foundational hypothesis to
the point of absurdity itself. If one wants fully to understand why Antiphon has given himself over to the everyday, then I propose, fully in the
spirit of the text, the utter and complete abandonment of what has been
memorized.

   Such utter and complete abandonment leaves us, of course, with
nothing and thereby with the hypothesis "if nothing is." If nothing is and
is so emphatically that nothing stands in relation only to itself, then all
talk of time and space, of parts and wholes, of the one and the many, of
time (either with or without beginning or end), of space (either with or
without boundary), will have to give way to the utter silence of no feel-
ings, no thoughts, no perceptions, no images, no anything whatsoever.
Nor is this the not yet of what will later be or the no longer of what once
was. As a nothing only in relation to nothing, it contains nothing within it
and has nothing to which it could give birth. Indeed, as a nothing only in
relation to nothing, it contains within itself even no nothing, for it neither
contains nor does not contain, neither gives birth nor refrains from giving birth. It neither begins nor ends, neither moves nor rests. The same
holds for every possible nameable opposition. It is as little outside as it is
inside. It can be found neither before the beginning nor after the end,
for it is the utterly simple nothing in which neither beginning nor end is
even as much as possible. In the nothing, we ourselves have never been
born and never will die: there is neither consciousness nor the object of
consciousness nor the possibility of either. Having neither beginning nor
end, the nothing is in every way unlimited, for it nullifies all boundaries
and eradicates all opposition. It is not empty time but is instead empty of
time; it is not empty space but is instead empty of space. It lies nowhere,
not even in itself. It moves as little as it rests. It can be identified with nothing whatsoever even as it is nothing whatsoever. The pure unbounded,
it is the free and always enduring, for no possible eruption of anything
could ever limit its sovereignty. What, after all, could a world be for the
nothing? For one who is dead the universe is dead as well. As such, as

the absolutely nothing beyond the possibility of determination, nothing cannot even be said to be. The nothing that is, is the nothing that is not. Nothing nothings, eradicating itself eternally as nothing, and in its self-eradication depositing as its corpse everything that is.

This brings us, then, to the second question: if nothing is, what are the consequences of its being for everything that is not nothing? Larger than everything, it is smaller than anything. Towering above everything, it cowers below what is lowest, for there is nothing that is brighter than the brightest and nothing darker than the darkest. There is nothing more red than red, just as there is nothing more white than white. Indeed, nothing is outside of everything and inside of anything. Beyond what is extreme in any direction there is nothing: nothing is stronger than the strongest; nothing is weaker than the weakest; nothing is better than the best; nothing is worse than the worst. Nothing is before the beginning and nothing is after the end. Both before time and after time, it is the self-dividing of nothing that gives birth to time. Nothing is greater than infinite space and nothing is smaller than the most infinitesimal fragment of that space. Simultaneously the absolutely beyond and the absolutely within, it is the self-dividing of nothing that gives birth to space. Before I was, there was (for me) nothing, and after I cease to be, there is (for me) nothing; it is the self-dividing of nothing into before and after that gave birth to me. There is nothing older than a universe without beginning and nothing that could possibly come after a universe without end; it is the self-dividing of nothing that gave birth to the universe. Similarly, nothing comes before the God that is the beginning and nothing comes after the God that is the end; it is the self-dividing of nothing that gave birth to God.

Self-divided, the nothing both generates all things and consumes all things. If such a nothing is, everything is.

What is, *is*—so emphatically, that it is, even if nothing is. The irrevocable necessity of being is the inevitable conclusion of the dialectic, regardless of whether one proceeds from the hypothesis that something is or from the contrary hypothesis that nothing is. As Fichte, Schelling, and Hegel correctly noted in response to Kant, the antinomy is not where reason breaks down but where it begins. Indeed, it is where the world itself begins. And because it is rooted so deeply, it leaves no space for a counterpossibility. Whether things are or are not, they are. Release from being is impossible. The dialectic ends with an intuition into necessity that one who is thoughtful might regard as an invitation to hell. Yet within this, the deep source of the utterly irrevocable necessity of being, there is perfect freedom. For the nothing that incessantly gives birth to what is, is in itself, as nothing, absolutely undetermined. This, the "now" that is, exists only as the ever-changing now. Bound by nothing, it is that which no conceivable logic could anticipate. As such, it is the utterly and completely new, that which commands full attention and awakens spirit from the void: for Antiphon, first the securing of a bridle bit, and then the telling of a thinking that stuns the mind to silence; for Socrates, the unique destiny of carrying this silence into thinking. The reduction of thought to absurdity is what delivered Socrates over to nature. Parmenides's task completed, we now turn our attention to Socrates's other great teacher. The next two chapters are devoted specifically to the education he received from Diotima.

4

Socrates and Alcibiades

"Warum huldigest du, heiliger Sokrates,
   Diesem Jünglinge stets? kennest du Größers nicht?
    Warum siehet mit Liebe,
      Wie auf Götter, dein Aug' auf ihn?"

Wer das Tiefste gedacht, liebt das Lebendigste,
   Höhe Jugend versteht, wer in die Welt geblikt
    Und es neigen die Weisen
      Oft am Ende zu Schönem sich.

***

"Holy Socrates, why always with deference
   Do you treat this young man? Don't you know greater things?
    Why so lovingly, raptly,
      As on gods, do you gaze on him?"

Who the deepest has thought loves what is most alive,
   Wide experience may well turn to what's best in youth,
    And the wise in the end will
      Often bow to the beautiful.
      —Hölderlin, "Sokrates und Alcibiades"

The erotic Socrates is so passionately in love with life that he is willing to defy the dead-world Sophists, those who choose to cling to life instead of live it, whose fear of losing life becomes the source of the anger and the will to punish that leads them in turn to impose a regime of death on others.[1] The life that Socrates loves is a life intensified by the ever-present possibility of death—that strangest of possibilities that, while more certain than anything else in life, can never be fully realized as long as one is alive. Conventional wisdom, the wisdom that sees in death only an enemy, cannot but mistake the adventurous flirtation with death for its converse: the life-denying will of the Gnostic. Even Nietzsche, the bohemian of all bohemians, could only discern despair at the basis of Socrates's willingness to die.[2] It is a possibility that has to be taken seriously, for if Socrates did in fact despair, this would have profound ramifications for how we are to understand philosophy and the metaphysical impulse that lies at its core. Does the philosopher courageously stand up to life—or is he burying his head in the sand of conceptual illusion? Is the metaphysician merely seeking a foundational support for conventional assurances—or celebrating the dissolution of all ground in the open expanse of transcendence?

And, were Socrates in fact to be deemed life-affirming rather than life-negating, what exactly did he love when he loved life? Was his eroticism already so modern that its object was itself freely constituted, the fantasy of beauty and wholeness engendered by the spirit's revolt against finitude? Or was it, rather, a much saner eroticism, one utterly Greek and still plainly pagan, an eroticism fired by a beauty actually present in the world?[3] To move forward with these questions, we will have to be attentive to Plato's text. But because the texts do not truly speak until imagination is brought to bear on them, we will have to place real trust in what we ourselves have before us: teacher and student, face to face. What does it mean to liken this relationship to the relationship between lover and beloved? Where is philosophy most alive? Where the teacher, engaged in philosophical "research," turns away from the student—or where research concerns are rendered secondary by the simple fact that the student presents him- or herself as real and alive—and in need of something that can only be delivered to the degree that one is prepared to reach beyond what one has to offer, to offer what we all in fact need: the capacity and willingness fully to encounter one's own monstrous strangeness. The impossibility of receiving this gift is what holds Alcibiades in an abiding sense of shame over against Socrates (*Symp.* 216b). Alcibiades knows that he is incapable of being who he is. And thus he remains a stranger to himself and all those around him. For all that, Socrates loves him.

Let me begin with a few words on the dialogue that depicts the love affair. The *Symposium* took place in 416 B.C. (the year Agathon won the tragedy contest, but also the last glory year of the Athenian democracy, the year before Alcibiades engaged in his own bit of madness that culminated in the disastrous siege of Syracuse). Yet the narration did not occur, if we are to follow Martha Nussbaum's surmise that it was occasioned by Alcibiades's death, until 404 B.C.[4] The narrator, the enthusiastic disciple

Apollodorus (the one who cried so violently at the death of Socrates), wasn't at the original symposium but narrated what he himself had heard from an older enthusiast, Aristodemus, whom he closely resembled. The story is fresh in his mind, however, because he had recently been asked to relate it by Glaucon, Plato's older brother, who, once again according to Nussbaum, may have wanted to hear it in response to a rumor that Alcibiades was returning to Athens to restore the democracy. The story itself, in other words, was resurrected after having been set aside for many years. Thus re-created, it is a work of poetry, a myth: it tells of speeches made long ago, not through direct narration of what was said, but through a spontaneous re-creation of what must have been said, by one whose enthusiasm renders him a vehicle not of the actual events but of the truth behind them.

Apollodorus, gently called mad, *manikos* (173d), accepted the abuse by repeating it himself. The word he used, *mainomai* (173e), is, if anything, even stronger. In 1 Cor. 14:23, Paul used it to characterize those who speak in tongues. The *Phaedrus*'s depiction of philosophy as a form of divine madness (249d) lies, of course, even closer at hand, for with the word "madness" we are reminded that every story that lives out of memory lives simultaneously out of forgetting. The root word, "mania," can be taken as a case in point. Socrates reminds us that it is closely related to the word *mantis*, which refers to the seer and to his prophecy (244c). The imagination lives out of such prophetic power, though in its divining we can by no means be assured of anything resembling "objective truth." Poetic re-creations are, as the great nineteenth-century philologist Max Müller often pointed out, as much works of forgetting as of remembering.[5] Before the advent of writing, goddess Memory (*Mnemosyne*) ruled supreme, relying heavily on the poetry of meter and rhyme—and thus on the magic of homophony: words that sound the same can have vastly different roots and meanings. But because sounds do matter, they fade into one another in moments of forgetfulness. This is why Müller regards mythology as the "dark shadow which language throws on thought."[6] Mythology is a reminder that mishearing a word can make possible a creative rehearing. Let "mania" be a case in point. If the ear alone is free to hear what it will, there is no reason to limit its range to its objective history. What if "mania" had been bequeathed to the Greek by the older Sanskrit *mantra*, the magical word of words itself, whose repetition, if carried out long enough, is said to open the door to the divine. Even with this, the history may not be exhausted, not if all we are doing is playfully hearing whatever can be heard. The Japanese word for "magic" is *majinai* (or *majutsu*). The magical word of words, even across the great divide between

East and West, may be the word "magic" itself, floating lightly above the kind of madness that makes language speak. As Martin Heidegger liked to show (and very much in the spirit of divine madness), fanciful etymologizing can be as fruitful for thought as the real thing.[7] Against the logician who yearns after the purity of the concept freed from words, the magician of thought can milk insight from words misheard and misspoken. The very name Apollodorus reminds us that beside the madman stands Apollo himself as the secret guardian. The account Apollodorus provides, in dramatic contrast to an alternative account that was first mediated by a man named Phoenix (*Symp.* 172b), is notable not only for its depth and beauty, but for its *lucidity*. I can think of two explanations for this. First of all, in contrast to his unnamed companions, who are men with important business on their hands (173b–c), Apollodorus was an idler. He had time on his hands. The story he delivered had undergone a long and leisurely incubation. But the other explanation of his lucidity may lie in his very madness. In times of sickness or distress, one finds oneself hoping that the mind will sink into a torpid slumber. Often just the opposite occurs; the mind awakens; thoughts take on an energy and life they never had before, so that the full contingent of internal observers is present to memorialize one's pain and misery. Lucidity (and clarity) is surely not a condition that stands fully apart from madness. If it were, instead of representing a metaphor for hell, madness would be thought of as a kind of safe haven. But of course the madness of Apollodorus is not a tortured one at all. His lucidity is the font of recollection.

The dialogue as a whole is a story of events from a fairly remote past. Its most significant speeches—those of Socrates and Alcibiades— reach back even further. Socrates provides one of his rare stories about his early youth. His speech is a memory, concentrated and distilled, of conversations he had had, perhaps even as a boy, with his "teacher," Diotima, the mysterious "priestess from Mantinea," whose magic had once saved Athens from a plague (201d). "Mantinea" itself we could translate, in accord with the etymology Socrates gives in the *Phaedrus* (244c), as the "land of prophecy and magic." It is the land of an archaic past, the morning in which the world was still young.

The poetic nature of philosophical recollection is, of course, paradoxical. The *Symposium* is presented as a competition between poetry (represented by Agathon) and philosophy (represented by Socrates). Dionysus, in the form of Alcibiades, is supposed to decide whose wisdom should prevail (175e). His choice of Socrates was an ominous one. Rationality rules the world to this very day. Yet philosophy, the mother of reason, is itself strangely allied with its competitor. This is the lesson of the *Symposium*, philosophy's most poetic work. Its introduction and conclusion read more like a novel than a work of philosophy. The speeches that make up its middle, speeches in honor of Eros, the god of poetry and love, also rely heavily on images. We move from a battlefield to scenes of lavish decadence, in which middle-aged pederasts chase young boys. In the most brutally graphic image of all, Zeus is depicted hacking apart the circle-men of old, who ever since hop about seeking sexual union with their lost halves. Even Socrates's speech is eerily pictorial. In part, this results from his free use of myth: the story, for example, of a noisy party of drunken deities and, just outside, Eros being conceived in the bushes. More significantly, though, the arrival of Beauty itself, despite its supposedly being "invisible" (the philosophical alternative to mythical representations), is so poetically presented that we can still speak of an "image." Beauty leaps out at us from the supercelestial clarity of what lies beyond all image.

That "beyond" awakens life. Immediately after the unveiling of Beauty, Alcibiades arrives on the scene. Decked out as Dionysus, crowned with ribbons and ivy, he is followed by a band of flute girls and drunken devotees. He lavishes praise on Socrates without really saying anything about his beliefs or ideas. Instead, he gives us a series of vivid images, including that of the philosopher wrestling naked with Alcibiades in the gymnasium—or embracing him as he lies naked in bed.

The most vivid image of all is the one that comes at the very end of the dialogue. After a long night that finally degenerates into wild partying, the remaining symposiasts lie asleep on the floor. Aristodemus wakes up and sees that Socrates is still seated on a couch, in conversation with Agathon and Aristophanes. As Aristodemus watches, the poets nod off and fall asleep. The young disciple is the only one left to witness the actual moment of transfiguration: Socrates, triumphant over his competitors, is crowned, not by Dionysus, but by Apollo. Behind him, the sun has started to rise. Light and beauty break forth upon the noble head. Only a Raphael could have done the picture justice.

With regard to the love affair between Alcibiades and Socrates, Kierkegaard's understanding generally prevails: the love was one-sided, with Alcibiades falsely seduced by Socrates's ironic remove. The philosopher himself felt little or nothing for the young man.[8] This is a view shared by Gregory Vlastos and Martha Nussbaum, as much as they otherwise differ in their understanding of Platonic Eros.[9] The same observation also forms the basis of Stanley Rosen's book-length commentary on the *Symposium*.[10] He interprets the work as presenting Plato's critique of his mentor. Plato is the erotic one; Socrates is ultimately to be criticized for possessing an unerotic nature.

There is, of course, evidence to support this view, starting with the fact that the young Socrates needed Diotima to awaken in him what everyone else arrives at easily and naturally: an appreciation for the power of erotic desire. Indeed, Diotima seems positively amused at how bewildered Socrates becomes when she delineates the world of animal passion (207c). She ends by expressing her doubt as to whether he can penetrate to the final vision of Beauty itself (210a). It has become a commonplace among Plato scholars to assume that Socrates in fact couldn't come so far, that Plato was using Diotima's skepticism to show where Socratic thought ends and his own thought begins. This accords once again with Aristotle's way of distinguishing his two predecessors (*Meta.* 1078b17–32). He portrays Socrates as caught up in the search for definitions, concerned only with what things are "in general," whereas Plato had a thirst for vision, positing a metaphysical world of separate and intuitable ideas somewhere above our own world, thus transforming reason into an erotic affair that departed completely from Socrates's cold (and utterly empty) logic. Plato's love affair with Dion has the ring of truth to it.[11] Socrates's affair with Alcibiades, however, seems contrived, an exercise in Socratic irony.

To a certain extent the *Symposium* does support this conclusion. Diotima first tries to get Socrates to understand that Eros is a daemon rather than a god—that is, a spirit that, instead of abiding in pure light and truth, mediates between heaven and earth, between god and man. The need for such a spirit arises once the divine is regarded philosophically as absolute perfection, goodness to the exclusion of all else. This "purified" conception of divinity, as the *Republic* makes clear (377b–382c), is incompatible with traditional Greek polytheism, which was based on the deification of cosmic powers, many of which (such as light and darkness) are caught up in interminable conflict. But none of this posed a problem for Socrates. The notion of a unified, self-consistent godhead he seemed to regard as expressing a simple command of reason. He seemed to have difficulty accepting that the metaphysical Absolute might require the retention of at least one cosmic spirit of the traditional kind: Eros. In the same way that Christianity regarded Christ as the necessary mediating link to a fully transcendent god, the newly emerging philosophical religion—an outgrowth of the post-Homeric mystery cults—required its mediating agent as well. Indeed, according to Gerhard Krüger, this was the actual purpose of the *Symposium*: to initiate a new Eros cult as a way of providing a religious solution to the "remoteness" of the transcendent god that thinkers like Xenophanes and Parmenides were gesturing toward.[12] If we accept the image of Socrates as a man of pure reason, we will have good reason to suspect that he must be the odd man out at such a party: why search for a mediating link between the human and the rational, if rationality itself adequately expresses the essence of what it means to be human? We start then with the suspicion that Socrates lacked even that measure of pagan sensibility that might help reconcile the divide between experience and metaphysics. If we reduce metaphysics simply to the assertion that reality itself is implicit reason, it would be Socrates, more than Plato, who will appear to be "lost" in metaphysics.

And indeed Socrates does express the typical mistake of those too enamored with logic. When told that Eros is not divine, he concludes that Diotima must be saying that he is evil (*Symp.* 201e). He forgets that real-world relations are relations of contrast and opposition rather than relations of formal contradiction. Whereas contradictory propositions exclude even the possibility of a middle option, contrary propositions frame a wide and open middle. Formally conceived, not-A can never be identical with A. Yet in the real world, the child (not adult) is forever growing to adulthood. The logic of form, which excludes the possibility of change, is not the logic of the world we live in. Socrates, the young man who spoke with Diotima, seems to have forgotten that he himself was ever a child.

But Diotima made him remember. The Socrates we encounter in the dialogue is after all capable of conjuring up the image of his young and naïve self in order to provide a parody of the speeches that preceded his own. Within the circle of speakers from Pausanius to Agathon, all were incapable of comprehending an Eros who was both ugly and beautiful. Typical Sophists, they addressed the problem of a complex deity by the simple device of making a distinction. After separating the "heavenly" Eros from the "earthly" one, they could go on, pretending that their own desires were pure to the degree that they could be distinguished from the desires of crude and vulgar people (180c–d). Socrates clearly intended to reclaim this excluded dimension (which Aristophanes alone had the courage to articulate and defend) by taking it back into his own understanding of Eros. Philosophy distinguishes itself from enlightened rationality through its awareness that nothing great is achieved without passion. This is not to say that it begins with a Faustian pact with the devil. Philosophy never goes that far; it never gives the devil the upper hand, never chooses intoxication without a sobriety that surpasses it. But it has sufficient knowledge of the devil to successfully transform the would-be master into a dutiful servant: Eros is daemonic power. Being precedes knowing.

"Until Diotima taught me better," Socrates confides, "I'd been telling her pretty much what Agathon has just been telling me—how Love was a great god, and how he was the love of what is beautiful" (201e). In other words, he did in fact remember that he was once a child. He too had once insisted that questions have to have clear and unambiguous answers. His tutelage at the feet of Diotima represents the disruption of his juvenile insistence on dogmatic simplicity through the violent encounter with Eros itself. He discovered that the world is far more awake and alive than he ever could have realized. Without question, this idea that the nonerotic Socrates is the adolescent Socrates flies in the face of our contemporary assumption that the sober view of the universe is the adult one. But a caution is in order: "adult" sobriety, work ethic conformity, represents little more than a retreat into the prosaic viewpoint of childhood induced by an inability to withstand the erotic revelations of adolescence. Adulthood need not reduce itself to the anxious demand that reality be always "less"—that is to say, more pliant and easy to manipulate—than the World Alive of the pantheist or the mystic. We can be taught better.

That Socrates himself learned his erotic lesson is indicated first by Diotima's description of Eros as an unattractive, shoeless vagrant, determined by great courage and devotion to knowledge (203d). This is none other than Socrates. The language of pregnancy and birth, moreover, far from representing an incursion of an element utterly foreign to the cerebral Socrates, corresponds instead to the very substance of the Socratic project: philosophy as "midwifery" (*Symp.* 209a–e; *Tht.* 149a–151d). These are points that are obvious enough that I assume they will be quickly conceded. I want, however, to add the more controversial assertion that Socrates's eroticism was not simply metaphorical and ethereal. We have to take seriously his claim in the *Phaedrus* that he carried within himself a monster (*Phdr.* 230a). To that we can add Diotima's plain assessment of his response to beautiful boys "whose aspect now so astounds you and makes you . . . ready to do without either food or drink if that were any way possible, and only gaze upon them and have their company" (*Symp.* 211d).[13]

Eros, Socrates said, is the "only thing" he really understands (*Symp.* 177d, 198d; *Lys.* 218b). Although we can ask whether he came to the end of his erotic quest, there is no reason for doubting that he had begun it: "every man should honour Love, as I myself do honour all love-matters with especial devotion, and exhort all other men to do the same; both now and always do I glorify Love's power and valour as far as I am able" (*Symp.* 212b). Diotima's skepticism about whether Socrates could go "all the way" has to apply to Plato just as thoroughly as to Socrates. One of the most important features of the philosophy of Eros is the understanding that one can never go all the way. The act of satisfying a desire is too deeply implicated in the process of awakening desire. Philosophical Eros belongs as decisively on this side of the fall from innocence as it yearns to reconstitute innocence anew. The passion for nature is always more than a natural passion.

At the same time, we should avoid assimilating the Socratic experience into modernity's sense of a goal that is infinitely far removed. A ceaseless and ultimately absurd form of striving is the result of Eros's becoming its own object. For Socrates, the goal of Eros is the vision of Beauty. In fact, on this account erotic fervor can be maintained only under the condition that the goal is achievable. Intercourse with the Absolute must constitute a genuine possibility.[14] It is, however, precisely within such union, not outside it, that the elusive "more" shows itself. Just as Dante still longed for the empyrean after he gained the paradise of the lunar sphere, so Beauty itself, by itself and for itself, leads us up the ladder of its manifold manifestations.

Even the empyrean must be understood as incorporating never-ending folds of erotic transcendencies: eternal life would sink into eternal stasis if this weren't the case. Divine vision must be a beginning as well as an end. The key to understanding pure beauty always lies in the appreciation of its elusiveness: perfect form has to be fully immanent in the concrete experience of beauty while at the same time withholding itself in absolute transcendence. Beauty is the epiphany of the beyond. Access to such beauty is afforded only on the side of sheer immanence: one must begin by being completely and *physically* captivated by the erotic allure of a specific human body (210a). Dante has his Beatrice; Socrates his Alcibiades. To attain full force, passion must begin from below, awakened by beauty in a form that is physical and near.

We must take Socrates at his own word. He loves Alcibiades but finds his jealousy hard to bear (213c). Even so, it is jealousy that confirms the intensity of the erotic engagement.[15] At the same time, Alcibiades could not have initiated the affair: his youth and good looks speak too strongly against this possibility. Socrates was the seducer. He intended to awaken the boy's passion. He could philosophize only in the face of life: a dead world gives rise to dead and mechanical thinking. Of course, Alcibiades could never be sure about this. He assumed that Socrates was teasing him. He warned everyone that Socrates is a Silenus-like figure who is really the opposite of what he pretends to be. He pretends to fall in love with good-looking people, but in fact doesn't care anything about them. He is contemptuous of their beauty and of everything they stand for. The wealth and good name they seek, he finds debasing, even despicable. And he likes to say that he is ignorant when instead he is filled with knowledge and self-control. He is a god masquerading as a simple man. He goes through his whole life "chaffing and making game of his fellow-men" (216e). It is a theme that echoes through Alcibiades's entire speech, which ends with him accusing Socrates in the name of all who have "found his way of loving so deceitful that he might rather be their favourite than their lover" (222b).

The charge is a grave one. Indeed, if it is true, it is utterly damning. Remarkably, it is almost universally believed. Kierkegaard built his whole conception of Socratic irony around this passage. Rosen and Nussbaum accept it without question. Vlastos, even while holding Socrates up as a model of virtue and sincerity, has no trouble believing that Alcibiades has put his finger on "the real Socrates." None of these modern commentators seem bothered by something Aristotle saw clearly: deception is deception, whether it is the desire to make one appear better than one is or whether it is Socrates pretending to be worse than he is (*Nic. Eth.* 1127a29–b31).[16]

Another possibility should be considered. Socratic irony may simply refer to the fact that, for those who haven't thought a great deal themselves, the proclamations of thinkers appear to be charged with paradox and untruth. In other words, Socrates may be telling the truth when he says he appreciates "good looks." Indeed, he may even have had an appreciation of wealth and a good name. More to the point, Socrates may have been sufficiently human to feel an inordinate passion for Alcibiades. There are several reasons for asserting this. First of all, we have the word of Socrates for it, not only in the *Symposium* but elsewhere as well (e.g., *Grg.* 481d). Second, the dramatic impact of Socrates's withstanding the temptation of a naked Alcibiades is brought home only under the assumption that the temptation was real. That he may have loved something else (goodness and beauty) so much that he was able to resist what was offered him provides evidence of a passion that has been redirected, not one that has been destroyed through starvation (see *Rep.* 485d for a description of how such sublimation is achieved).

Further, the Vlastos-Nussbaum assumption that Socrates got stuck somewhere toward the top of Diotima's ladder presupposes something that neither of them is prepared to take seriously: he could only have arrived at the top by starting at the bottom. One *must* begin by falling in love with "one particular body" (*Symp.* 210a).[17] And Socrates, himself, was a body sort of person. Not only was he strikingly ugly and distinctly on the portly side, but he was remarkably strong and healthy. When he was an old man, he continued to father children. When younger, he walked barefoot over ice and snow, which I regard as a sign of health and vigor, not (as Nussbaum has it) of "detachment." Shoeless feet are closer to the earth, not further from it. It is Eryximachus who was afraid of drinking wine—not Socrates (214a–b). To the response that Socrates was too rigidly sober ever to be affected by wine, one can counter that he was perhaps always already drunk, so that wine could never make a difference.[18]

If indeed an eroticist, why then did Socrates turn down Alcibiades's offer? The answer can be given in a word: because he so loved the boy. That Socrates made Alcibiades feel shame is proof of his love, not evidence of the contrary (216b). Alcibiades was completely infatuated with himself (218c). Anyone who truly loved him would have been required to cut through his hubris. Socrates was the only one who even tried. In fact, according to *Alcibiades* (1:103a–d), Socrates left him alone during the years when Alcibiades's sexual appeal was at its peak. Only after he grew bearded, so that his other suitors began to lose interest, did Socrates make his move. When he did so, he spoke in the name of love. It is for this reason that, instead of playing to the boy's vanity, he tried to make him realize his ignorance—his need to grow in virtue and wisdom. What Alcibiades was suggesting to Socrates ("I'll give you sex if you teach me about virtue") was simply wrong (*Symp.* 218c–d). As the Lysias speech in the *Phaedrus* (and to a certain extent the Pausanius speech in the *Symposium*) makes clear, this kind of contractual approach to love (which is regarded as the mark of enlightened sexuality in our own age) is appropriate only in the mouth of the nonlover, not the lover.

It is helpful once again to call Lysias's speech to mind—and Socrates's response to it. The argument that one should beware the excesses of a lover was an argument that Socrates could repeat—but only by placing it in the mouth of a cunning lover who was intent on disguising the intensity of his love. But even this pretense of the lover, rendered conventionally acceptable by the urgency of love, was enough to make Socrates hide his head in shame (*Phdr.* 237a). Alcibiades's charge that Socrates "pretends" to love is a more serious one than commentators have noticed. Without even the excuse of love, the lie is only shameful. The lover is the only one who has the right to proclaim his love. In the mouth of anyone else, such a proclamation would be not only dishonest but (given the extent of human vulnerability) evil and cruel.

What Alcibiades didn't realize was that there was nothing for which he could bargain. Socrates was already "teaching" him about virtue, to the degree that the lesson can be taught, whenever he tried to lure him out of his hubris—that is, whenever he treated him to elenctic refutation. Openness to the Good is the primary condition of its realization.[19] When Alcibiades demanded a positive account of just what constitutes goodness, he was asking for something Socrates could never give. Rather than displaying his "typical irony" (*Symp.* 218d), Socrates was being completely honest when he suggested that he himself had nothing to give—beyond, that is, exactly what he was already giving, an example of what it means to be virtuous in conjunction with a revelation of Alcibiades's great hubris.

Within that hubris lies, nonetheless, not only the explanation for Alcibiades's blindness but also the reason Socrates fell in love with him. Hölderlin (who once contemplated writing a play under the title *The Death of Socrates*) grasped the issue fully. To the question why Socrates loved Alcibiades, he provides the answer: "Who the deepest has thought loves what is most alive."[20] Life comes, however, with a shadow side, which only the living dead lack. As Plato has Socrates put it in book 5 of the *Republic*: "the best endowed souls become worse than the others under a bad education" (491e). The one with the highest potential for good is the one who is most vulnerable to the corrupting conditions of a democracy. Unless protected (as was Socrates) by poverty and an ugly face, a youth with a high potential for philosophy and leadership will almost inevitably be led astray by the pandering of the crowd (494b–e). Socrates clearly has Alcibiades in mind when he sums up the issue: "Such, my good friend, . . . is the destruction and corruption of *the most excellent nature*. . . . And it is from men of this type that those spring who do the greatest harm to communities and individuals, and the greatest good when the stream chances to be turned into that channel, but a small nature never does anything great to a man or a city" (495b; emphasis is mine).

Vlastos and Nussbaum are united in their belief that the *Symposium*'s conception of Eros only allows one to love actualized instances of goodness: mere mortals get left behind. But Socrates's love for Alcibiades reveals another possibility: what one loves in another person may be his or her *potential* for goodness. What one tries to provide the beloved, on the basis of that love, is help toward the actualization of that good. The ultimate proof that Socrates's love for Alcibiades was well placed is, sadly and ironically, the completeness of Alcibiades's failure. Only one with the potential for real greatness could have erred so completely and tragically.

Another mistake shared by Vlastos and Nussbaum is the implicit belief that, because Socrates did not have sex with Alcibiades that night, he never had sex with anyone but his wife. This would, of course, be entirely consistent with his virtue, but it cannot be inferred from the episode with Alcibiades. What it fails to recognize is that under the condition of Alcibiades's proposed "agreement"—and under the condition of Socrates's love for the young man—it would have been a catastrophic error to give in to this particular young man, to thereby gratify his monumental conceit, to confirm him in the belief that by sheer trickery he had come into the possession of something Socrates didn't have: a secret doctrine, a key to becoming even greater and more powerful than he already was. The only thing that Socrates could do was to grant Alcibiades the gift of recognizing his inadequacy and need. As Socrates points out in the *Lysis*, the true lover does not pamper his beloved but instead tries to "humble and check" him, nudging him constantly toward the acquisition of knowledge and virtue (210e).

Nussbaum relies much on Plutarch's glowing description of Alcibiades.[21] If he had been able to lend his support and leadership to the Sicilian expedition, which had been his idea in the first place, Athens might have usurped the position later attained by Rome, and Alcibiades would have been caesar. But, as is well known, he turned traitor instead, because—justifiably or not—he was accused of profaning the Mysteries and of vandalizing sacred images. His history of parading through the streets like Dionysus reborn awakened too many suspicions for his own good.

What Nussbaum and other admirers of Alcibiades should add to their Plutarch is an appreciation of the full force of Thucydides's report. In his Melian dialogue, he told the story of how Alcibiades, elected general the year before the *Symposium* was supposed to have taken place, not only violated the neutrality of Melos, but had its entire population executed or sold into slavery—all within the context of a purely Machiavellian maneuver.[22] To lament the fact that Socrates did not gratify the wishes of such a man is preposterous. All Athens joined to gratify his desires and to serve his pleasure and whim. Socrates alone tried to make the man suffer the shame of self-recognition. And why? To bring him, through an act of love, to virtue and truth. That such an attempt was unsuccessful is no proof that the attempt was never made. Even the love of Socrates is hard put to undo the harm inflicted by the pseudolove of the masses. The more one acknowledges the limit to what Socrates could have done for his beloved, the harder it is to defend Nussbaum's position.

Before proceeding onward, I want to take a quick inventory of how far we have come. Nussbaum follows Aristotle and very many others in regarding Socrates as essentially nonerotic. To her, he represents the disembodied, totally self-sufficient intellect that is in need of no one. Against this, I make essentially two claims. The first is that, if indeed he has achieved such a height, he had to get there from somewhere. Diotima's thesis is compelling. Only the urgencies of desire have the power and intensity that are necessary to carry one toward the ideal, which entails "self-sufficiency" only in its fulfillment. The view from the bottom is easier to depict. Socrates had a body, was drawn to beauty, and presumably experienced the various joys and pains of sexuality. Given how often Socrates is depicted as the lover of Alcibiades, we might as well assume that he was.

My second claim is that there is no justification for dismissing the claim Socrates makes to ignorance. Reason may have provided him with a very deep conviction that things separate can be brought together—that is, that unity is ontologically real. But it could never have yielded him any kind of final proof that reality is thus unified, that it is fundamentally good, and/or that it conforms to reason. This lack of proof was, moreover, a real problem for him. Socrates was not Kant. He did not insist that one should lead an ethical life even in the event that the world itself (and not simply the human community) is irrational. His conception of the Good was *eudaimonic*: what verifies the goodness of the Good is that it leads to happiness (if only in the world outside the cave). Indeed, when one considers that Kant himself, after completing his ethical writings, added the *Critique of Judgment* in an attempt to rescue at least a regulative notion of teleology, so necessary for providing morality with an incentive, one can conclude that not even Kant was consistently Kantian on this issue. The world must be good, either here or in the beyond, before we can be good. But its goodness stands in such sharp opposition to appearances that one is always left wondering how it could possibly be demonstrated.

Socrates constantly emphasized his fundamental ignorance because he was aware of the problem of demonstration. When he insisted on the truth of what he was arguing (e.g., *Grg.* 472b, 473b, 479e), he did so only in terms of what has been clarified and established by rational argumentation. He had no way of knowing that reality itself is at bottom rational (although he did know that it surpasses its phenomenal show). His insistence on his ignorance and need for knowledge were not self-consciously donned masks but the honest recognition of the desperation that anyone faces who has thought his way to the abyss. So too his habit of always looking for people with whom he could talk. Instead of regarding this as the higher mission of one endowed with the ability to see into and reform other people's souls,[23] it is once again better simply to take Socrates at his word: the man needed friends (*Lys.* 212a).

But what could a dangerous fool such as Alcibiades possibly have had to offer him? The answer has two very different sides. As a man of passion and intelligence, Alcibiades added to commonplace human ignorance an intensity that a philosopher could rightly regard as a "great gift." Thus, in the *Gorgias* Socrates described even Callicles as a "godsend": "I am certain that whenever you agree with the opinions held by my soul, then at last we have attained the actual truth" (487a).[24] The philosopher requires, in other words, discussion with someone who is both willing and capable of giving voice to the diabolical whisperings that almost everyone follows, but few have the courage to defend.[25]

To realize how central this is to Plato's whole vision, one might consider the significance of the fact that the *Republic* opens with Socrates's descent into the hellish port city of Piraeus, where he was intent on worshipping Bendis, a goddess of the underworld (327a).[26] Under one of her other names, she is Hecate, the goddess of sorcery and witchcraft, rank with the fumes of hell. Just as a man like Alcibiades stands in greater need of a critic than a flatterer, so philosophy requires its critic as well. Accommodating a devil's advocate is a step in the right direction. The worship of Bendis suggests that philosophy, the culmination of the path of moderation and balance, must ground itself by acknowledging its own origin in the volatility of radical questioning. The cloven hoof is not simply the challenge of what vacillates in uncertainty. The thoroughness with which Alcibiades, strong and capable as he was, surrendered himself to desire, provides evidence that desire masks a positive power of its own.

Bendis is not Hecate alone, but also a name for Persephone. The child of God, she had been dragged down to hell against her will. The desire that rages in Alcibiades is the desire of the god, caged within him, to be returned to the light. Human consciousness has behind it a long and brutal evolution through the immeasurable darkness of nature. It is a movement comprehensible only under the assumption that it rises out of the desire for something real and good that was lost and can one day be regained.

Socrates, we are often told, was chilly and aloof. As we have already been reminded, whereas Christ wept for Jerusalem, Socrates shed no tears for Athens.[27] Although he did go about conversing with everyone, he seemed more amused than horror-struck by their refusal to change their minds. When unable to convince them, Socrates simply shrugged his shoulders and went on his way. Behind this image stands a familiar critique of the Greek conception of friendship. True friendship, according to Aristotle (echoing themes from the *Lysis*), must take place among equals, for we can only love what is good (*Nic. Eth.*, bk. 10). Absolute love is found only in God and has that same God as its only adequate object (*Meta.*, bk. 12). Such love leads ultimately to solipsism. It took Christianity, we are often reminded, to transform Eros into agape so that love could be shared with the downtrodden.

I doubt, however, that the pagan-Christian opposition is this stark. Not only does it finally confine the consummately happy pagan to a life of solitude, but it also implies an internal limit to happiness itself, as if it is hemmed in by the fear that entanglement with the unhappy might be all it takes to disrupt one's semblance of calm. Socrates, I like to think, was not so fearful. It may be a token of strength that he had room for Alcibiades—whose potential for greatness lay hidden in the fever and insanity of his desire. This is not to say, however, that Socrates was motivated alone by an altruistic need to liberate caged Persephones. Painfully ostracized by his community, he was engaged in an honest, and consistently futile, search for friends (*Lys.* 211e–212a). Alcibiades's famous celebration of Socrates's uniqueness, that he is "unlike to anybody else" (*Symp.* 221c), has its dark side: such a man is lonely.

Nussbaum believes that Socrates was "protected" by his self-sufficiency. Instead of sympathizing with his predicament, she relegates him to his closed sphere and denies him the need for friends. This is presumably what allows any of us to justify our unremitting exclusion of the "arrogant." For myself, I find Socrates a more melancholy character, with a melancholy that is intimately woven into the brilliant splendor of his unforgivable happiness ("How dare he smile when we have withdrawn from him our collective favor!"). Luminosity of the twofold is one of the primary things we regard as beautiful. To uncover it in Socrates, the issue of his suffering has to be broached. Not only does it add depth to his notorious cheerfulness, but, more important in the present context, it renders plausible the idea that his concern for Alcibiades could have been genuine. In the *Lysis,* Socrates says there is nothing in the world he would value more than a true friend. He expresses envy of the boys around him who have so easily found their friends, "whereas I am so far from acquiring such a thing, that I do not even know in what way one person becomes a friend of another" (*Lys.* 212a). Socrates is not speaking "ironically" here, but stating the plain truth. One can reread the *Crito* to be reminded of how little a friend Socrates had even in his best friend. The man would have done anything for him—except what he was incapable of doing, which was to give him real understanding.

Socrates was a flirt because he was always in search of something (or someone). The only component of his irony that he could have intended as such is the element of exaggerated politeness that shines forth when he so consistently calls his interlocutors "dear" and "noble" and "wise"— but, above all, "my friend." The irony, when understood to be patronizing, may have a purpose: the various Callicleses and Alcibiadeses of the world will never improve themselves until they are sufficiently reminded of their worthlessness. Viewed from the perspective of Socrates, however, there is even in this irony no irony: he could only welcome that fictional Alcibiades who, instead of endeavoring to be caesar, might recognize a far better option and, seizing on it, become Socrates's friend. This does not mean that Alcibiades should have become more clever and insightful. All Socrates asks of him is that he join him in his quest. What he loved in

Alcibiades was the strength of his passions and his mental vision. What he deplored was the entanglement of that vision in the sphere of a narcissistic ego. In a gesture of true love, he offered the young man a way out. But when Alcibiades understood all that he would have to give up, then (like the rich young man in the Gospels) he responded with anger and refused the liberation.

In one regard, I agree with Nussbaum wholeheartedly. She understands the richness of the *Symposium* as a text and realizes how absurd it is to extract from it its metaphysical core, the short "ascent passage" of Diotima, christening it "Plato's doctrine of love" in order then to set it in opposition to the competing conceptions of Christianity, romanticism, or Freudian psychology. Freud was right to express enthusiasm about the speech of Aristophanes, which, after all, was part of Plato's composition. Its identification of Eros with sexuality is fully Freudian. The image of "halved circle men" seeking their other halves (191a–192e) also comes close to the romantic conception of love. Even the Christian doctrine is not wholly unanticipated: Phaedrus focuses on sacrifice and on lovers who descend even into hell to save their loved ones, themes that Diotima does not abandon entirely (207b, 208d).

Nussbaum falls into the very error she criticizes (detaching the doctrine of Platonic love from the rest of the *Symposium*) when she separates the various passions that are celebrated in these other speeches from her understanding of Socrates: his love, she maintains, was for the "universal" alone. It was dispassionate. To insist on this is to fail to see that Socrates must have *become* Socrates; in other words, he began where we all began— with his soul bound to the beauties of this earth—and if he somehow transcended these primary desires, he never could have abolished them. In some sense, he contains within himself the entire gallery of speakers: Phaedrus, Pausanius, Eryximachus, Aristophanes, Agathon, and Diotima (how else could he display such superb understanding of what his interlocutors have to say?).[28] Against the mediated view of Socrates, Nussbaum (in the *Fragility of Goodness*) regards him one-dimensionally as the prototype of those who find the contingencies of this world too painful to bear. Instead of loving what can disappoint (his friends, his family, his city), her Socrates has replaced it all with the abstract conception of the "lovable as such," fooling himself (for the purposes of therapy?) into believing that the abstract could live apart from the concrete things from which it is abstracted. Worshipping the universal, he remained oblivious to the entreaties of Alcibiades. He was "deaf," even worse, a "stone."[29] But this cool detachment is what attracted Alcibiades, who, yearning for release from his own stormy emotional life, sought refuge in Socrates's calm. Even more, however (at least according to Nussbaum), Alcibiades found Socrates a challenge: he wanted to "tear open" the self-enclosed sphere of Socrates's perfection and lay bare the "divine images" hidden inside the man.[30]

With the rape and destruction of Melos in mind, it is hard to ignore the violence of such language. For this reason, I do not share Nussbaum's sense that Alcibiades was "determined to care for Socrates's individuality."[31] One who profanes the Mysteries, smashes sacred objects, and destroys cities is not likely to have been one with a genuinely caring attitude. It is Alcibiades, not Socrates, who loves only himself. My objections to Nussbaum's interpretation go further. I can get at them by first conceding her point that Alcibiades wanted something from Socrates. Presumably his purpose was not just to tear him open. He wanted access to his secrets. In other words, he wanted something very similar to what contemporary scholars are searching for when they try so hard to determine Socrates's "true beliefs." He wanted to lay hold of those ideas that answer our deepest questions and that explain the philosopher's moral strength. When Nussbaum comments on the relevant passage, the one that depicts Alcibiades's "offer" and Socrates's response to it (*Symp.* 218c–e), she finds it necessary simply to omit the primary point. She indicates that Socrates refused Alcibiades's proposal because the young man displayed greed in seeking the philosopher's beauty, which so "surpassed" his own.[32] This would have been a rather odd refusal for Socrates to make, given that Diotima's ascent is based on exactly this kind of movement toward progressively greater beauties. A thirst for "more" is what he admired in Alcibiades, not what he tried to correct. The only thing Socrates criticizes in the passage Nussbaum highlights is the contractual language Alcibiades uses. Eros cannot unfold as an exchange. It does not proceed from "my beauty" to "your beauty" but from a "lack of beauty" to "beauty." It must fulfill itself, in other words, in a gift rather than a trade.

This is not, however, what I mean by suggesting that Nussbaum sets the main point of the passage aside. Her mistake is to pretend that Socrates really thought he possessed a "surpassing beauty." Socrates, who has transcended his Agathonian belief that humans can be gods, insists that he does not. Alcibiades's refusal to take him seriously on this point is echoed by nearly everyone, from Kierkegaard to Nussbaum. The result is that Alcibiades's anger appears to be justified. He was searching (just as he was "supposed" to) for the secret. Socrates disappointed him by saying he didn't have one to reveal. What was the young man to do?

If we assume, in contrast to the prevailing interpretations, that Socrates in fact loved Alcibiades, we discover ourselves with a remarkable proof of the legitimacy of Socrates's claim to ignorance. If he had been able to tell Alcibiades the secret of virtue, he would have done so. Alcibiades would then have become a very different kind of person from the one he in fact became. The impossibility of teaching virtue (*Meno* 89d–94e) is nowhere more convincingly shown than in Socrates's failure to teach Alcibiades.

At the same time, there was an important piece of knowledge Socrates had to share: the knowledge of ignorance itself. That knowledge, in combination with the positive example Socrates set, was all Alcibiades needed to turn his life around. In other words, if Alcibiades had been more open, he would have responded better to what Socrates wanted to share: his own openness. To call Socrates "deaf" is preposterous. His exuberant flow of words is only understandable if one assumes that he concentrated himself into a pure listening—and that he did so successfully. The "stability" that Alcibiades found in Socrates is not to be accounted for, as Nussbaum assumes, by supposing that Socrates had taken possession of an absolute form (either fictional or real). Instead, it is the same order of stability he displayed on the battlefield. Where danger loomed, he took his stand.

Although insanity would be the price of the disclosure that reality is in fact irrational and essentially evil, Socrates never gave up his inquiry (which is sustained by keeping open even that possibility). He made no leap of faith and he embraced no false absolutes. His steadfastness reflects the resoluteness of his questioning and nothing else. Socrates's mind was so far from being closed that it is the very paragon of openness. He was so far from being a stone that he endeavored constantly, with everyone he met (but above all with his favored ones, the "beauties"), to communicate his openness and to live the communal life of philosophy.

Callicles and Alcibiades sought to command reality in order to assure the availability of whatever their voracious appetites desired and to ward off death as long as possible. In contrast, Socrates sought only the power of knowledge. This does not mean that he became a "contemplative" and turned away from the world. Socrates conceived himself, after all, as Athens's only genuine statesman (*Grg.* 521d). True, he was not "political": he did not endeavor to control the city for the sake of himself and his friends. He was a "statesman" nonetheless, for he earnestly sought the one thing that can truly consolidate a human community: knowledge of the Good, of what makes life meaningful. The "passivity" of knowledge is inseparable from the positive affirmation of what appears to be radically contingent: recognizing the goodness of reality is the only thing that allows us to accord each and every thing its own sphere of being. This is what Socrates called *justice*. The love for what one cannot replace, body and life, family and friends, city and country, is not to be pursued through the eradication of what someone else will also deem irreplaceable. It is for the sake of justice that we are urged to find our beauty somewhere "beyond" the specific things we love. This beyond is not, however, something detached and aloof and apart, for its recognition supplies us with beautiful words and beautiful deeds. The beauty Socrates had in mind is, after all, the beauty of the world itself. Glimpsing that beauty is what prepares us for life in the world, not what removes us from it.

Nussbaum would have seen this for herself if she had been more sensitive to what really awakened Alcibiades's passion for the philosopher. Socrates's words, according to Alcibiades, have the ability to "entrance" and overwhelm (*Symp.* 215c–d). They made him "worse than the Corybantes" (215e). He compared them to the flute playing of Marsyas but found them purer and better. Under the surface, his words are filled with the "divine" (222a). They divide the initiates from the noninitiates (215c). Those who are open to the beauty of Socrates's speech are capable of working toward the vision of Beauty itself. Alcibiades was, in this sense, one of the initiates. He heard the power of the word and felt its enormous life and vitality. He himself could never have called Socrates a stone. He knew what force was required to create words that command the attention of everyone, whether of a "woman or a man or a youngster" (215d). The fact that he himself heard with such clarity and precision shows that he was in a position to move upward.

The rhapsodist Ion says reciting Homer "fills his eyes with tears and makes his heart leap" (*Ion* 535c). In so doing, he anticipates the precise words used by Alcibiades to describe the effect on him of Socrates's speeches (*Symp.* 215e).[33] In the *Ion* Socrates suggested that there is only one explanation for this kind of effect. A god pours his spirit into the Muses, who transfer it to the poets and anyone they touch. All are held together as by a magnetic attraction. The enthusiasm of the Corybantes has the same origin (*Ion* 536a–c). The theme of divine madness, which is explicitly discussed in the *Phaedrus,* is thus central to the *Symposium* as well. The assumption that Socrates is the master of self-control and self-sufficiency has to be radically revised. His Eros is more erotic than that. He "hears" his arguments, he told Crito, just as the Corybantes hear within themselves the music of the flute. Socrates is internally silent, but far from being deaf.

Alcibiades was cognizant of a daemonic Socrates who was nothing at all if not openness and ear. He resisted his allure because he felt he had too much at stake. He resisted because he was aware that the basic message was true: one should not neglect oneself to attend to the affairs of the city (*Symp.* 216a). But Alcibiades said that he shut his ears "as from the Sirens . . . for fear I should go on sitting beside him till old age was upon me" (216a). Like anyone today who has a share of wealth, power, or simply "important work" to do, he had too much at stake in the maintenance of a godless world to ever devote himself to the advent of a god. Philosophy is for children—or for the hopelessly alienated. Anyone with enough intelligence and insight to hear its message will be well enough occupied to reject it. Visible and attainable goods always win out over remote and invisible ones, regardless of how well the latter are described by enthusiasts. Alcibiades is the mirror in which we are supposed to recognize, if not ourselves, then our hopes and ambitions. If he needs "saving," perhaps we do as well.

The final proof of Socrates's capacity to love is given in the work of the one who was capable of receiving it: Plato. The Socrates who speaks in the dialogues is never anything like the disembodied voice of reason: he is, in the most decisive and positive sense imaginable, a *personality*. It is the achievement of authentic selfhood, not the dissolution of character in abstract universality, that Plato celebrates throughout the dialogues. To recognize this is to recognize the need to reinterpret the metaphysical core of the *Symposium*, the famous ascent passage of Diotima. There is no reason to accept without scrutiny the general consensus that it portrays a steady movement away from the individual toward the sphere of abstract universality. Diotima's first word of advice, that the initiate should fall in love with "one particular body," should be taken seriously.

If this seems hard to do, it is because the advice is so quickly withdrawn. We are told to forget the one who has captured our heart. One beautiful body, Diotima assures us, is not much different from another. We should turn our attention to all the beauties of the world, wherever they are to be found, to prepare ourselves for an encounter with the beauty of the soul. After finding a beautiful soul to love, we should then turn our attention to customs, laws, and institutions. From there we are urged to explore the beauties of science. Only when we are able to recognize the beauty of ideas and systematic constructions are we ready for the last step. A final act of abstraction places us before the splendor of beauty itself, shorn of all particularity, totally void of content. In love with the universal, our hearts will never again be broken by the loss of what is finite.

This, at any rate, is the standard reading of the ascent passage. What happens when we endeavor to be more attentive? Although the passage seems to represent a steady movement from the particular to the universal, a closer look shows that there are important twists and turns. Moving from an infatuation with one person's body to an appreciation of beautiful bodies in general certainly represents a movement away from the individual, but discovering a beautiful soul reverses the direction back to the individual. At that point, the movement seems to lead in both directions at once. We are not asked to abandon the beautiful soul for the sake of a gregarious interaction with a multiplicity of such souls. Instead, we are directed toward customs, laws, and institutions—that is, toward all that has helped form the beauty of that one beautiful soul. The same point can also be made about the next two stages of the ascent. Human laws reflect—and in some sense are grounded in—the laws and harmonies of nature, as is the individual. The movement outward is thus simultaneously a movement inward. The last step of all makes this completely clear: it is philosophical recollection, not the evidence of our eyes and ears, that leads us to the threshold of beauty itself. If we are still to speak of experience, we will do so only in terms of what is disclosed to us through an inner sense.[34] The reason for this is simple: if beauty is "not anywhere in another thing" and is genuinely "by itself and with itself" alone (211a–b),[35] then it can in no way stand apart from the self that glimpses it. The movement "upward and away" has rebounded back into our own particularity. It is the movement of the soul.

The movement has its correlate. The beauty that love clings to must itself have roots and depth. Once the sea of passion has been stirred within an individual, of itself it will seek the more genuine beauty that arises from the depths of another's "within." This is what necessitates the turn toward the soul. Because the interiority of the body is irrevocably hidden, bodies are able to meet only along surfaces. The frenzy of sexuality, so superbly depicted by Aristophanes, has its roots in the exasperating impossibility of overcoming this condition. Even the deepest penetration leaves one still stranded somewhere on the outside. Only when the heart is captured, not by a body but by another soul, does the possibility of true love begin.

The meeting of souls is also the point where the enslavement of physical infatuation begins to give way to a form of attachment that is freer: the soul of the other can join our own soul in the adventure of self-transcendence and growth. Taking up a common object of concern ("how are we to raise our children?") reflects a greater dimension of love than the obsession of one partner for the other. The former is as liberating as the latter is suffocating. Indeed, soul mates face no ultimate limit to their love. As Aristotle declared in *On the Soul*, "the soul is in a way all things," by which he means that it has the potential to unite with anything and everything.[36] To love a beautiful soul is to prepare for the actual ascent. Friendship with another person does not fall outside the quest for unity. The Ultimate One is never the "night in which all cows are black,"[37] but the unity in which any conceivable consciousness can converge, internally rather than externally (as in conversation), with any other consciousness. In this connection the passage (*Symp.* 209b–e) that immediately precedes the ascent passage is tremendously helpful: the sphere of culture unfolds—in its entirety—as a confirmation of friendship and mutual love. Diotima never demands that the beautiful soul be abandoned. Indeed, even the preliminary love, the one that has the body as its object, may not have to be abandoned. It is possible that one has chanced on someone who is not only physically beautiful but "who in their souls still more than their bodies conceive those things which are proper for the soul to conceive and bring forth" (209a).

It is important to realize (in opposition to the view of Nussbaum and others) that the purpose of making the ascent is not to escape the possibility of pain. In fact, the person who clings to adolescent love (the infatuation with the appearance of beauty) is the one who is motivated by the fear of pain, not the person who, recognizing that there are "many beautiful bodies," is capable of carrying through with a painful break. It is Alcibiades, not Socrates, who makes the hazardous suggestion (in an aside to Agathon) that one should be able to live life without experiencing pain (222b). The willingness to endure pain (Socrates walking barefoot in the snow) is the hidden but necessary condition of all erotic ascent. Such ascent is not the soul's achievement of radical autonomy through its realization of its own ultimate desire but, quite the contrary, its final release from the tyranny of such desire. The full disclosure of Beauty manifests itself only to the soul that has been carried (by desire) beyond desire. Ascent does not encapsulate and isolate the self in the sphere of an impenetrable Absolute; instead it strips the self of every form of encapsulation so that, thus purified, it extends outward to meet what is most inner in all of us.

The emptiness of the Beautiful is not the emptiness of conceptual abstraction, for it contains within it everything that exists. This is true on at least two levels. First of all, everything that exists has been born out of the craving for the Beautiful and is contained within it—in very much the same way that the universe is contained within the ultimate "beyond." The relationship to beauty is, however, at the same time far more intimate. By virtue of not appearing "in the guise of a face or of hands or any other portion of the body, nor as a particular description or piece of knowledge" (211a), the Beautiful attains the purity that enables it to actually enter into the life of the existent. Every instance of organic unity derives its unity from the Beautiful itself. The "beyond" is itself the deepest soul "within." Diotima's ultimate determination of the Beautiful is that it is "in itself and by itself" (211b). This "by itselfness" has usually been understood in terms of a radical separation from the physical. If one recalls, however, an instance in which one has actually been affected by the sight of something profoundly beautiful—a sunset, a painting of Cezanne, the face of a woman—one realizes that abstraction from the physical is hardly what is at issue. The decisive point is simply this: what is beautiful holds itself apart from all that surrounds it. It stands, in a very radical and decisive way, "by itself." Nothing can explain it, for nothing can reduce it to the elements that surround it. As she smiles, all else disappears.

And in this disappearance, time fulfills itself. In that breath-taking moment when Beauty steps forth in the form of Alcibiades, all else fades into the background. The Divine is there—and there in Alcibiades— whether or not Socrates ever succeeds in getting the young man to live up to its command. The competition of those with poorer vision, the flatterers, who are convinced that the beauty is simply worldly adornment, makes Socrates's task difficult, but never impossible. What the many proclaim is always the same: that the project of living "beyond" the world and its seductions is life-denying flight into the chilly distance of abstraction. It is a proclamation that bespeaks a kind of stunted sensibility that obscures the fact that such a beyond manifests itself fully within this life. Acts of noble courage—and works of beauty and originality—are seldom recognized when they are encountered. And even when they are recognized, they can fill us, as they filled Alcibiades, with such a strong sense of shame that we turn our heads downward and let pass the offer of awakening.

5

Love and Philosophy

In philosophy, love is everything, for what else is philosophy but the attempt (rendered so seemingly impossible by the great monstrosity of evil) to learn how to love reality itself? Although "beliefs" form the focus of so much attention in contemporary philosophy, in fact they are of interest only insofar as they serve the task of love. The ultimate Socratic belief is that reality itself is good. Yet this belief is at once the most central, most vulnerable, and most questionable. It represents not a piece of knowledge Socrates has but one he is looking for—with all the urgency that sends the lover looking for the beloved.

Although the goodness of reality itself remains hidden from the world, there are yet beings that, enshrouded in beauty, offer the promise that goodness can be realized. Socrates's capacity for love was genuine and the dialogues of Plato are the proof that his love bore fruit. But unless we are to regard someone like Theaetetus (who would have been about Plato's own age) as a mask for Plato, there is no text we can rely on that directly portrays Socrates's love for his successor. This is why I now shift my focus to Plato's love for Socrates, apparent in everything he wrote.

If Socrates was such a strange and unique man, what did Plato—whose obsession is with universal truth—see in him? With this question before us, let us once again ask why, in Diotima's ascent passage, the initiate, after being exposed to the full force of physical desire, was asked to turn outward to discover how many beautiful faces there are in the world. This act of disengagement is not necessarily an anticipation of other similar acts that are to follow. It may instead be regarded as a preparation for finding someone—someone in particular—who, more truly beautiful, is more worthy of our love. The beautiful body, unlike the beautiful soul, may be tinsel and glitter, beauty without substance, beauty without an inside.

One may then, on the basis of appearance alone, choose a totally unsuitable object of love. Besides being a truism, this is a hard lesson to learn, especially because beauty is more thoroughly released into the world of appearances than are goodness and truth. What I mean by this is straightforward. Though hypocrites and liars are neither good nor true, a woman who paints her face well may achieve a genuine beauty that would have been absent without the artwork.[1] Even so, that beauty in appearance carries with it no guarantee of the still fuller beauty that also would step into appearance, if she, for instance, displayed harmony between her appearance and her conduct, if she were a woman of true charm and grace. In that case, she would have to be free of the problem that plagues Hollywood, the embarrassing disclosure that someone who is physically well-proportioned may not know at all "how to act." This holds as well for whatever we deem beautiful. A flower, for instance, is not beautiful on its surface alone, for it is genuinely beautiful only to the degree that it shows forth its essence.[2] Similarly, a work of art must go deeper than the thickness of paint on a canvas. It is beautiful only if it succeeds in bringing to light something characteristic (yet inexpressible) within the artist—in immediate conjunction with the characteristic truth of what the artwork displays from its own autonomous field.[3]

It is for this very reason, however (and not so that he can learn the cruel art of abandoning the particular), that the initiate (for Diotima always a male) is referred to a beautiful body in the first place. He has to learn how to act. To do so, he must learn to love, not with his mind alone, but with his entire self. His movements must be governed not by general principles (the commands of some external director) but by Eros itself, rooted as deeply as possible in the nerves and sinews of his own flesh. To awaken the inner life of the body, the encounter with the beauty of someone else's body is indispensable. As Eryximachus had pointed out, love begins already in the preconscious, indeed, in the preanimate, layers of nature (*Symp.* 186a). Authentic love is deeply grounded. A life grounded in such love is touched and directed less by verbal commands than by the music and harmony of nature itself (187c).

Eros, we can say, is earth torn open to greet the sky. As such, an erotic ascent must have its ground in the flesh. The beauty that love clings to must itself have roots and depth. John Sallis, in a series of books published after *Being and Logos*, traces out the descent of Eros, its clinging to the darkness of the sensual and the particular, as a call to an ever-renewed beginning—one rendered necessary by the inexhaustible nature of the world that stands before us, the world we are trying to understand and, indeed, ultimately to love.[4] What is torn open here is the wellspring of culture, first in the form of seductive speech, words that celebrate the object of our erotic desire, but finally in the form of a poetic celebration of the entire interplay of natural forces, from the awesome power of the lightning bolt to the alluring charm of spring's first blossoms.

As the beautiful soul is impelled upward to "customs and laws," it is slowly relieved of the burden of its particularity, discovering again and again that the monstrosity of its strange eruption is mitigated by every-thing that makes it belong to a world. Consider briefly an ascent motif from an entirely different tradition that is supposed to constitute the "un-bridgeable divide" between Jerusalem and Athens. The salvation history of the Jews is portrayed as beginning in Egypt. This represents the indis-pensable grounding that also starts with sensual attachment. Even the Jews must have their pagan escapade. From Egypt, salvation history moves toward progressively higher attachments, first to the Promised Land, and then to the holy cities of Jerusalem and Zion. As a land "flowing with milk and honey," the Promised Land represents the restoration of the sensu-ous condition that once enslaved a people.

The Biblical narrative has its correlate in the Diotima speech. The one with a beautiful soul must also have at least a spark of sensual allure (*Symp.* 210b–c). The way upward does not involve anything as simplistic as an abandonment of one's sexuality, although it does in fact promise liberation from sexual enslavement. "Egypt" represents not sensuality as such, but enslavement to it. The reality of that enslavement is so brutal and intense that it requires a tremendous effort—and obedience to ex-acting commands—to become free. Between Egypt and the Promised Land, while engaged in the long and tortuous trek through the desert, the Jews received their laws. The point of the law was to discipline a people who would gladly have returned to Egypt at any time. Plato's ref-erence to "customs and laws" has to be read with an appreciation of the tremendous difficulty of "forming" the beautiful soul by redirect-ing its instinctual desires. The hidden moment in Diotima's words, what we have to "carefully" attend, is the history of the pain involved in any genuine process of learning. After experiencing the joys of first love, in which mighty Eros tears apart the veil of innocence, one has to be taken through the desert, so that the awakened monster might be subdued. Nor is the process ever one that is simply "over." In the form of Baal, the Jews encountered Egypt even in the Promised Land. "No one can be a saint," Christians used to say, "who stands above temptation." Socrates flirted with pretty boys until the end of his life (*Phd.* 89b).

To highlight erotic desire in Socrates and thereby answer the old Aristotelian critique of Socratic intellectualism was the primary purpose of chapter 2. By keeping his focus on "beliefs," Vlastos missed Socrates himself, a man drawn in every way to Alcibiades. Erotic attraction to youth makes the ascent difficult—but it is also what makes it possible. The force of law is required to check the force of desire. The love that is involved in the discussion of good political and social institutions is the love for what we, together with our friends, can become. As Alcibiades bemoaned, how-ever, it involves hardships and sacrifices—but only for those well enough endowed to actually have something to sacrifice. In the *Gorgias*, this observation that humans are reluctant to sacrifice what they have leads to a prediction of Socrates's tragic fate. Because he alone is the true statesman (concerning himself with what people need rather than what they want), he will be put to death—after a trial that will be "like a doctor prosecuted by a cook before a jury of children" (521e). Good medicine does not always taste good. Under such circumstances the one who embodies true love will not be easy to recognize. The prevailing view of contemporary scholars that the Diotima speech proves that Plato (or Socrates) was willing to abandon his fellow human being for the sake of a more "reliable" love for the Absolute suggests that nothing has changed. Only those who themselves lack the desire to make the climb could fail to recognize that the very presence of the ladder proves the love of the one who put it there. Self-satisfaction remains now, as always, the greatest barrier to advancement: "The man who does not feel himself defective has no desire for that whereof he feels no defect" (*Symp.* 204a).

Desire itself is the instrument of the ascent. Because desire must be given before it can be educated, its political formation remains secondary. As Diotima makes clear (209e–210a), the creation of laws, presumably even good ones, takes place well before the approach to the highest Mystery. The perfection of the state does not resolve the problem of existence. The mere survival of a nation, the physical and cultural propagation of the species, is a lofty enough goal to engender laws and institutions that set limits to the pursuit of desire. What is good for one's community should not, however, be confused with the highest good, for communities can thrive whether or not their members achieve true happiness. Indeed, the immortality of the species requires that the erotic energy of its members must serve the task of reproduction (both biological and cultural). Where nature miscarries in its ultimate attempt to give birth to its own formative principle, it commemorates its failures by permitting them to duplicate themselves before going into the death they deserve. Noneternal form "eternalizes" itself through the mechanism of erotic reproduction. This is the "eternal recurrence" of Nietzsche—or the "never-ending cycle of rebirth" referred to by the Hindus and Buddhists. Where survival is the only issue, a hellish kind of absurdity lurks, unrecognized, just below the surface. Neither political order nor "prosperity" do anything to modify such absurdity. The goal of life has to be sought higher.

Breaking through to the highest Mystery requires a deeper grounding than can be attained through even the best institutions. This is shown by a remark in the *Republic* that had as its primary intent the justification of Socrates's apolitical stance. After the famous assertion that those who are educated to an understanding of the Good must be forced to return to "the cave" in order to free others, a qualification is immediately added: "men of similar quality who spring up in other cities should not share in the labors there. They grow up spontaneously from no volition of the government in the several states, and it is justice that the self-grown, indebted to none for its breeding, should not be zealous either to pay to anyone the price of its nurture" (520a–b). The "beauty of institutions" is an ideal one only. Socrates devotes himself to the articulation of this ideal out of a genuine love for his fellow man. His own nurture, however, has taken place, in very essential respects, outside and apart from the state. His only teachers are his daemon, his conscience, and his sense of urgency and mission. In the *Symposium*, these forces are concentrated into the idea of Eros—as personified in Diotima. The roots of Eros lie deep in nature (the speech of Eryximachus forms the philosophical background of the entire Diotima speech). The rhythm and harmony of nature itself, its implicit *music*, is the real principle of the soul's formation. Thus, Socrates's own allure, his own beauty and goodness, are not the result of a universality imposed on him from above. Instead, his erotic qualities have welled up out of the hidden depths of his embodied and earth-bound self. Socrates's daemonic formation is the source of his remarkable uniqueness, which is what Plato obviously loved. The dialogues do not give honor to a Socrates who, by subordinating himself to universal structures, has become cleansed of character and personality. Instead, the dialogues focus (lovingly) on what is characteristic in Socrates, his passion for the truth, his almost eerie otherness, his unquestionable authenticity.

It is for this reason that Plato's love for Socrates (and thus the literary project of the dialogues) assumes a priority over his work in the Academy.[5] Plato recognizes the superiority of virtue (and insight) that is attained despite, rather than because of, one's discursively mediated education. This is a crucial point, for it will otherwise appear that the Academy, symbolizing the desire to teach, is the abyss that separates Plato from Socrates (who always insisted that he had no "teachings" to share). If Plato teaches, therefore, it is with full knowledge that he has chosen the second-best path. This is dramatically demonstrated by the story that comes at the very end of the *Republic*, when Plato's Socrates depicts the fate of souls who were to choose new lives. They had all just gone through a thousand years of either reward or punishment for lives lived long ago. The worst choice of all, the life of a tyrant, was the very first choice that was made. Having "the most options to choose from" offered no help to the poor soul who chose simply what appeared to be the biggest and shiniest form he saw. Nor did it help that he happened to be a soul who had just come down from heaven, "a man who had lived in a well-ordered polity in his former existence, participating in virtue by habit and not by philosophy" (619c). In fact, most of the bad choices were made by those who had come down from heaven, "inasmuch as they were unexercised in suffering," whereas the souls coming up from the belly of the earth, where they had experienced horrible sufferings, fared much better (619d). The very last soul to make a choice, despite his severely reduced options, did better than anyone else. It was, in fact, the soul of Odysseus, who, having suffered much in both his own life and during his thousand years in the underworld, chose the soul of "an ordinary citizen who minds his own business" (620c).

The reference to Socrates himself is in my mind clear. The mystery of Socrates's education lies buried deep within the past of his own preexistence. Odysseus reborn, he had behind him the only education that leads to genuine goodness: a long path of pain and suffering. The man who had suffered it all emerged purified, with neither fear nor pretension. His soul, sufficiently humbled, was prepared to reach upward toward the light. Having learned the hard way the futility of attachments, he became fully engaged in the project of self-transcendence, slowly transforming himself into the medium of the sublime indifference of beauty itself. For this, he was rewarded with the friendship of the gods (*Symp.* 212a). He had achieved detachment—but not in the sense of being delivered of every form of care and concern. What he was free from was slavish attachment. What he was freed into was the possibility of a love that is free, in the double sense that it is freely given and freely received. Socrates's own ascent has to be understood in terms of a kind of prodigal son motif.[6]

The way Socrates evinced the reality of the love he himself felt was through his own noncoerced return to the cave. Only one who has suffered—and who somehow escapes the spirit of *ressentiment*—feels compassion. The freedom with which Socrates entered into his conversations with those around him stands in contrast to the philosophical guardians in the *Republic* who have to be forced to interrupt their philosophical studies in order to engage themselves in the governance of the state (519c–520e). In his freely chosen activity as a questioner, a gadfly, and (in a radically alternative sense of the word) a teacher, Socrates lived out his own intense awareness of how difficult it is to live a virtuous life. The sensitivity he derived from his own suffering was combined with the confidence of one who has discovered that suffering can be overcome. This double relation shows itself in the fact that Socrates was not the kind of teacher who betrayed his own insecurity by trying, with the help of doctrines and "answers," to shield others from the pain of their own paths. He was instead the teacher who did not teach, the philosophical midwife who delivered others into the educational process of their own suffering, until they became able to give birth to the light that they carried, unrecognized, hidden within their own darkness. Alcibiades revealed the tendency to reject such baptism by fire. Plato was the one who, by bringing forth his own light, gave testimony to the love owed the true teacher, who, instead of teaching, allows learning to take place.

It may be helpful to reinforce the reminder that the ascent passage has to be read in conjunction with the complete speech of Diotima and with all the speeches that precede it. Phaedrus's allusions to an Eros as old as the cosmos itself (and in fact the principle of its generation) and to the themes of self-sacrifice and descent into hell are, as I've already pointed out, reappropriated into the fabric of Diotima's speech. The same holds for Aristophanes's myth of severed bodies and a cataclysmic fall. Recovery of forgotten light presupposes a fall just as much as the frantic search for one's "lost half." Eros descends into the world (as the child of Poverty) in the same moment as the Divine is elevated above it. Diotima's insistence that Eros is not divine is hard for Socrates to accept, because, spanning the full and awful divide between heaven and hell, it embodies all the power and force of nature and of human spirit as well. The thesis that Eros is not divine is thus predicated on a new understanding of divinity as extending beyond natural force and power. The paradox is that this elevation of the conception of divinity, while reducing Eros to a daemonic status, simultaneously elevates him to a dignity and importance he had never previously possessed. As Eryximachus points out at the beginning of the dialogue (*Symp.* 177b), Eros has never before been the subject of a poet's praise. Only when the Divine is fathomed in its awesome sublimity does the relation to the Divine disclose its erotic fervor. What is humbled is thus simultaneously elevated.

An actual event in the history of consciousness stands behind the Platonic doctrine of Eros. The dialectic that elevates the humble is not something uniquely Christian, for it is grounded in the nature of reality itself. There is mud at the root of anything that blossoms. The image of the seed that "dies in the earth" is universal, binding Jesus Christ not only with Persephone but with religion as such. The image (and this is to be found within paganism itself) conveys the epochal shift from the deification of nature to the possibility of its transcendence, the shift from paganism to the religions of salvation. Nature, the sphere of unending and seemingly insatiable lust and longing, the desire for life and more life, regardless of its pains (207b), is granted the possibility of putting an end to the insanity of its own eternal recurrence.

But salvation is not suicide. The need for salvation involves something different from the cynicism of a Schopenhauer, according to which our real dilemma is that the youthful desire for sex outweighs the reflective realization that arrives always too late: the realization that the pain of life is just not worth the fleeting moments of pleasure that keep the wheel turning. Were this the dilemma, salvation would involve simple escape, universal sterilization perhaps. True salvation, however, is the recognition that such escape is not even an option: what springs forth from nature is condemned to recurrence. Suffering itself has to be redeemed. But for suffering to be redeemed, it must demonstrate its capacity to become the vehicle of what is good.

It is of utmost importance that Diotima uses the language of the mystery cults (210a)—and that the language recurs throughout the speech of Alcibiades. The caesura in the middle of the Diotima speech is the key to the entire *Symposium.* It is based on the distinction (209d) between lower mysteries that are readily accessible to Socrates (and could make him as great as Homer or Hesiod!) and higher mysteries that hold a far greater promise (but require correspondingly more effort to comprehend).[7] On the one side of the caesura falls not only the longest portion of the Diotima speech but the speech of every symposiast, from Phaedrus to Agathon, who spoke before Socrates. Each of them was visibly motivated by the desire that Diotima places at the center of the lower mystery: the desire for vicarious immortality, to be attained through one's children or one's words or actions. In each speech, the speaker endeavors to project the best possible image of *himself.* The "Eros" honored is consistently nothing but the glorified image of the speaker in question. Diotima maintains that this is not only natural but something very good. Poets, motivated by the desire for fame, are the begetters of "wisdom [*phronēsis*] and virtue in general" (209a). Homer and Hesiod, even though they were responsible for the "nonelevated" conception of divinity that Socrates set out to overcome, are not the victims of a heavy-handed poetry critique (such as we find in the *Republic*). In the *Symposium* we find instead something that is much more subtle, much more profound, and much more interesting.

Socrates himself delivers (in the name of Diotima) the "defense of poetry" that, according to the *Republic,* every poet or "lover of poetry" should strive to make (607d). But the rehabilitated form of poetry is fundamentally different from the poetry that precedes it. In other words, Socrates stands on the far side of Diotima's caesura. Instead of honoring himself in his speech, he honors Diotima, his teacher, his *daimon.* By removing himself from the center stage, Socrates is the first truly to honor Eros. The condition for being able to do this is that he be freed from the most common form of erotic compulsion, the necessity of projecting and affirming an image of himself.

By coming to the realization that there is no longer a need to "eternalize" the finite, Socrates shows that he had in fact penetrated the "highest Mystery."[8] Absolute Beauty may be unknowable to us mortals, but its unknowable nature—which amounts to our own erotic constitution—is thoroughly knowable. This is why Socrates so often insisted that he knew the "truth" about Eros (177e, 198d, 199a–b, 201c). To know this truth is (among other things) to know the vanity and futility of all attempts at "self-immortalization." For man's deepest desire, previously hidden, is not that he be bound forever into the world but that he be released from it. The same can be said with regard to the self: a profound enough realization of its erotic nature will lead us to the attempt, not to immortalize it (at least as it stands), but to rise beyond it. The new project is one of constant self-transcendence.

The mystery cults disclose the secret behind all previous Greek religion, indeed, all paganism as such: the manifold beauties of mythology (Diotima's "lower mysteries") presuppose the descent of a yet "higher beauty." Persephone, the spirit of beauty divine, had been pulled down into Hades. The tremendously complex mythologies that underlay every culture were refractions of one and the same light, entangled now in darkness. Her release, which amounted to the end of the mythological process (the recognition that all gods are faces of one God), is what the cults set out to celebrate. This is why their ultimate secret seems to have been that the reign of Zeus will prove to be as limited as the reigns of Uranus and Kronos before him: a Dionysus yet to come, one born out of the womb of a mortal woman, will one day come to establish a new order.[9] Zeus binds within himself the whole polytheistic order. His death and resurrection in the form of a future God signifies the necessity that human beings undergo a corresponding transformation. The human spirit has been granted, after all, a higher goal to strive toward (Persephone resurrected). At the same time, it has to come to terms with the correspondingly greater impoverishment of the world itself that accompanies the disclosure of the absurdity of "eternal recurrence." As Heaven was revealed above the heavens (compare the prologue to Parmenides's poem on Being), the earth sank down toward Hades.

The image of the cave is in fact the correlate of the doctrine of Eros. Its import extends far beyond the subject matter of the *Republic*. From Samothrace to Judea (the resurrection of Lazarus!) to India and Tibet, mystical initiates were being buried under the earth as the prelude to a dramatic "liberation." What the god has undergone, we ourselves have to undergo. The pagan attention to the sublimity of natural forces and the power of beautiful appearances led, of itself, to a dramatic turn toward the transcendent "beyond." The sheer love of life culminated in the love of death as its hidden but real condition. Mystery religion gave birth not only to philosophy but to the sublimity of Aeschylus and Sophocles. Eros made his appearance as the rescuing deity first when the world itself was understood in its finitude and insufficiency. Thus, the wisdom of Silenus that Nietzsche refers to in the *Birth of Tragedy*: "The best of all things is something entirely out of your grasp: not to be born, not to *be*, to be *nothing*. But the second best thing for you—to die as soon as possible."[10] It is in this context, the most important turning point in the history of religion, that Plato's doctrine reveals its full meaning. Generations of Indian yogis, using ascetic and tantric means to redirect their erotic impulse, form—together with legions of Corybantists and Pythagoreans—the historical precursors of the ascent that Diotima had in mind.

Socrates-Odysseus, humbled by a thousand years of labor somewhere deep in the belly of the earth (the penalty paid for Odysseus's "cunning"), is a far different Socrates from the arrogant ironist we are usually presented with. Plato does not repeat Alcibiades's mistake of imagining divinity as something that Socrates commanded within himself. His Socrates is above all a human being, living into death, never certain of what lies beyond appearances. What makes him a consummate human being is the humility with which he lives within his humanity, renouncing the will to order and control everything around him. Socratic wisdom, the knowledge of ignorance, can be understood with the help of a New Testament gloss: "You have shown to the unlearned what you have hidden from the wise and learned" (Matt. 11:25). These "wise and learned," the *sophoi kai sunetoi*, are essentially the same as the Sophists whom Socrates combated. Satisfied with the power of human intelligence, its capacity for securing existence and fulfilling desires, they are the ones who most persistently combat the idea that our true desire remains unfulfilled. They resist, above all else, any deeper understanding that would justify trading comfort for happiness—and power for beauty.

The celebration of disempowerment is of course highly paradoxical. The first problem is that one is always tempted to question the authenticity of humility. After all, what was asserted with regard to the other symposiasts, that they each sculpted Eros in accord with their own image, could be said about Socrates as well. Commentators have always pointed out that the picture of Eros that Diotima presents, that he is "poor," "hard and parched, shoeless and homeless" (*Symp.* 203d), is one that seems to have been crafted in the image of Socrates. There thus seem to be grounds to reject my previous suggestion that the (prephilosophical) poet seeks fame while the philosopher-poet, indifferent to a good that depends so much on the opinion of other people, devotes himself purely to the pursuit of truth. Indeed, Socrates did ultimately go on to achieve the same kind of "immortality" that Homer attained. To what may appear to be his greatest act of humility, his acceptance of his execution, one could apply the same words that Diotima used with regard to the deaths of Alcestis and Achilles: "Do you suppose they ever would have died in this manner, if they had not expected to win 'a deathless memory for valour' which now we keep?" (208d).

Because this suspicion turns on the possibility of a "hidden motive" (which, as Kant pointed out, one can never definitively dismiss), one can do little more than suggest an alternative: instead of regarding the image of Eros as crafted in the image of Socrates, one can also reverse the relationship and suggest that Socrates, through an act of self-transformation (more or less the ascent that Diotima depicted), succeeded in sculpting himself in accord with the image of Eros. Those who are poor because they lack the strength and intelligence to break out of their poverty may as a matter of fact decide to celebrate that very poverty as a virtue. If, as Nietzsche pointed out,[11] they are able to do this in sufficient numbers, then it may even be possible for them to have a profound impact on the generalized conception of morality. In such a situation, to appear "good" may require identification with the oppressed (though preferably from the vantage point of middle-class comfort). The case of Socrates, however, is something completely different. It has nothing to do with the dynamics of self-justification or with hypocrisy. Socrates could have pursued a career as a travelling Sophist if he had so chosen. His poverty was thus both real and self-imposed. Given normal human ambitions, this is a fact so remarkable that Socrates used it as testimony at his trial (*Ap.* 31c). His poverty was the proof of his authenticity. It is his poverty that awakened the love of Plato, the young aristocrat.

If the true "rites of initiation" into the Mysteries involved something as bizarre as locking people underground, it would seem that there is little evidence for anything remotely similar in the ascent passage of Diotima's speech as narrated by Socrates. And unless there is evidence within the central text, it is poor scholarship to try to prove the case by looking elsewhere—for instance, in the allegory of the cave and the myth of Er, both found in the *Republic*. I have tried to counter this obstacle by arguing that the ascent does in fact begin with a prior descent. If the point of the passage, as commentators have generally assumed, is to preach the importance of a thoroughly desensitized love, it is hard to understand why Diotima would begin with the insistence that one has to first fall in love with someone's beautiful body. This active encouragement of a purely carnal connection makes sense only under two conditions: first, if the entire ascent requires the passion that such a relationship unleashes; and second, if the subsequent demand that one surrender what one has enjoyed (by giving up the carnal connection) makes a necessary contribution to the humbling of the spirit. Both of these possibilities point really in the same direction: the initiate has to be pulled out of his habit of thinking and planning solely on the basis of his conscious self. The burial is the establishment of the erotic condition of ascent.

We are asked ultimately to sacrifice our infatuation with any "single instance" (*Symp.* 210d). A scholar who refuses to surrender his passion for a specific area of research in order to inquire into the nature of reality would be as guilty of cultivating a demeaning form of attachment as anyone else. This demand that we always be prepared to surrender something we have come to love is what undoubtedly has awakened the most persistent objections to the text. In sacrifice, it is hard to discern anything but loss. Diotima's real art lay in her ability to overcome this resistance. "Growth through humility" is paradoxical enough to require an external guide. According to Socrates, Diotima began her activity as a priestess by convincing the Athenians to make substantial sacrifices in order to hold off the onslaught of a plague (201d). She successfully demanded, in other words, that sacrifices be made to ward off a hypothetical future evil for which there presumably was no evidence. To appreciate the accomplishment, we might imagine the difficulty a contemporary Diotima would face convincing people to make even minor sacrifices (perhaps a reduction to one car per family) on the basis of future evils (such as total environmental collapse) for which there is considerable evidence indeed. Despite its glaring irrationality, one might still regard this as the sign of a significant advance: rational individuals are those who carefully guard their own self-interest, even when the encroachment is generated by the good of the collectivity. This rule masquerades as something universal ("it's human nature"), making it difficult to understand why a man as profoundly skeptical as Socrates lets himself be talked into sacrificing sexual enjoyment, material prosperity, and the goodwill of his neighbors for the sake of a "possible" spiritual vision somewhere at the end.

The case in the *Symposium* is actually quite different from that in the *Republic*, which also raises the issue of "sacrifice." After Socrates's attention to the demands of justice, Glaucon's "luxurious city" begins to look like a replica of Sparta (*Rep.* 419a, 449d). Asking the guardians to surrender family life and private property for the sake of the community seems "too much." Socrates's answer is that good leaders can educate the guardians to do what is right. Such leaders will be those who have seen and comprehended the Good. They will be in control of the instruments of power and thus in a position to enforce its dictates. The movement, on the assumption that the Good can be known, will come from above. In contrast, Diotima relies only on a certain air of authority. Instead of aiming at the Good, which carries with it a strong sense that an unambiguous something would be "right" for us, she aims at the Beautiful, which seems somehow more nebulous (*Symp.* 204d–e), hard for even Socrates to attain, in part because it will require a great deal of self-sacrifice on his part. To place himself on the proper path, he will first of all have to *believe* what Diotima was saying. Yet she lacks anything like a convincing scientific description of the Beautiful—that is, the kind of conceptual delineation that would allow an intelligent listener, capable of mentally reconstructing the object, to intuit it intellectually. To convince Socrates she relies on nothing more than the beauty of her own words. Diotima makes a rhetorical and poetic kind of appeal. In terms of her own division, her attempt to reveal the highest Mystery itself structurally belongs to the order of the "lower mysteries." The lower is there, in fact, "for the sake of" the higher (210a).

This is the real justification of poetry. To argue that the stringencies of a spiritual path are worth the effort appears to be a hopeless task in light of the incommunicability of the goal. To comprehend the Beautiful no description will ever suffice; the initiate will have to see it for himself (as Diotima has presumably seen it for herself). To come so far, however, one has to be tremendously motivated. The goal simply has to be brought into sight. Yet by its very nature, its absolute simplicity (211b), it cannot be regarded as the product of a conceptual synthesis (which is why it can be known only in the immediacy of a vision). The dilemma would indeed be as hopeless as it appears, if there did not exist another possibility, what the German idealists (Schelling in particular) later referred to as an *aesthetic intuition*, the intuition of the Absolute in its diffraction.[12] This is indeed the mystery of the poetic word: the fullness of being that lies at its root, which it can never find a way of adequately saying, is revealed not only in its absence but by its absence. Diotima, who spoke so well, could only evoke the Beautiful by stringing together a long series of negations (211a–b). Eros is thereby granted more dignity than one could ever have thought possible on the basis of the beginning of Socrates's speech. The negative determination of the Beautiful is the direct function of that withdrawal that maintains the erotic nature of any attempt to appropriate it. Eros is thus taken into the heart of the Beautiful. The "always more" reflects not the frustrations of a cognitively limited subject but the inner fullness of Being itself.

With Eros, poetry and mythology enjoy a new splendor. They are no longer one-sidedly tied to appearances but have attained a new dignity as the bearers of a hidden mystery that requires the full effort of interpretation. The meaning of philosophy also undergoes a transformation. It remains, as always, insistent on the necessity of delivering explanations, but because it also insists on being brought before the sanctuary of the highest Mystery, it must be prepared to communicate through a foreign instrument. In its moment of silent gazing (the culmination of the cognitive effort in an unalterably private affair), philosophy flows back into its poetic condition. The refusal to accept its alliance with the poetic (like Wittgenstein's resolve to "keep silent" about everything that resists the language of science) is self-destructive. Without the "silence of the word" that poetry grants, philosophy dies. It dies, first of all, because only poetry can awaken it to its highest quest. But it dies a second death as well, for only poetry is capable of making the public communication (delivering the explanation) that is philosophy's own innermost demand.

Socrates the philosopher awakens Plato the poet.

The structure of Diotima's speech should now be clear. It first outlines the "lower mysteries." Individuals seek immortal fame; societies seek stable foundations that will enable them to survive indefinitely. To fulfill these desires, human beings look for beauty wherever they can find it. Their purpose is not the attainment of beauty as such but, as already noted, "giving birth in beauty" (206b–e). The dimension that I indicated was "left out" of the standard account of the ascent passage is the emphasis on the creative response to beauty, which is actually a carry-over from the lower mysteries. The ascent itself is sustained by everything that preceded it. Although those who seek fame draw their inspiration sporadically, wherever they can find it, the initiates to the "higher mysteries" move systematically up a scale of beauty until they finally draw their inspiration specifically from the beauty that was generated by creative response to the lower mysteries. Dante requires his Beatrice before he can give birth to the sublime vision he has stored within himself. The philosopher requires not Beatrice but the poetic vision that she inspired.

The need for a creative response is evident in each step of the ascent. On the lowest level, the sight of a beautiful body is important above all because of the language of seduction it awakens. First in the beautiful words that the lover whispers to the beloved do we find the expression of the "inner soul" that shows the way to the next level that has to be attained. "Do you mean what you say?" "Does it matter what I mean?" "Of course it matters, I don't want to be hurt." In such a conversation one already finds oneself talking about the conditions for living a good life. By articulating the implications of their own little community, lovers are drawn into a still higher discourse about the larger community in which they find themselves embedded. Responding properly to the beauty generated by such discourse, new speeches are added. The polis is itself situated in nature. To understand it, one will have to understand the world as such. The realization of how beautiful bodies and souls emerge, and how they all fit together to form the "great sea of beauty" which is the cosmos itself, is likewise a love that bears a tremendous creative potential. Words finally emerge that are so noble and expansive that the self itself acquires "strength and increase" until, like a great mountain god, it has attained sufficient stature to bear the highest revelation (210d). Even then, however, when the passage beyond words and epistemic knowledge is made (*oude tis logos, oude tis epistēmē*, 211a), our attention is drawn not only to the beauty one will see but also to what will be inspired by it. All of reality can be understood as an ecstatic reaching upward to the ultimate light. One who directly encounters such beauty will be left speechless, but in this silencing he will find his way to true virtue (212a). Virtue and knowledge are one, but the knowledge that gives rise to virtue is the knowledge that we ourselves do not—and cannot—know, for we cannot comprehend the mystery we have seen. When the soul has carried its ascent into the highest sanctuary, in which holy chamber its compulsion to speak finally gives way to peace, it is prepared for its own most glittering birth: in the moment of self-abandoned rapture, the Good itself becomes *incarnate*. One thus "touched" becomes worthy of true love.

Diotima may have "stolen" Socrates's heart. She may, indeed, have succeeded in silencing his strong sense of "self." But in doing so, she stole away only with a ghost and a fiction, whereas in overcoming himself, Socrates found his true self. The highest Mystery can certainly tolerate a biblical kind of formulation: Those who hold on to their life (and everything they regard as essential to it) will lose it. Those who lose their life (for the sake of the True, the Good, and the Beautiful) will gain it, transformed and renewed by the holy source into which they have delivered it.

Michelangelo and Shakespeare, Mozart and Goethe, undoubtedly made tremendous sacrifices for the sake of their creative work. But that work itself gives tangible proof that they were rewarded by the gift of authentic selfhood. Of course, one might object that the ascent passage privileges scientific discourse (210c–d) in such a way that the kind of dialectic embodied by the great artist is irrelevant. Poetic utterances awaken a personal response; scientific laws, on the contrary, are to be understood objectively. Good science is not the stage on which one displays authentic selfhood.

But what Plato called "science" is not altogether what we call science. The Platonic Idea is a mysterious affair that (already by definition) can never be discursively clarified. But if we are to judge on the basis of what is contained in the dialogues, we can make one claim without any hesitation whatsoever. Whereas modern science fashions its ideas everywhere in accord with the model of a mechanism, Platonic philosophy relies instead on the model of an *organism*. The simplest proof of this is that whereas modern science focuses solely on efficient and material causality, Platonic philosophy explicitly rejects such causality in favor of the teleological conception of the Good.[13]

The organic conception I have in mind is embodied, for instance, in a tree, whereby unity emerges precisely through a differentiation of parts so complete that, as the saying goes, "no two leaves are exactly alike." Properly understood, the organic can only be captured in an aesthetic intuition, one grounded in the uniqueness of what holds all those leaves apart from one another. Plato's thinking is everywhere guided by this kind of intuition. In the *Timaeus*, the material universe is portrayed as a massive organism, bound together by a great cosmic soul. In the *Republic*, the state is presented in a similar fashion. It is in fact this organic dimension that lies at the basis of the *Republic*'s conception of justice, in which members of a society are brought into harmony by a wisdom that assigns to each his or her own place.

The injunction that each "mind his own business" is more powerful than it might first appear. Mechanical unity subordinates things identical (atoms, "interchangeable parts") to an overarching form of unity (universal law), whereas organic unity unfolds as its members, each unique, find their way into whatever place allows them to unfold their full potential. Heart and lung tissue have to be organized *differently* for the human organism to function.[14]

The unity of "abstraction" is empty to the degree that it comprehends all that lies under it. What is unique, what stands apart from the "common" or "universal," is, for the purpose of completing the act of abstraction, simply eliminated. The emptiness of the Beautiful is something entirely different. It is not attained by completing a conceptual "act." For the Beautiful is itself primary insofar as all that "comes to be and perishes" exists first by virtue of participation in it (*Symp.* 211b). The Beautiful is the ultimate source of existence, not the dead husk of universality that is left behind after reflection has painted its "grey on grey."[15] As we have seen, each stage of the ascent gives rise to a new creation. The Beautiful itself gives rise to all that is, for "all that is" is what arises from the erotic craving of nonbeing for the fullness and completion of being.

This self-articulation of the Beautiful has to be understood not only in terms of spatiality but of temporality as well. The moment in which the beautiful one appears is removed from the temporal sequence that stands before and after it. This is why it occurs "suddenly" (*exaiphnēs*, 210e).[16] Beauty delivers us thus into the full presence of the present. The past passes totally out of sight. The future withholds itself completely in its futurity. The present discloses its innermost secret: that it always is. It is *aei*, eternal, all-being: One. The telos of the Good, which ordinary consciousness must always view as withholding itself into the future, even into the absolute future of an always absent God, flashes forth in the now. Because of the reality of pain and suffering, this truth breaks forth but rarely. When it does, it necessarily takes the form of a secret disclosed: the breaking forth of a hidden "within."

It is a "within" found even in the "without." Philosophy and mystery religion do not contradict the pagan relationship to reality. They complete it. This remains clear when we shift from the lower to the higher mysteries. Diotima is not the only mysterious priestess that Socrates alludes to. In the *Meno* we are referred to priestesses who can do something unheard of: "they can give a reasoned account of their ministry" (81a–b). They are the stewards of a new philosophical religion, a religion that understands itself. It is they who introduce the Platonic doctrine of recollection, whereby the "beyond" is truly shown to lie "within." The doctrine is the hidden presupposition of the *Symposium* as well. The Beautiful can be experienced only in an act of anamnesis precisely because it is "in itself." Unless we bring our own interiority into a correspondence with this "in itselfness," the Beautiful will be locked forever from our sight. But once the correspondence is achieved, the vision is a real possibility. In the *Meno*, Socrates defends the doctrine with a quotation from Pindar: "Those from whom / Persephone receives requital for ancient doom / in the ninth year she restores again / their souls to the sun above / from whom rise noble kings / the swift in strength and the greatest in wisdom" (*Meno* 81b, quoting Pindar's fragment 133).

The final proof that the ascent passage does not destroy the possibility of human love is that the knowledge of the Beautiful (which is one with the knowledge of our own ignorance) does not refer to the destruction of the self so much as to its completion. A death of sorts has occurred, but only as the prelude to a new awakening, a resurrection of lost light, stored in the darkness within.

In Anders Nygren's *Agape and Eros*, we find (in the spirit of Martin Luther) a set of bald contrasts that have now been effectively undone:

Eros is acquisitive desire and longing. Agape is sacrificial giving. Eros is
an upward movement. Agape comes down. Eros is man's way to God.
Agape is God's way to man. Eros is man's effort: it assumes that man's
salvation is his own work. Agape is God's grace: salvation is the work of
Divine love. Eros is egocentric love, a form of self-assertion of the highest, noblest, sublimest kind. Agape is unselfish love, it "seeketh not its
own," it gives itself away. Eros seeks to gain its life, a life divine, immor-
talized. Agape lives the life of God, therefore dares to "lose it." Eros is
the will to get and possess which depends on want and need. Agape is
freedom in giving, which depends on wealth and plenty.[17]

The list goes on, but the point is clear: there is nothing that we human
beings can do to merit the love of God. There is no erotic ladder to climb.
No method that will lead to salvation. Either God bestows his grace or
he does not. If he does, his love will reflect not our merit, but his bounty.

There is clearly a problem in Nygren's conception, quite apart from
the false interpretation of Plato that derives from it. If he is right, the
bounty of God's love is a strangely limited one. Not everyone is the re-
cipient of divine grace. As Ivan Karamazov made clear in his story of the
Grand Inquisitor, a compassionate soul can only be left horrified by the
revelation that, in the end, only twelve times twelve thousand souls are
to be saved.[18]

Another model works better. It can be found in its purest form in
the sermons of Meister Eckhart.[19] God's love is taken to be universal. We
are kept from realizing it by our attachment to ourselves. If Satan himself
could for one moment free himself of that attachment, he would discover
that he was in heaven with God. In other words, hell is the attempt to
overcome fear with pride.

Grace and action are not mutually exclusive. Divine grace is already
there for us. To receive it, we have to recognize our own nothingness,
which is different from *wanting* to recognize our nothingness. In other
words, we have to overcome the very fear of death that makes us cling
to ourselves. The only way to do this is through humility, the free acceptance of the death that is always being bestowed on us. God's wrath is in
fact God's love, for ultimately it will remove the barrier that separates us
from the beatific experience. Presumably, even the pride of Satan will ultimately be overcome. In the end, he will once again assume his rightful
position, above everything but God Himself ("the first shall be last and
the last shall be first").

We have to understand as genuine the humility that leads Socrates
to place all his best insights in the mouth of Diotima (not to speak of the

humility of Plato that leads him to place all his insights into the mouth of Socrates). The entire erotic ascent is predicated on the dialectic of sacrifice, of death and rebirth. I will try to provide a fuller account of this in the following chapter.

For the moment, I want to return to the initial point I made in introducing the ascent passage: Plato clearly conceived his own dialogues as a hymn of love to Socrates. Socrates commanded Plato's attention because, besides speaking powerfully and well, he gave every sign of being a man who embodied genuine virtue. As we have seen, the ultimate creative response to the Beautiful is not an outpouring of words but the attainment of good actions (212a). The calm and dignity with which Socrates faced his death gave Plato eloquent proof of Socrates's achievement. No fewer than seven dialogues—the *Theaetetus, Euthyphro, Sophist, Statesman, Apology, Crito,* and *Phaedo*—have dramatic dates that cluster around the time of Socrates's trial and execution. An eighth, the *Philosopher,* was projected but never written. Moreover, in the dialogues as a whole, Socrates's character is always portrayed as outweighing in importance both his deeds and his thoughts. The only knowledge that is of real interest to him is the knowledge that makes one good.

It should be completely clear by now that such knowledge is not propositional in character. This is why its avowal must include the notorious "I know that I do not know." The general issue has its correlate in the inadequacy of legal strictures: "for the differences of men and of actions and the fact that nothing, I may say, in human life is ever at rest, forbid any science whatsoever to promulgate any simple rule for everything and for all time" (*Statesm.* 294b). "If a man, whether rich or poor, by persuasion or by other means, in accordance with written laws or contrary to them, does what is for the good of the people, must not this be the truest criterion of right government, in accordance with which the wise and good man will govern the affairs of his subjects?" (296e). The same holds as well for the individual with regard to the matter of his own internal governance. The point is not to learn the right thing to say or the right thing to think. Propositions and slogans do not reach far enough into the interstices of the self. Ultimately, one must *see* something—and see it so well and so clearly that one's nature is transformed. Yet in order to see, the impediment to sight, the thoroughgoing attachment to self, has to be overcome. To see, we have (in some manner) to die.

The preparation for this inner death is the persistent and ever-repeated "passing from view to view of beautiful things, in the right and regular ascent" (*Symp.* 210e). To view what is beautiful is, for that moment, to be lifted up out of oneself, to "die." Constant repetition is necessary, for it is only when the entire hierarchy has been sufficiently internalized—that is, when one can view within oneself what goes so far beyond oneself, the long and sublime movement from the physical to the spiritual, progressing slowly through the elements, from earth to water to air, then fire, until through the light of that fire one is delivered into the pure ether of a strictly intellectual vision—that one becomes ready for what might, or might not, occur, the sudden and all-transforming eruption of what takes the place of the now humbled self: the Beautiful. These are, of course, themselves only words. As such, they belong to the lower mysteries, not the higher.

But Plato's most fundamental disclosure is that Socrates went beyond words: he in fact had the vision and emerged transformed. Plato's response to the Beauty manifested in Socrates is perhaps the most sophisticated form of philosophical poetry the world will ever witness. In this way, he renewed what was at stake in the relationship between Socrates and Diotima. The dialogues, in other words, are works of art. Just as Socrates's personality, his strange admixture of physical resiliency and intellectual obsession, of irony and seriousness, of harshness and goodwill, leaves its stamp on everything he says, so Plato's characteristic personality shines forth in the dialogues as a whole. In this too we are faced with an apparent meeting of opposites. In Plato, the erotic enthusiast comes together with the politically minded aristocrat and the contemplative schoolmaster. Above all else, Plato represents the meeting point between philosophy and poetry. It is Plato's art, not Socrates's, that is responsible for Agathon's speech. I have hardly alluded to the speech because for the most part it is no more than a lovely piece of fluff. Agathon's climax should, however, be brought to mind, for it tells us much about an art that was all Plato's own. Socrates was not being ironic when he commented on the climax by saying: "The beauty of the words and phrases could not but take one's breath away" (198b). Agathon's speech did in fact culminate in a piece of pure music (197c–e). The timing goes notably into verse with a tight cluster of rhymes that marshal out the typical Greek endings: *os, es, ai, oon, ois*, etc. There is moreover a complete correspondence between form and content, for Agathon wanted only to say of Eros: "He is so beautiful, in every conceivable way, he is so beautiful." What Agathon has brought to words is the entire spectacle of beauty that was Athens at its peak.

But recall once more (from chapter 4), the timing of the *Symposium*, only a year or more before the disastrous siege of Syracuse. Agathon's ode to an Eros that is eternally beautiful and eternally young is in every way appropriate to the splendor of a city that could crown itself with the Parthenon, but for those of us who come after, the irony is undeniable: the glorious vision came undone. Empires are glorious—and notoriously short-lived. The Athenian empire was the most glorious—and the shortest lived. When Diotima introduces need and lack into her conception of Eros, she is addressing this truth, which at times takes an earthquake to disclose.

Even so, in one respect Agathon's speech seems to coincide well enough with the Socrates-Diotima speech: both depict Eros as above all else the god of poetic creativity. Agathon certainly anticipates Diotima's emphasis on "procreation in beauty," insisting that Eros is the principle not only of all artistic and poetic creativity (196e), but the procreation of animals as well (197a). But whereas Agathon celebrates the creative principle as the privilege of eternal youth, Diotima again and again makes clear that its necessity is grounded in the fact that *we are mortal*. Procreation in beauty is "what mortals have in place of immortality" (207a). It is what makes it possible for an animal to die for its young (207b). People live by being renewed as they pass away (207e). We study to make up for what we forget (208a). We glimpse beauty eternal, but only for a passing moment. Our job then is to resurrect her by giving birth, and in the world of time, to virtuous deeds (212a).

The real reason for calling Agathon to mind is that the entire *Symposium* is cast (as is the *Republic*) as a contest between poetry and philosophy. If Alcibiades placed crowns on the heads of both Agathon and Socrates (212e, 213e), Apollo, as we have seen, ultimately decides in favor of Socrates, who goes forth to a new day as the poets fall asleep. Of course, in Socrates's speech too we often detect a musical quality. It should not surprise us when Plato—using his art—let this musicality show forth. The climax of the Socrates-Diotima speech reproduces the pulse and rhythm of Agathon's climax (211a–b). There is, however, an important difference. The tight cluster of rhymes is a repetition always of the same ending: *on.* It constitutes a kind of mantra that flows into the heart of the primary definition of the Beautiful: *auto kath'hauto meth'hautou monoeides aei on.* The final *on* carries the weight of the whole. It is the Greek word for Being, the majestic One out of which all things flow and into which they always return, a constant coming and going that leaves the source itself pure and unchanged. The poetry of the lower mysteries is the poetry of the Many, which is why its verse forms are diverse. The poetry of philosophy is, however, the poetry of the highest Mystery. It knows not only the power of music but the possibility of tracing that power to an origin before and beyond all sound: *Nada Brahman,* the unspeakable *Logos* that stands rooted in the origin itself—that *archē* that can only be called God. Its actual name must remain forever shrouded in silence.

6

Standing in Death

For thus it is, men of Athens, in truth; wherever a man stations himself, thinking it is best to be there, or is stationed by his commander, there he must, as it seems to me, remain and face the danger, considering neither death nor any other thing more than disgrace.

—Plato, *Apology* 28d

You should hear what else he did during that campaign, "The exploit our strong-hearted hero dared to do." One day, at dawn, he started thinking about some problem or other; he just stood outside, trying to figure it out. He couldn't resolve it, but he wouldn't give up. He simply stood there, glued to the same spot. By midday, many soldiers had seen him, and, quite mystified, they told everyone that Socrates had been standing there all day, thinking about something. He was still there when evening came, and after dinner some Ionians moved their bedding outside, where it was cooler and more comfortable (all this took place in the summer), but mainly in order to watch if Socrates was going to stay out there all night. And so he did; he stood on the very same spot until dawn! He only left next morning, when the sun came out, and he made his prayers to the new day.

—Plato, *Symposium* 220c–d

Alcibiades's depiction in the *Symposium* of Socrates's twenty-four-hour standing trance is well known. Despite illuminating commentary from none other than Hegel, its meaning remains obscure.[1] My own interpretation will proceed from the observation that the great trance took place on a battlefield. It thereby becomes the trope not so much of self-reflection as of crisis and inner transformation.

In the *Apology*, Socrates concludes his defense by assuming a warrior's heroic guise. He compares himself to Achilles, who, with full knowledge of his impending death, fought his battle to the end (28b–29b).[2] In the same spirit, Socrates promises that he would go on philosophizing, even if the activity were deemed punishable by death. Apollo, through the oracle at Delphi, had assigned him to his post. Socrates would not budge.

Indeed, constancy and steadfastness form the foundation for the whole list of virtues that are associated with Socrates: self-restraint, sobriety, moderation, resoluteness, courage, justice, and wisdom. It is the very need for constancy, for the reliability that must accompany any virtue whatsoever, which introduces the turn toward the idea of the Good in the *Republic*. A mind that is "fixed" on the unchangeable is not led astray by prudential concerns; it is not torn one way and the other by the attachments that cause strife and discontent. It does not lose itself in anger and despair once suffering becomes its lot. By virtue of its indifference to the finite, it is impartial, it is just. It lets everything find its own appropriate sphere. Moreover, by clinging to nothing but the Absolute, it rises above the attachment to life itself. It has nothing to fear, not even death (*Rep.* 486a). Wisdom, the abiding intuition of the eternal, is the font of true courage.

Yet this same image of constancy awakens suspicions. We are, with justification, leery of what is rigid and closed. Nietzsche was surely right to worry about the passivity of stoic resignation, insisting instead that "strength" and "vitality" be added to the list of virtues. The indifferent mind is a dead one. And intransigence in itself is hardly a virtue. Indeed, by refusing to budge at his trial, Socrates discredited his avowal of ignorance and humility. His stubbornness evinced arrogance and hubris. The outrage of his Athenian jurors is not hard to understand. At the same time, for all our discomfort with rigidity, we are equally suspicious of its opposite. Plato's description of the "flexibility" of the true statesman as one who somehow stands above the law (*Statesm.* 293d–297a) quite rightly awakens our fear of tyrannical excess. The idea that it is the "good" that hovers above all legal pronouncements even seems contradictory: what is good must be something that we can determine and articulate, for how else can it facilitate a consensus, how else can it establish harmony, if not by uniting people in a common understanding of what is right? An inexpressible good can only be the source of confusion and arbitrariness. As such, it would be the ground of evil.

The problem with accepting a nondiscursive form of understanding is that we will then have to accept the validity of it merely on the authority of the one who has "seen." This may have sufficed in earlier times, but it is not appropriate for the present age. As Kant asserted, the time for enlightenment has dawned: we have to accept the responsibilities of adulthood.[3] We must live by our own insight. If the insight is one we can share, it will be determinable and rational. In other words, it will be fixed and closed. Reason, our only defense from tyranny, will itself appear tyrannical for anyone who fails to follow its logic. There seems no end to the infuriating antinomy. We cannot help but be confused.

But given the severity of our confusion (are we perhaps supposed to be confused?), and the impossibility of finding a logical way out of the dilemma (wouldn't a fully realized Good spell the end of the very freedom that renders goodness "good" in the first place?), we find ourselves in a double bind. We are torn between the need to think and the fear that thinking will only make things worse. In such a situation, we have no choice but to come directly to terms with confusion itself. This is impossible, however, if we persist in identifying confusion with evil. We shall at least have to consider the possibility that we have no answers because the Good, in its goodness, withholds them from us.

Such divine silence damns us, to be sure, but to no hell greater than human freedom itself.[4] Out of that hell there is at least hope for release. This is what freedom is.

Somewhere in the background, the voice of Meno can be heard, complaining that he once knew the difference between right and wrong and that Socrates has robbed him of his certainties (*Meno* 80a–d). Socrates's reply also hovers in the air: "I feel the same perplexity you do. I have reason to hope, however, that this very confusion is a good thing. Questions come before answers. Pain precedes birth." To measure the full depth of Socrates's own perplexity, the genuine nature of his famous declaration of ignorance, we have no choice but to abandon the discursive order. Instead of critiquing an argument, I propose a long look at the often cited but never adequately explained passage from the *Symposium* that I quoted as an epigraph to this chapter (220c–d). It provides the vivid image of the loquacious philosopher rendered fully silent. Alcibiades describes him standing motionless, barefoot on the battlefield of Potidaea, for a full twenty-four hours. At the end of the trance he says his prayers to the rising sun and goes on with his life as a soldier. The only thing we are told about what occupied him so long is that he was caught up in a problem, which he stood "considering." In other words, he was perplexed. Yet this perplexity itself delivered him into his stand.

Of course, stands are ceaselessly being taken, even too often and too relentlessly. They are taken with the slightest of justifications and used to shield their bearers from a perplexity that would otherwise prove overwhelming. But the stand that Socrates took was different. It was a stand taken *in* perplexity. It was a stand taken on a battlefield. Ending as it did in prayer, it is reasonable to infer that it was taken on the command of a god. Indeed, the god is not a hidden one and should thus be named. Appearing with the rising sun (both the beginning and the end of the twenty-four-hour stand), he is none other than Apollo.

The name of the god suffices. Alcibiades did not say what problem had stopped Socrates in his tracks. But perhaps it can be inferred from the fact that the bout of reflection began at sunrise. If so, the problem may have been posed by the rising sun itself: how is it that out of darkness light suddenly emerges? How is it that out of the subterranean abyss, the majestic orb of light suddenly lifts itself into the sky?

We know that the young Socrates regarded this, the simple fact of becoming, as a problem. Diotima had cautioned him not to perceive it as a problem, but, despite her caution, he was still filled with wonder (*Symp.* 201e). How can Eros span the divide between ugliness and beauty? How can being emerge from the abyss of not-being?[5] Parmenides had already founded metaphysics with the very rational assumption that it cannot: nothing comes from nothing. Thus, what is must always be. The senses, by offering us the spectacle of constant change, lead us astray. Becoming is an illusion. What is, is—and is eternally. Never changing, it remains always the same. Pure, unadulterated self-identity is the only true reality.

Yet against this proclamation of reason, Socrates found himself standing face to face with the dawning face of God. It seems reasonable to suppose that he stood through the day trying to decipher the mystery of day's renewal, the rebirth of a god that by all reason should simply be, beyond all comings and goings, all deaths and rebirths (*Rep.* 380d–381c). He stood until the mystery repeated itself, this time by day's mysterious disappearance into night. Thrust into the heart of darkness, he stood throughout the long night, waiting for a revelation. An answer was given to him only at dawn, as the sun rose once again.

Socrates gained insight, if we are to judge on the basis of what everyone "knows" about Platonic philosophy, from the completion of the celestial cycle: the sun's rise is necessary. Behind the appearance of an event is hidden the enduring form of cyclical closure. A circle that turns in on itself is the closest image of form as such (any idea is bound into the circle of self-identity: $A = A$): thus the divinity of the celestial spheres (*Tim.* 34b). The sheer perfection of Absolute Reality awakens from the abyss of Eternal Night the desire to be—and through that desire the pale imitation that is the veil of appearance and becoming, the veil of world. Being itself is beyond the veil, accessible only to the inner eye of the understanding. Socrates's trance, so understood, is an anticipation of that other twenty-four-hour journey, the one that is presented in the *Phaedrus* in the beautiful image of the great procession of the gods, all driving their chariots on the outer rim of the celestial sphere itself, drinking in the splendor of invisible truth shining forth from the Absolute beyond, a movement that occurs easily, effortlessly, as everything is carried along by the sky's daily rotation around the earth far below (246c–247e). This feast of truth, the intuition of which makes the gods divine, can also be understood as the unveiling of the forms, pristine structures of pure reason that are located in the vast open field of eternal luminosity. In the luminous open lies reality itself, towering above the cosmic order of change and appearance.

This is the conclusion of more than two thousand years of Platonism. Yet if we are to judge solely on the basis of what Alcibiades tells of the event, another interpretive possibility presents itself. Instead of intellectually comprehending self-evident structures, revolving as it were in the realm of the mathematical a priori, Socrates may have comprehended something very different indeed: the very incomprehensibility of his problem. By coming to know why he lacked knowledge, Socrates may have become Socrates. To do so, however, he simultaneously had to be freed from the very human need to feign knowledge where knowledge does not exist. To cease supporting himself with lies, he had to discover something else that offers all the support we need. Such a discovery one must liken to the discovery of the Divine, for standing truly in a god, one would receive the support one needs to be oneself. The self is mediated, to be sure, but, as authentic and true self, that mediation occurs only through immediacy. Spontaneity is possible only where the need to invent the self is overcome.

But if the god thus discovered now turns out to be Apollo, the spirit of the rising sun, we will have to drastically alter our entire conception, dispensing altogether with the vision of transcendent forms. From the new point of view, instead of asserting that the form of perfection awakens the circular movement of the cosmos, we might do well simply to dispense with the idea that something "caused" the sun to rise. The sun rose—without cause. Or, saying the same thing, Apollo, in defiance of all gravity (earth clinging to earth), drove his flaming chariot into the sky. The "god" is not a self-contained structure that lies beyond the appearance but rather the self-unfolding into visibility that is the appearance itself. And, indeed, the text suggests this reading by the way it concludes. Socrates abandoned his reflections and offered a prayer to the rising sun. At this point it is necessary to make a small correction to the translation, according to which Socrates prayed to the "new day." In the Greek (*Symp.* 220d) he leaves only after offering his prayer to the "sun" (*proseuxamenos tō hēliō*). He did not pray to an idea that hovers somewhere above the sun, not even to Apollo as something apart from the sun, but to the sun itself, the miraculously rising sun. Divinity is what awakens wonder. The sheer impossibility of it all is what commands awe and devotion.

Years later, shortly before his death, Socrates tried to direct Euthyphro, the alleged "expert" in all religious matters, into an elementary understanding of piety: we are, as human beings, ignorant in the face of things divine (*Euthphr.* 6b). The one who shares this recognition—together with the realization that ignorance is not always negative—is more religious than the self-righteous ever could be. Ignorance that is positive, that is to say, that knows itself as ignorance, is the indispensable condition for recognizing the miraculous nature of the miraculous. There is no presence, including the presence of the material universe, that can simply be taken for granted.

Yet a sense of mystery is surely not all that is at issue. A fuller version of the story would stress the role of beauty. As suggested in the last chapter, beauty is the mode of the Absolute that most fully shines forth in appearances. It is the solution to the riddle posed in the *Phaedrus*. Wings are nourished only by a vision of the forms. Yet without wings, the soul can never attain the heights necessary for the revelation of the forms. Whence, then, does a soul sprout wings?[6] This is an urgent question for human beings, those bipeds who have lost their wings. The *Phaedrus* answers the question in this way: if wings are nurtured solely through a vision of forms, at least one form must make itself manifest in appearance; this is the form of the Beautiful (255c–d). Apollo not only gave Socrates a problem worth thinking about, he captivated him by his stunning display of light and color. He is the god not simply of understanding but of light and sky and heavenly beauty. Any contemplation of higher forms, any exercise of the "pure understanding," requires that one has already been carried aloft by an experience of beauty.

Beauty both lured Socrates into his reflections and, twenty-four hours later, released him from their hold. Absolute understanding (the foundation of rationality) exists only *within* the disclosure of beauty. A sense of wonder about what is inexplicably given is only the beginning of philosophy. Its completion is the realization that what is has no need of justification. Thinking is awakened by what presents itself as irrational. Evil, for instance, is what most emphatically requires an explanation: it should not be (indeed, it cannot be), yet it is. The question "why?" betrays inner torment, fury at what is but should not be. Goodness, however, carries its justification within itself. Its occurrence moves one to marvel but not to ask "why." Disease awakens the search for causes. Health has no such concern. Indeed, that existence poses itself as a "problem" is already a symptom that something has gone profoundly awry. If one asks why God exists, one has not understood the first thing about God.

Yet the question does pose itself. What is . . . cannot be. The reassuring tautology of being finds itself shattered by an eruption that begins in the darkness of earth, far below the cold clamminess of mud and slime, there where the infernal fires melt the elements and beget as ill-wrought catastrophes living beings that grasp and struggle and crawl toward whatever glimmer of light shows itself. At the shrine of Apollo at Delphi, within the very center of the Holy of Holies, was hidden (according to Plutarch) the grave of Dionysus, the god who could be born, the god who could die.[7] This is the great mystery, the genesis of the Olympian out of the earth-enclosed abyss, which Euthyphro, on the authority of Hesiod, claimed to understand (*Euthphr.* 6a–c). Socrates knew that, on the contrary, this mystery was incomprehensible. The release of day out of the bowels of night is the mystery of Being. Only in the beautiful illusion of the sun hung midday in the sky is the mystery released into the light of self-evidence. Yes, what is beautiful requires no explanation. I see that it is beautiful, I appreciate that it is beautiful, and I have no need to ask why it is beautiful. And yet this too, the possibility of happiness, unquestioning enjoyment of the act of being, is incomprehensible. Socrates knew not only how to pray but why to pray. Denied devotion, God does not so much rage and punish as he sheds a tear for those who, by their blindness to their own blindness, have eluded the possible gift of his grace.

Hegel advanced a very different interpretation of the trance scene. The context for it is to be found in two different sections of the *Phenomenology of Spirit*. The first outlines the transition from the ethical community of the ancient Greeks to the Jewish, Christian, and, ultimately, Kantian conception of morality. The second outlines the transition from the Greek "religion of art" to the "revealed religion" of Judaism and Christianity. What is remarkable is that the figure of Socrates is in both instances located on the Christian side of the divide. Socrates is unable simply to act as the community has always acted, as the gods have always already commanded them to act (beyond the possibility of question). His insistence that one act only if one knows that what one is doing is right is thus the foundation of morality.[8] The necessity of personal insight corresponds to the Christian understanding that the individual, although a creature of God, is yet mysteriously independent of God. Socrates thus represents the emergence of the idea of freedom within the development of pagan religiosity. For this reason he also signals the end of the religion of art. The Greek contribution to that religion is the god who appears in human form. This is at first fully external (the column of a temple), but in time yields dramas in which human beings can actually portray the gods on stage. With comedy, a fully human world is attained. It is in this world that Socrates emerges—"the return of everything universal into the certainty of itself which, in consequence, is the complete loss of fear."[9] The god that appeared in artwork is now a thought in the mind of the philosopher: the Good, the Beautiful. A religion that finds divinity in nature comes to its end by discovering divinity in human nature. Socrates thus opened the way to Christ.[10] The moment of incarnation represents the fusion of the natural religion of the pagan with the salvation history of the Jew. In contrast to my own portrayal of a Socrates stunned by the riddle of becoming, Hegel understands him as representing the disappearance of the riddle. Socrates, for Hegel, is the attainment of "the fullness of self-certainty."

The penultimate section of the *Logic*, which portrays the formation of the idea of the Good, can also be read as a commentary on Socrates. The clearest document of Hegel's understanding of Socrates, however, is the long narrative of his life and thought recorded in Hegel's *Lectures on the History of Philosophy*. Because I am not concerned with Hegel's full interpretation, I will limit my observations to the depiction of the trance at Potidaea, which Hegel uses to introduce his discussion of Socrates.[11] The reason he stresses the importance of the trance can be gleaned from the *Logic*. The idea of the Good, Socrates's contribution to the history of thought, is the ultimate expression of practical philosophy, which is limited by its own fundamental subjectivity. The Good is what should be, not what is but what we always strive for in the form of an ideal. In the idea of the Good, the reality of the actually existent world is effectively negated.[12] The practical imperative is rooted in the realization of the insufficiency of reality as such. The subject alone shows itself to be truly real.

This emphasis on subjectivity yields the basis of Hegel's understanding of the trance scene. Socrates has turned his gaze fully into himself. Far from following the movement of the sun, he has encapsulated himself in a form of self-consciousness so pure that the outside world has altogether vanished. Surprisingly enough, and despite Hegel's strong commitment to the "labor of the concept," he completely ignores the struggle to come clear on something, to *think*, which is just the word Alcibiades used to describe what Socrates was doing. On this issue the various translations concur (I will withhold comments on the Greek text until the end of this chapter).[13] Referring to the Nehamas and Woodruff version cited in the second epigraph to this chapter, we find that Socrates was "thinking about some problem, . . . trying to figure it out." Unable to "resolve" the problem, he stubbornly refused to "give it up." In this description there is nothing whatsoever of Hegel's twice-mentioned "cataleptic state,"[14] no evidence in the actual passage for Hegel's insistence that Socrates's sense perception had "died away entirely," leaving him utterly "abstracted" from his "concrete physical being."[15]

The importance of the scene for Hegel is that it provides a vivid image of the depth of Socrates's turn inward. It is in this very moment, he suggests, that Socrates's position as a "world-historical" personality was attained, whereby he embodied the "primary turning point" of Spirit, away from the externality of pagan culture, back into the interiority of its own self-consciousness.[16] In other words, what took place in Socrates on the battlefield of Potidaea can be likened to the proclamation of the Judaic God that he is Yahweh, the pure "I am that I am," that underlies all reality, or, in another cultural context, the Upanishadic revelation of the identity of Brahman and Atman. Hegel's Socrates thus represents far more than the culmination of pagan consciousness. He represents its transformation into a totally new form, the beginning of the philosophical development that would ultimately comprehend within itself the revealed God of Christianity.

What makes this claim problematic in my mind is the immediate context in which Hegel locates his reading. He regards Socrates first and foremost as a response to the breakdown of values that occurred during the Peloponnesian War. If the gods once determined what is right, the descent into chaos made it necessary for men to investigate for themselves. What this means is that the interiority of self-consciousness, the epochal coming to itself of Spirit (an "image" of which we find in the Potidaea incident), is for Hegel nothing apart from Socrates's own subjective consciousness. Of course, in my own account, I have also suggested that the image should be used to represent the completion of the famous *gnōthi se-auton*, or "know thyself," of the Delphic Oracle. The difference, however, lies in how the self-discovery was mediated. According to Hegel, what was essential was the insecurity of the historical moment, which no longer allowed Socrates to thoughtlessly follow the customs of his community.

In contrast, the mediation to which I want to point is an internal mediation. Self-discovery is made possible by the God that lies within. I have already tried to articulate what this means in the previous two chapters. I have not, however, advanced far enough. A self-discovery that is mediated by the simultaneous discovery of a God within us is evocative of Saint Augustine.[17] To understand it in this way is, however, to anticipate the Hegelian figure of Absolute Spirit. I have two reasons for rejecting this. The first is that it is rooted in a "worldless" understanding, one that has no place for Apollo, a god who appears (if at all) in the world of nature. The second is that it is irreconcilable with Socrates's emphatic insistence on his own ultimate ignorance.

To these observations I can also add a bit of textual support. In the *Charmides*, Plato records a conversation Socrates was supposed to have had immediately on his return from Potidaea. Not only does Socrates stress the matter of his own ignorance in that dialogue (165b, 166d, 175b), but he pointedly rejects the conception of wisdom that Hegel was ultimately to make his own, whereby wisdom is the science simultaneously of all other sciences and of itself (166c). In contrast, Socrates repeatedly emphasizes in the *Charmides* the impossibility of that pure relationship to self that, according to Hegel, had been his essential discovery. It is, of course, possible that Socrates was not speaking his full mind at the time. Perhaps his real objection was to Critias's pretense that "self-knowledge" is an easy attainment. Even so, he says enough to make it clear that, were self-knowledge a possibility, it would have to be a most paradoxical affair. Mystery still cloaks the whole.

I omitted something crucial in my preliminary interpretation of the trance passage. The scene is introduced by a quotation from Homer that, in the context of Alcibiades's drunken speech, might easily be mistaken for parody: "what a valiant deed that was which the mighty man dared and did!"

The quotation can be found at two junctures in the *Odyssey*. The first describes how Odysseus made his way into Troy by assuming the disguise of a beggar (4.242). It is evocative of the way Socrates, who like Eros (*Symp.* 203d) often has the appearance of a beggar, entered the party of Agathon, disguised as a respectable man (he was wearing shoes!). Odysseus, the master of cunning deceit, was the genius who brought the Trojan War to a successful conclusion. His famous subterfuge provides the context for the second occurrence of the line in Homer (4.271). "What a valiant deed that was which the mighty man dared and did" opens the story of how our hero, locked away in the Trojan horse with the other Achaean chieftains, managed to keep his accomplices silent while Helen, standing outside, artfully imitated the voices of the wives they so missed. The episode also anticipates the famous image of Odysseus tied to the mast of his ship where he withstands the song of the Sirens.

Steadfastness in the face of sensuality's powerful allure is what binds Odysseus immediately to Socrates. After all, the context of the passage in the *Symposium* is Alcibiades's account of Socrates's "awe-inspiring" resistance to his own sexual advances. The resistance takes on a new dimension when linked to the manner in which Odysseus achieved steadfastness: by "silencing" the multifarious voices of desire. The passions that drive men to war, in this case, the love of every man for Helen, are in themselves incapable of achieving victory. War begins when the passions are stirred. An end is found only when a spirit emerges that is capable of maintaining sobriety and calm amid the slaughter and devastation that is the reality of war. In the face of this maelstrom only silence can prevail. If the silent hero is Odysseus, in some mysterious way it is Socrates as well.

The deeds of Odysseus were valiant because in each instance they transported him into the very heart of enemy territory. If Socrates's trance is to be understood in a corresponding fashion, it is inappropriate to interpret it, as Hegel did, in the guise of homecoming, as the return of consciousness to itself. Instead, we will have to interpret it in the opposite direction, as the courageous encounter of consciousness with the full intensity and strangeness of the radically "other." The silencing of desire, the first moment recovered, cannot be understood as the simple attainment of inner serenity. The "deed" occurred not only amid the general confusion of war but at the place of greatest danger. It was, moreover, most emphatically a deed—and not a prolonged state of quietist stupor.

As I have already mentioned, the image of Socrates-Odysseus is a recurring one in Plato's works. The *Republic* both begins and ends with it (from the opening "I went down" to the figure of Odysseus reborn at the end of the myth of Er). Although we cannot discount the possibility of parody from the point of view of Alcibiades, we certainly can from the point of view of Plato. Socrates was, after all, his hero. Further, the memory of war-weary Odysseus is strangely appropriate in this passage. Socrates's "valiant deed" also took place against the background of a long campaign of war. Although not the ten-year siege of Troy, it was a two-year siege of a city almost as far away, Potidaea, located in the northernmost reaches of the Aegean. Warrior-philosophers abound in the *Republic*. In the historical Socrates we have their prototype. We find him on a field somewhere outside the besieged city, thinking long and hard about we know not what for sure.

If Socrates is to be understood as having somehow appropriated Odysseus's weariness with war, we might assume he was contemplating the irrationality and evil of the bloodshed he had encountered in a year on the battlefield. The mature Socrates decried war and its cause—the pursuit of unnecessary wealth (*Phd.* 66c). At the same time, however, his freedom from desire may have relieved him of the fear that war awakens in others. Alcibiades is not the only one who depicted Socrates's exemplary courage on the battlefield. Laches, the general under whom he served at Delium, confirmed and added to the story (*La.* 181b). Whether Socrates had already achieved such a state of Odysseus-like dispassion at the time of the trance is, however, unclear. Perhaps this was what he was seeking.

Another possibility is compatible with Hegel's general statement that the chaos generated by the Peloponnesian War led to moral uncertainty. The *Republic* spells out rudimentary limitations to be respected when Greeks fight Greeks (469b–c). One might speculate that, had the time been right, these conditions could have been unfolded into a full-blown theory of just war. The siege of Potidaea, a Greek city, populated not only with soldiers but with their families, would not have met such conditions. Not only did it wrongly involve innocents, but it was carried out for purely strategic reasons. Athens sought a base of power from which it could strike out to the East. Socrates, the very symbol of the just man, may have been seeking insight into the morality of what he himself was doing. The internal battle would have been made all the more severe by virtue of his prior decision to follow whatever orders his commander might give (*Ap.* 28d–e).[18] If he had reservations about his participation in the campaign, and according to his own conception of justice he should have had very serious reservations, his position was far more interesting than that depicted by Hegel. Hegel's Socrates had already detached himself fully from the ethical community. He was the moral man who was committed to following the dictates of his conscience. The dilemma of the real Socrates was both more complex and more tragic—for he was clearly torn between two competing commands. The question he faced thus penetrated more deeply than the purely speculative question about the possibility of Being's first emergence. Instead, the question penetrated into the root of his own existence and disclosed the horror of freedom and choice. Freedom is a problematic affair.

The reference to the "mighty man's valiant deed" cannot serve as the introduction to a philosopher's bout of contemplation or self-absorption. It is particularly inappropriate to the empty state of catalepsy that Hegel assumes. The phrase puts us squarely on the field of battle. Because there was a lull in the fighting at Potidaea, the battle could only have been an internal one. Furthermore, because it was a battle within the heart and soul of Socrates, it has to be construed as going beyond the internal wrangling any of us may undergo over a question of choice. The normal human being is appeased once a preference has been established ("this is what I *want* to do"). Socrates's question, however, as the moral question ("what is the right thing to do?"), pushes relentlessly beyond itself. Insight into what is right presupposes an understanding of what we human beings are in the first place. The moral question, seriously posed, transforms itself into the metaphysical question about the nature and truth of reality. Understood in this way, the metaphysical question is no longer a purely speculative or theoretical one. To know what to do is to live directly out of what I have referred to as the root of one's existence. For this to be possible, the root has first to be exposed. The premise of this book is that this might require an earthquake. In any event, the philosophical soul finds no rest until truth, the ultimate truth about what is, has been disclosed.

What battle can be more intense than the one that rages when a human being decides to cast aside lies and pretense to face the truth of existence? For existence, cut loose from the conceptual net we cast upon it, constitutes a maelstrom. As noted earlier, the *Phaedrus* connects philosophy with madness (249d). Although Socrates goes on to say that the insanity of the philosopher is tantamount to possession by a deity, he neglects the issue of what kind of insanity one has to endure to become open to such possession. In posing the question of truth, the philosopher in effect dares reality to shed its mask of everydayness and show itself for what it truly is.

The question is never posed without the suspicion that things are not as they appear. If, however, they are not as they appear, they will not fall into the predictable and customary patterns we have come to anticipate. Raising the question of truth thus requires the readiness to be brought—suddenly—face to face with a reality one has never been prepared to encounter. The issue of sanity and insanity has thus been broached. Socrates's "valiant deed" is the deed of a warrior. The genuine philosopher cannot hold on to *any* presupposition about reality. If reason is the instrument for knowing what is, and if what is, is ultimately the Good, these things will have to be revealed on the field of truth. Having abandoned even the last hold on reality, the philosopher (Schelling tells us) must know what it is to tremble before those awful words that, according to Dante, adorn the gates of Hell: "Abandon every hope, all you who enter here."[19]

This disturbing reflection reveals the inadequacy of my initial interpretation of Alcibiades's story. I assumed that Apollo, as the beauty of the rising sun, was there from the beginning and that Apollo bestowed directly on Socrates the gift of his speculative interlude. This interpretation, however, merely repeats the mistake of Anders Nygren, to which I referred at the end of the last chapter. It accords no space for significant human action; it leaves us with nothing to do. The decision to cease supporting ourselves by lies is *not* founded on the discovery that something else is already supporting us. If faith were understood as providing us with that kind of prior support, the revelation of truth would require that we first put in place a new lie. Such faith would not be a very impressive commodity. It is too easy to let go, if we know that something is going to catch us. True faith, the faith that makes a master, is the faith that allows us to consider the possibility that reality itself might be hell. Indeed, a prior descent into hell is the condition for any genuine ascent into heaven. What other measure could the ordered rightness of being have beyond the depth of pain and confusion that it rescues us from? Is not the very divinity of the Divine the full extent of despair and chaos that it is capable of overcoming? Whence the awesome display of ethereal light, if not from the raging fires of hell below? We need to deepen our interpretation.

Nothing in the passage we are examining seems to warrant this sudden marriage of heaven and hell. At the same time, the theme is one that does sporadically surface in Plato's dialogues. In addition to the talk of madness in the *Phaedrus,* there is Socrates's worry that he doesn't know whether he is a "Typhon" or a gentler spirit. The *Meno* lays great stress on the confusion and perplexity that give rise to philosophy. Talk of "labor pains" or the pain of "unfolding wings" is characteristic. In the *Phaedo,* after commenting on the pleasure he feels after removing the chains that had bound him during the night, Socrates draws the conclusion that pleasure and pain always follow one another, "as if the two were joined together in one head" (60b). The image sets the tone for the great death scene itself: life, because of the countless desires that chain us to the finite, is essentially suffering. It is death that provides the great release. At the same time, the image has something profoundly disturbing about it. If pleasure follows pain, pain also follows pleasure. Even the redemption made possible by death cannot be a lasting one. Christian mythology hides the same awful secret: the highest salvation possible would be to stand where Satan stood before his fall.

The *Republic* confirms this vision. There are the central "underground" myths: the discovery, after an earthquake, of the Ring of Gyges; the myth of the metals; the allegory of the cave; and the myth of Er. Just as surely as the ideal state must reject (even if they are true) myths and poems that depict the soul's fate as a return into darkness (386c–387a), Socrates fashions a new set of myths that reverse the direction and point from darkness to light. Yet at times the movement seems to go downward as well as upward. The philosopher who is forced to return to the cave is able at least to maintain contact with a vision once enjoyed. In other instances, the reversal is more catastrophic. The myth of Er depicts souls that come down from heaven only to choose lives that will ultimately condemn them to hell: "a majority of those who were thus caught were of the company that had come down from heaven, inasmuch as they were unexercised in suffering" (619d). The problem of health and happiness is that they lead to the sins of hubris. Philosophers can acknowledge this unfortunate truth, for they are not bound to the foundational myth of the state (the assurance that order and goodness must prevail in the end). In this, the philosopher shares something with the gods. According to the

Phaedrus, even the processions of the gods do not spend eternity gazing at the forms but periodically return "home" to Hestia, the goddess who never leaves earth (247a).

Glaucon, after naming Socrates a "snake charmer" (for taming Thrasymachus), insists on the importance of playing the devil's advocate (*Rep.* 358d). He implores Socrates to "strip him [the just man] bare of everything but justice" (361c), making him "endure the lash, the rack, chains, the branding iron in his eyes, and finally, after every extremity of suffering, having him crucified" (361e–362a). The point is to discover whether the just man really is just or simply appears that way. The issue is a serious one. According to the Book of Job, God himself needed the help of Satan to discover whether Job's goodness was real. As for Socrates, he had gone down to Piraeus to pay his "devotions to the goddess" (*Rep.* 327a), which is unremarkable until one discovers that the goddess in question is Bendis, a Thracian form of Hecate, goddess of hell.[20] John Sallis, as I have already pointed out, reads the entire first book of the *Republic* in light of the fact that its opening word is *katebēn*: "I went down."[21] It is also the word with which Homer's Odysseus, in conversation with Penelope, begins to tell of his descent into Hades. Socrates in Piraeus thus becomes Socrates in Hades. The world of politics is the world of shadows. The philosopher descends into it, but only to prove that escape is possible.

As to why Socrates would have offered prayers to the devil-goddess of the Thracians, two observations might suffice. First of all, philosophy distinguishes itself not only by its great faith but also by its great doubt. Indeed, the very measure of philosophy's faith is the degree of skepticism it will tolerate. Without the *advocatis diabolis*, philosophy would not be possible. That the philosopher knows something about the Faustian contract does not, however, account for Socrates's devotion to Bendis in particular. To understand this requires a second observation: Socrates, thanks to the campaign in Potidaea, was no stranger to Thrace. He had direct knowledge of the Thracians, who, given as they were to intoxication (*Laws* 637d–e), were the originators of the cult of Dionysus.[22] Socrates may have felt that, as the earliest custodians of the Mysteries, they had something important to teach. Indeed, in the *Charmides*, he indicates that he used his time in Potidaea by studying at the feet of a Thracian shaman (156d–157c). He even indicates that the Thracian is the one who initiated him into philosophy, which he learned "with so much pain, and to so little profit" (175e).

This assertion, however, is difficult to understand. Why would Socrates, of all people, disparage philosophy for being the source of pain? And why would he have sought an initiation to philosophy? Two dialogues, the *Parmenides* and the *Protagoras*, depict Socrates before he marched off to Potidaea. He was clearly already adept at philosophy. He had studied with Anaxagoras (and Prodicus) and argued with every philosopher he could find. Why would he, approaching forty years of age, apprentice himself to a Thracian shaman? What could he have been looking for?

If we trust the hints provided in the *Charmides*, the question can be answered: Socrates was looking for a *cure*. Greek physicians practiced a holistic form of medicine to the degree that they concerned themselves with the regime of the whole body (156c). The Thracian shaman, however, occupied himself with both the body and the soul. "For all good and evil, he said, whether in the body or in the whole man, originates, as he declared, in the soul, and overflows from thence, as if from the head into the eyes. And therefore if the head and body are to be well, you must begin by curing the soul" (156e). The cure, moreover, can be specified: by use of beautiful words as "charms," temperance can be engendered in the soul (157a). Whatever Socrates was suffering from, its roots were psychological and its cure required that he learn temperance. As the image of Odysseus in the Trojan horse reminds us, it requires strength and valiancy to silence the passions. Was Socrates, during his twenty-four-hour stand, carrying out a shamanistic exercise, seeking to follow his anxieties to their ultimate root, thus making the metaphorical "descent into hell" to expurgate them in the only way this is possible, by holding them in a steady gaze, by taming them and, using "fair words as charms," making friends with them? Was this then his first devotion to Bendis?

Is it possible that the serpent-monster can be tamed by pulling the tail, once and for all, out of the mouth? If pleasure is bound to pain in the form of an escape, what happens when pain itself is accepted? What salvation is gained by the philosopher's stoic recognition that no final salvation is possible, that the way upward and the way downward are the same? And what of temperance itself? What of the pure pleasures that are free of the pain of hunger and desire, the pleasures of aesthetic and intellectual contemplation (*Phil.* 51b, 52a)? The idea of a "disinterested" pleasure was not first discovered by Kant. Nor was Schopenhauer the first to suggest that it holds the key to breaking free of the tail-in-the-mouth cycle of rebirth. The philosopher seeks a cure. Finitude itself must be overcome, even if the path to its overcoming goes through the hellish recognition that it can never be overcome. Not every intuition has to serve the whims of desire. The mind can be freed, if only because it must be freed.

A. E. Taylor offers a helpful clue for discerning how Socrates could have worked himself into the state of frenzy necessary to give birth to so high a hope.[23] According to his reconstruction, Socrates gained a reputation for wisdom well before the campaign in Potidaea. He points for evidence to the *Protagoras*, in which Socrates puts himself forward as a rival to the most eminent philosopher of the day. It was in this period, according to Taylor, that Chaerephon must have posed his question to the oracle of Delphi, "Is Socrates the wisest of men?" The disclosure that he was indeed the wisest initiated the crisis that came to a head during the twenty-four-hour stand. The famous account in the *Apology*—in which Socrates confesses that he initially tried to prove that the oracle was wrong by cross-examining those with a reputation for wisdom—shows that a dramatic reversal took place. The *Protagoras* represents this first phase. Socratic ignorance shows itself as the arrogant self-certainty of the skeptic. The young Socrates is convinced that he has the intelligence necessary to overcome the older and wiser Protagoras in a battle of words. He is guided by a noble intuition, the identity of knowledge and virtue, but his actual contributions are decisively negative, whereas his tendency to lecture Protagoras is an embarrassment. One sympathizes when Protagoras indicates that Socrates needs more time and life experience before he will ever be a true philosopher (361e). Even a Sophist such as Protagoras realizes that it takes more than "keenness" and "argumentative skill" to make a philosopher. He may even need to go off to war, for arrogance must be tempered through suffering. And that Socrates's brashness in the *Protagoras* masked a more serious hubris becomes evident, once we recall that the will to refute Protagoras was the will to refute Apollo.

But in Potidaea something must have happened. Once again, we can recall the account in the *Apology*. Socrates confessed that he came to the realization that the oracle was right. No one is wiser than he, for no mortal can truly be called wise. Instead of challenging the authority of Apollo, Socrates has come to accept it. He is now a gentler spirit, who, guided by the god, attempts to instill in others the temperance and piety of a philosopher. The *Charmides* represents the new beginning. Socrates is aroused by the young boy's physical beauty. But instead of trying to seduce him with a fearsome dialectical display, he takes seriously his complaint (the boy suffers from headaches) and sets out to complete the cure. The new modesty, the willingness to live out of the life of the gods, instead of the self-certainty of self-consciousness (represented by Critias), is something that can be taught. But because the form of virtue is humility, it cannot be taught by transferring a positive and determinate knowledge of what virtue is. Negative dialectic is thus retained, but instead of representing a device for asserting the superiority of the skeptic, who prevails over every conceivable positive assertion, it has been transformed into a kind of cathartic medicine (*Soph.* 230b–d). The Socrates of the *Charmides* uses the same forms of argumentation as the Socrates of

the *Protagoras*. But there is an essential difference. He has become a better man. If he continues to humble his interlocutors, he does so only to
facilitate their elevation by a power greater than himself. He has become
the servant of a god.

This, at any rate, is Plato's account of the matter. That Aristophanes
still found it necessary to administer a public spanking to Socrates as late
as 423 B.C. (seven years after he returned from Potidaea) would seem to
indicate that the turnabout into the kindly old Socrates may have taken
longer than Plato imagined. This does not, however, detract from the
importance of Potidaea. The Socrates caricatured by Aristophanes is not
the quasi-aristocratic chaser after young boys that we find in the *Protagoras*
but a floating-on-the-clouds ascetic, who seems to have lost all touch with
his own erotic nature. This is still compatible with the basic intuition that
I have been pursuing: "something happened" in Potidaea. If it did not
constitute an immediate and full cure of Socrates's hubris, it (to follow
Aristophanes on this point alone) certainly catapulted him into a new
and strange form of hubris. To reduce it to a word, Socrates's new arrogance is the arrogance of a saint.

Taylor is right to suggest that the twenty-four-hour trance holds the key
to Socrates's dramatic reversal.[24] But to turn the key, we need to take seriously the assertion in the text that Socrates threw himself, body and soul,
into the resolution of a problem. I include the "body" because Socrates
not only vowed never to "give up thinking" until he received an answer,
but he also showed a determination to keep his body perfectly erect for
however long this took. The importance of standing erect is affirmed at
the end of the *Timaeus* (90b–d), where it becomes a symbol for the orientation toward the celestial origin that elevates man above animal concerns. Standing erect thus represents the possibility of securing true happiness (90c). In this way, standing on the battlefield is a preparation for
the kind of standing that is portrayed in the *Timaeus*. What we have before
us is not so much an image of harmony with the cosmos as a portrayal of
the intensity of the desire to achieve such harmony. Why else would Socrates so stubbornly persist with his endeavor? The upright figure in the
Timaeus is free to follow the heavenly movements of the sun and the stars.
Socrates, however, is obstinately fighting to break through to the root of
his existence. He is not caught up in quiet contemplation. Instead, he
has delivered himself, body and soul, into the activity of thinking. This,
at any rate, is the consensus of our translators. To test it, we need to take
a look at a bit of the Greek.

First of all, with regard to what Socrates was after, Agathon already said the essential at a very early stage of the dialogue (175d), when he pointed out that he would never have given up his fit of contemplation and joined the party if he had not been able to fix on some wisdom (*tou sophou haptomenos*). Yet what captured Socrates's attention on the battlefield certainly did not manifest itself as wisdom from the beginning. Instead, we find Socrates standing and "scoping" some vague "it" (*ti eistekei skopon*). This is not yet so much a thinking as an intensive searching—a taking aim. An archer would scope a target in much the same way. And although the consensus among the translators is that Socrates himself made no progress (*ou pro-chōrei*), the absence of an explicit subject could take us back to that same vague "it" that Socrates had fastened onto in the first place: "it was not yielding to him," "it was not letting him in." Read in this manner, we get an intuition into what the "it" is, for the verb itself (*pro-chōrō*) makes reference to *chōra*, to space.[25] Socrates is staring into empty space. Or, more precisely, he has stationed himself before the abode of empty space, awaiting entry. Although at first glance this would seem to resurrect Hegel's contention that he was lost in a cataleptic condition, we need to recall that Socrates has thus stationed himself with the intent to break through to wisdom.

What lay under such resolve? What, if not the firmness of the very earth on which Socrates took his stand. In Socrates, earth seeks sky. The seed surrenders the hard shell that protects it in order—through its death—to strive upward to light, openness, and the perfection of its own swelling blossom. Feet planted on the ground, Socrates must will just such a death. He began his morning, let us surmise, by cursing the god Apollo, for it was Apollo who had called him the wisest of human beings—and by so calling him had revealed the horrible truth that humanity is lost. None of us knows who we are or what we are supposed to do with our lives. The great sea of humanity has nothing more to justify it than the need of animals to mate and once again to mate. Unholy horror! Release this caged demon, thrust unknowingly on the battlefield of life, his hands freshly bathed in the blood of superfluous humanity.

Yet to curse the god who placed us here is nothing short of hell. Let us further surmise then that it is a Socrates in need, a Socrates at the foot of a besieged city, who seeks now delivery into the emptiness of pure space. This, a desire for death if you will, could yet represent the possibility of a new beginning. As Plato asserts in the *Timaeus*, something stood before and beyond not only all that is sensible but all that is intelligible. It is the mysterious "third nature," what was neither created nor destroyed but stood as a sanctuary for all things created. This, the holy of holies, origin of all origins he names *chōras aei*, eternal space (52b). The lost center, from which the whole mad spectacle ushered forth, is to deliver the redeeming word.

The word is first and foremost recollection of what is. In the void of the void is voiding, contraction, disappearance. And yet the completion of that very contraction is simultaneously clearing, the opening of the great empty open. Abiding within, always one and the same void, whether collapsed inward into the dark ground of self, or released outward into the empty open of space. The eternal yes and no, held together in the unity of simple essence. It is this unity of contradiction, the impossible and thus ever-fleeting, that creates time out of space. Eruption and cavernous appetite for being precipitates a flood of images without substance, swirling over the deep (52 b–c). Negation, severing itself in defiant opposition to what simply is, has thus always already created chaos, the material condition of a universe (52e). Irony of ironies: without the primal will not to be, nothing would be.

Fire of Heraclitus, hidden core of all that is, where is the yes that can soften your infernal roar? Neither expansion fighting contraction nor the two locked together, but somewhere, higher, above and beyond, there must be a yes that could silence the jumbled frenzy. Socrates has positioned himself *pro-chōros*, face to face with the open of the sky, the open of empty space. A Socrates in need gathers himself to hear the word born in silence. His silence weds itself to the silence of space. The deepest question falls away in the intensity of its need for an answer, leaving only the empty vessel of earnest listening. In this empty silence an answer slowly begins to dawn. The silence of the question meets the deeper silence of the answer. The flood of appearances unleashed by primordial desire is stilled by the yes that, having nothing to say, has no more to negate. *Chōros* lets the world be.

The awakening of Socrates had its beginning in the darkness of a night that merged with the darkness of his own soul, the very place where Apollo surrenders himself to Dionysus. Against the logic of history, in which good and evil are locked in mortal combat and the world is transformed into a battlefield; against the logic of revenge and counter-revenge, in which the snake is always chasing its own tail; against the senseless futility of "nothing new under the sun" (Eccles. 1:9), there stands the higher logic of divinity whereby the Good prevails by letting evil be. Or, what amounts to the same thing, through which God realizes his fullest possible existence in and through his nonexistence. It is a wisdom that no human could ever claim to understand. Thrust as we are into the battlefield of life, we have no option but to take our stand and fight. The truth of history is war.

Yet as unavoidably as life within the agora is given over to the various struggles, it is still possible for a human being to look elsewhere for the courage to face what every sensitive soul knows to be a nightmare. As the battles around us intensify, it becomes progressively clearer that our commitments, contingently formed as they are, lack the depth to sustain us. As the moment of crisis comes to a head, we are forced into a deeper stand, a stand in death. The refusal to accept the unacceptable, the heart of the great experiment of modernity, is finally trumped by nature. We are, after all, mortal.

Even so, we discern, in a far distance that transcends all tragedy, the laughter of gods. And above even that, the great silence of empty space. The Good, Socrates tells us, "transcends being" in dignity and power (*Rep.* 509b).

So what has our sudden fantasy-filled excursion into the Beginning, baptism in primordial void, brought us? And what, if anything, might it have to do with Socrates?

I have tried to imaginatively re-create the persistence with which Socrates, seeking assurance of a Good that is always beyond, stretches his nerves and "does gymnastics" (*gumnazomenō, Rep.* 504d). The purest expression of divinity is given in the form of transcendence. In turn, the purest expression of transcendence is atheism: God is so "beyond" that he simply isn't there. Without a reconciliation of opposites, philosophy can never realize its goal. If its goal is not achievable, beginning is impossible.

A more complete examination of the *Timaeus* would suggest that the origin always includes within itself the possibility of chaos. Plato's Demiurge is bound by this necessity, creating what is good, but only "insofar as this is attainable" (30a). It is good to know that God has his limits. And even more, it is good to know that God is crowned finally by an all-encompassing emptiness. What cannot be reconciled in history may yet be reconciled in eternity.

The struggle to produce, rather than discover, what is good is often hailed (at least in the modern/postmodern world) as the highest form of nobility. Yet if the attempt to eradicate human misery leads in fact to its intensification, stupidity has doubled for nobility. If the Walpurgis Night dance includes the moment of mutual renunciation and withdrawal, if calm reigns in the eye of the hurricane, another possibility shows itself. Where beauty can be discerned, the promise of the Good is delivered. This has less to do with achieving an alternative explanation for what is happening than with the realization that what cannot be understood can be accepted. Nietzsche was wrong to claim that Socrates embodies the principle of *ressentiment*.[26] Socrates embodies the principle of wisdom, which for human beings is the highest piety. Had Socrates represented the need to fight at all costs for justice, he would have agreed emphatically with Euthyphro that a man may have to prosecute his own father. The appropriate symbol for a purely political outlook remains the guillotine.

The point is not, as the purely political man believes, that Socrates's veil of poverty was a disguise and that he too labored on behalf of the powerful.[27] The point is much more that plebeian and aristocrat alike are doomed to suffer and ultimately to die—and that we need to discover how best to live with that fact. The philosopher who urges on us the need to purify our souls will always be deemed a reactionary. The suggestion that we withdraw from the struggles of the day is not taken lightly by those who are strongly committed to one of the factions. But ironically enough, the philosopher who made this suggestion, the purest philosopher of them all, was a plebeian and presumably had much he could have fought for.[28] Only in the midst of suffering does the need to come to terms with suffering reach its culmination. The reason the oppressed so often resist efforts to politicize them is because they fear dying amid unfulfilled dreams.

The twenty-four-hour trance, I have tried to stress, depicts not a quietist swoon but a desperate attempt to break through to a liberating new insight. It is the most concrete example we possess of Socrates literally engaging in the "practice of dying and death" that, according to the *Phaedo*, is the heart and soul of genuine philosophy (64a). The practice must appear as an act of insanity to anyone who knows how to live life. The Nietzschean "last men" who, having "invented happiness," look at Zarathustra and "blink," have no need of philosophy.[29] When the philosopher extends to such a person the offer of a ritualistic cleansing and purging ("you know less than you think you do"), the response is generally a dismissive one. What we have to see is that the philosopher has something more to offer.

According to Alcibiades's narration, the "Ionians" camped out to see how long Socrates would maintain his stand. This might be understood as a variation on the theme of the maiden who laughed at Thales when, eyes fixed on the flawless geometry of the stars, he fell into a well visible at his feet (*Tht.* 174a–b). There is an abyss that separates the philosopher from everyone else.

Socrates's behavior was undoubtedly strange enough to prove entertaining. Still, another interpretive possibility presents itself. The Ionians were mercenaries, a more desperate lot than the Athenians. They may have looked upon Socrates out of awe and admiration rather than curiosity and ridicule. Indeed, the Athenians might well enough have followed suit but for the truth that makes it impossible to recognize a prophet in anyone but an outsider. Socrates's fellow citizens had presumably seen quite enough of different things. As Alcibiades pointed out, it is hard not to feel insulted when, shivering though fully attired in winter array, one observes a colleague traipsing about barefoot in the snow (*Symp.* 220b). "Who in the hell does he think he is, anyway?" The dismissal, scurrilous enough to eventually place the philosopher's life in jeopardy, hides enough envy to reinforce the point: every one of us has reason to hope that the philosopher's wings will one day be unfurled. Cynicism is most dismissive of the very sense of meaning it itself secretly craves.

The true test of the philosopher is whether the jeers awaken anger or simple understanding. If there is no God (and in this world there is no God), the battle for power is what we are left with. Of course, the philosopher is the subject of ridicule. The competing insight, that if there is no God, there is a God, cannot be discursively communicated. To discern structure in the unity of pure and undifferentiated void (and thereby to understand that, in fact, there is no nothing) is for the first time truly to see. Yet truly to *see* in that manner may require more than the kind of dialectical facility that is so well represented in dialogues such as the *Parmenides* and the *Sophist.* The void that contains the one, that contains number, that contains the all, is not a speculative idea that amounts to solipsism. All idealism is solipsism, including that of Hegel. What Socrates attained cannot be discursively reconstructed. Instead of representing the final appropriation of the standpoint of the subject, he has to be understood as representing the possibility of its overcoming and abandonment. During the last hours of his courageous stand, Socrates was free of his frenetic will to know. Having glimpsed the faint outline of a smile, or half-smile, at the bottom of it all, we might profitably wager that Socrates found his moment of peace in an act of self-surrender so complete that all will and subjectivity simply melted away. Standing before the *chōros*—and this I call thinking—he gained entry. A depth of emptiness engulfed him. From this deepest and holiest of all depths, the sun climbed fierily aloft and painted in the loveliest of colors both earth and sky. Awakening thus into the splendor of creation, what better response could there be than to fall on one's knees in prayer?

Blessed are the poor in spirit, for they shall inherit the kingdom of heaven.

The Resurrection of the Body

Socrates's "valiant feat" of standing for twenty-four hours, silent and motionless, while totally absorbed in thought, may seem difficult to reconcile with his general eagerness for talk. Yet regarded simply as a formidable display of endurance and concentration, the episode is not unrelated to Socrates's love for dialogue, given that his conversations presuppose his uncanny ability to hold on to a question or idea. Plato's portrayal is at times so exaggerated that it makes Socrates seem superhuman. The general structure of the *Symposium* affords a good example of how this point is made. According to Alcibiades's depiction of the trance scene, Socrates devoted twenty-four hours to reflection and then said his prayers to the sun, the ritualistic beginning of a new day. The *Symposium* as a whole reproduces exactly the same time frame. After occupying himself for a day, Socrates attended an all-night party and philosophized until dawn. From there, he went to the Lyceum, had a bath, and went about another day pursuing his philosophical discussions.

We would be able to dismiss this repetition of the thirty-six-hour day more easily if the pattern were not repeated elsewhere. The most prominent example is afforded by the *Republic*. Once again, Socrates philosophized through the entire night. After he returned home in the morning, instead of sleeping, he spent a very full and long day recounting the conversation of the previous day and night. Elsewhere, Plato lets us know that after completing the narration of the *Republic*, Socrates still remained unexhausted. According to the *Timaeus*, he was not only awake, but, insofar as listening requires more concentration than speaking, he was more awake than ever. He sat and listened, over the period of at least the next day or so, to three lengthy narrations: the speeches of Timaeus, Critias, and Hermocrates (17a–c, 20a–20c).

To complete the parallel with the Potidaea episode, we find that Socrates's attempt to listen brought him to an ever-intensified capacity for silence. The effect of this silence is made greater by the fact that, as dialogues, the *Critias* remains a fragment and no *Hermocrates* was ever written.[1] In other words, there is a steady progression into wordlessness. Adding it all together: after an all-night conversation about justice and the ideal state, Socrates proceeded first to narrate the entire conversation to an initially undisclosed group of friends and then to listen to their long speeches in turn. Plato thus projects a seventy-two-hour period of nonstop philosophizing that began during the festival of Bendis, the underworld goddess, and ended, at the completion of the third day, during the festival of Athena, the goddess of light and wisdom (*Rep.* 327a; *Tim.* 21a). The three-day movement into the celebration of the goddess of wisdom can be understood as an enactment of the central event that stands behind the Mysteries, the release of Persephone from Hades, and thus the recovery of her original form as an Olympian goddess. The *Republic* and the sequence of dialogues that are to begin with the *Timaeus* are the philosophical reenactment of the rebirth of the goddess. The closer her approach, the more fully Socrates gives himself over to silent listening— and the more definitively Plato himself grows silent about what might have been said.

This movement into silence is not what one might anticipate on the basis of the contemporary understanding of the dichotomy between the rational and the irrational. According to this understanding, it should have been the night world of Persephone (Bendis) that was shrouded in silence. But in that realm, as represented by the *Republic*, words flow without cease. In contrast, the festival of Athena is celebrated with words that were never recorded (who really is this Hermocrates who should be speaking last?). This is not to deny the fact, made clear in the phenomenon of psychological depression, that there is a silence of darkness. Plato seems, however, to be suggesting that there is also a corresponding silence of light and joy, sealed by the holy name of Athena, from which the soul is able to draw nurture and strength.

The same thing can be inferred from the *Phaedo*'s striking image of the swan who sings most beautifully in the moments preceding death (84e–85b). Socrates recalls it only after giving himself over to a prolonged moment of silence (84c). The swan sings, it seems, the beauty of death itself. Socrates demonstrates the same mysterious talent through his remarkable display of energy, not only on the day of his death, but during the weeks that preceded it. Shortly before his trial, he was supposed to have engaged in the long conversations that are recorded in the *Theaetetus*, the *Sophist*, and the *Statesman*. They too are compressed into a fantastically condensed time frame. Similarly to the *Timaeus* sequence, the *Sophist* and the *Statesman* also portray Socrates as a silent listener. In addition, a fourth dialogue (to have been titled the *Philosopher*) was projected but never written.

It is tempting to interpret these fanciful allusions to bizarrely long conversations back into the Potidaea episode. The preliminary dialogues that depict Socrates himself actively speaking correspond, in the twenty-four-hour stand, to a preliminary period of active searching. The subsequent dialogues, in which Socrates remains a silent listener, correspond to a later moment in which Socrates delivered himself fully into his question—and the need to listen for an answer. Indeed, this can be concretized: if, driven by the urgency of his plight, he actively pushed along the first phase of thinking, the second period corresponds to that moment of philosophical consciousness in which words simply descend on the waiting and receptive mind. To extend the comparison even further, the unwritten dialogues can now be understood as representing the completed stage of consciousness, in which, as at Potidaea, Socrates is not only silent but has disappeared entirely. The dialogues that were supposed to represent this last phase were to be called the *Philosopher* and the *Hermocrates*. The first title lets us know that it is philosophy that is thrust into ineffability. The second title is more mysterious. It is simply a name. To read into it a play on words (the hermetic Socrates, Socrates as Hermes, Socrates as hermit) would be, perhaps, to go too far.

One does not go too far, however, by assuming that Plato may have had something to say by announcing two lengthy dialogues that he never delivered. Indeed, I would like to consider the possibility of speaking of a third "unwritten dialogue," the most mysterious one of all. According to the first sentence of the *Timaeus*, another speaker (whose name is never given) was supposed to have been in attendance (17a). He was presumed to be "ill"—the same excuse that Plato uses to account for his own absence on the day of Socrates's death (*Phd.* 59b). In other words, in addition to the two announced but unwritten dialogues, we can infer a third that was not announced at all, and that was to have been narrated by a man without a name. The last word is the word of that death into which even the "immortal" Socrates had to go. To name the philosopher one has to resort first to a hermetic name and finally to no name at all. The reason for this has already been suggested: the "philosopher" is the one who "practices for dying and death" (*Phd.* 64a, 80e). To penetrate, with words, into the heart of this practice is more than can be accomplished. The philosopher is more than what the philosopher either says or thinks.

This "more" cannot be measured in words, but it can be glimpsed in deeds. The "valiant deed" of Potidaea was an anticipation of the most valiant deed of all: the death of Socrates. If I have been at all successful in rescuing the deed on the battlefield from the images of "trance" and quietist self-absorption that are generally attached to it, then it is my hope that I will similarly be able to rescue the death of Socrates from the image of life-denying intellectualism that has so often been foisted on it. The kinds of superhuman thought marathons that Plato loved to depict cannot be understood as the accomplishment of a disembodied intellect. Instead, they represent the highest instances of endurance, strength, and vitality that the human spirit is capable of achieving. Plato's dialogues find their parallel only in those truly great works—Michelangelo's Sistine Chapel, Dante's *Divine Comedy*, the *Missa Solemnis* of Beethoven—that give testimony to the divinity that lies buried amid the depths of human confusion. The path from Bendis to Athena, from the disputations of politics to the lasting achievements of art and philosophy, is a path that leads through all of us and ends in the glory of an ever-unfolding awakening. Death, comprehended as deed and awakening, is the wellspring of what has been called eternal life. It may be worth our while to investigate the possibility that Socrates, in the wisdom of his ignorance, might have known something that could restore a semblance of meaning to the phrase.

The "disembodied intellect" requires a foundation on which it can stand. The Platonic doctrine of "ideas" was once thought to fulfill this need: mind can disentangle itself from the world of appearances, made visible through the senses, and ground itself once again in its true element, the supernatural order of pure form. Spirit and nature stand opposed. Their unification in the embodied being that is man is a tenuous and fleeting affair. This metaphysical doctrine is no longer accepted. Many of the best Plato scholars have even maintained that Plato himself never seriously espoused such a doctrine. Still, as we have seen, it lives on in the scholarly ideal of speaking "as if" one inhabited the perspective of a disembodied intellect—even when one's research assumes nothing more real than the existence of bodies alone. How else do we account for that naïve naturalism that construes the world as if it were fully contained in a textbook in physics, even when the author of the book, out of concern for objectivity, has stepped completely outside the picture?

The Socratic alternative to dogmatic naturalism is compatible with many things that we contemporaries have been conditioned to believe. Intellect, as always, continues to seek separation and "disembodiment" (the model of detached objectivity). But at the same time it has become enlightened enough to seek its grounding not in the preexisting ideational reality of the beyond, but in the always necessarily provisional order that the mind establishes for itself. For Socrates that provisional order is given in the form of "definitions," abstract determinations of what endures amid the flux and flow. For us moderns, such order is reflected in the paradigms that constitute science, the latest shorthand accounts of what we all experience as the truly real: the world of sensually perceivable bodies, located somewhere in space and time. Through our abstractions and constructions (including theoretical models that seem to have dispensed entirely with any connection to the reassuring solidity of the sensually perceivable), we are able to gain enough distance from that world to exert some degree of control over it. Although death ensures that each of us will return to dust in the end, life lasts long enough that we can still attain a high degree of autonomy, refashioning by desire at least our own isolated corners of the world.

Because desire proves to be inextinguishable (and often damaging to our health), it is deemed necessary to appropriate a second Socratic moment: the concern with discovering which desires are best, the concern, that is, with values. Priorities have to be established. The issue is particularly urgent when human beings, engaged in their great collective projects, require consensus. Because at this point science fails to find a way, the discussion is left in the definitional mode that Socrates gave it. What is the good we are trying to achieve? What is the highest degree of justice that human beings can attain? What, in a word, are the answers that will enable us best to refashion the world we live in? Because (with Socrates) we have to concede that the answers are difficult to decipher, and because consensus about values is nonetheless necessary, we seem justified in assuming that the definitions will simply have to be posited. If we cannot live by the truth, we shall have to live by the best conventions we can establish.

For additions to our lists of proverbs, however, Socrates provides us with no help. The Socratic quest for definitions remains a quest. This does not, however, mean that Socrates was fundamentally a skeptic.[2] It is in fact his very insistence on the absoluteness of the Absolute that holds his quest open. Instead of positing unity behind multiplicity, he sought to uncover it. In this sense, Socrates was not as far removed from the Platonic theory of ideas as some have supposed.[3]

Yet the commitment to ideas does not translate into a predilection for dogmatism. Quite the contrary: the very refusal to rest satisfied with counterfeit truths is what opens the mind to transcendence. The effable idea is not the idea in truth. The intensity of the desire to find the truly desirable serves to detach the will from false desires. To know the purpose of our existence presupposes that we are fully aware that we have no idea why we are alive—and in a double sense: to determine the indeterminable is always to lose it; not to have determined it, but to search for it as that which alone can satisfy us, is to live our way into it and thus to be guided and touched by it. By knowing, one does not know; by not knowing, one knows. The Socratic search for definitions, by remaining always a quest, cannot establish even a provisional foundation for a detachable intellect. It serves instead the tasks of purgation and purification. If it frees us, it is not from the world but into the world. It does not take our feet off the ground; rather, by deflating the hyperbolic claims of the disembodied intellect, it places them firmly on the ground. (Even the winged soul of the *Phaedrus* is not able to soar above the celestial sphere whose turning it rides.) By purging us of our mistaken opinions, Socratic method wants to enable us to live, with restored innocence, directly in the world itself. This goal cannot be accomplished, of course, solely through the instrument of a negative dialectic. If opinions are tossed aside, new opinions will quickly take their place—unless, that is, the need to generate them can somehow be eradicated. The attempt to do this I understand as the true (the Socratic) "practice of dying and death." Only by living into our vulnerability can we be freed from the need to overcome it. Another word for this attempt is religion.

Contemporary interpretations of Plato, whether analytic or Straussian, generally share the same fundamental (and unexamined) metaphysical assumptions. Material reality is the only reality. Or, what comes to the same thing, reality itself is "unknowable" or "irrational." Form is thus the provisional creation of the human animal. Reason is an instrument. The "disembodiment of intellect" is inevitably a flawed project, but this very fact underscores its importance, why scholars still regard it as a kind of existential imperative. Because we are animals, sharing all the vulnerability of animal life, we fixate ourselves on the illusion that reason can put things in order. Whereas the analytic philosopher is forthright about these assumptions, the Straussian is more cunning, maintaining that the noble lie of classical metaphysics should be supported. To the postmodern mind, there is no authority above the human authority of science and politics, but intelligent people know that it is best to pretend there is. Socrates's arguments for the immortality of the soul, for instance, have to be respected, for the disciples gathered around him were in desperate need of the fiction. Only the "close reader" knows the truth: Socrates was fully aware of the correctness of the modern assumption that death is the dissolution of consciousness.[4]

As an antidote to such tendencies, it might be helpful to call to mind the Kantian antinomies about the finite and the infinite. The soul is no less "obviously" mortal than it is "obviously" immortal. The fixation on one or the other side of the antinomy is precisely the inflated claim to knowledge that Socratic elenchus was supposed to free us from. The problem of death, and with it the problem of life, cannot be approached until one has the courage to face the irresolvable nature of the mystery it poses. Some seek solace in the certainty of dissolution, while others seek solace in the certainty of eternal life. Both camps fail to acknowledge the horrors hidden within their purported "answers." Socratic wisdom, the wisdom of a fully realized human ignorance, may constitute a subtle third path between (or beyond) the poles of the antinomy. Charting the path presupposes, however, that we have recognized Scylla and Charybdis for the dangers they are. The path "between" may require, moreover, that like Odysseus we run aground on the one or the other. If so, annihilation just might serve to open the abyss of consciousness. The eternal, as the openness of this "nothing," juts forth only where self disappears. Purification of the spirit thus holds the key to whether one can make sense of the subtle alternative.

What I am attempting to do, by evoking the metaphysical and religious, is to remove Socrates from the prevailing horizon of interpretation (humanism: in the guise of either science or politics). By doing so, I affirm my sense of Socrates as a stranger. This does not make him, however, a stranger to us, for we too are strangers. We are not only engaged in the great project of modernity, which rests on the separation of mind and nature, but we also have to live with its failures and its contradictions. Ultimately, it is our own finitude we have to face.

What stands in the way of this understanding is formidable: it is Plato himself. The death of Socrates, on which I have staked my entire interpretation, is the subject of that most "Platonic" of dialogues, the *Phaedo*. In this dialogue, as nowhere else in the history of philosophy (apart from Descartes), the doctrine of the disembodied intellect would appear to reign supreme. If the dialogue has always invited a "religious" interpretation, it is hardly religious in the sense I have suggested, as the acceptance of human finitude; rather, it is religious in the contrary sense of finitude denied. Socrates's goal, after all, as presented in the main arguments of the *Phaedo*, is to demonstrate the immortality of the individual soul. His argument does not come to completion until he evokes the theory of ideas. The philosopher who practices for death awakens to the forms only to the degree that the demands of the body can be silenced and overcome. "Separation" of the soul from the body is, according to the dialogue, the final aim of philosophy.

Against such a "Platonist" reading of the *Phaedo*, a number of contemporary studies can be cited.[5] Whereas traditionally attention was focused on the logical arguments that purport to demonstrate the immortality of the soul, the newer interpretations begin by taking seriously Plato's own emphasis on the poetic dimension of philosophy. He has Socrates, for instance, using his time in prison to compose a hymn to Apollo and set several of Aesop's fables in verse. Socrates does this in response to a recurring dream that bids him to "make music and work at it" (*Phd.* 61a). Although philosophy itself partially satisfies this command (Socrates calls

it the "highest form of music"), he has suddenly realized that its conceptual form might also be a limitation: music requires rhythm and rhyme.
Before the word comes the elusive wind that bears it aloft. Swans do not
talk, they sing.

Nor is this a peripheral point. Throughout the dialogue, Socrates
suggests (in the spirit of the *Charmides*) that his arguments are to be
understood as "incantations" or "charms" (*Phd.* 77a–78a, 91b, 114d). He
is interested not only in concepts but in the musicality of language, in its
ability to create a certain *mood*: the mood of confidence and calm with
which he chooses to face death. Indeed, as the same commentators have
noticed (at least since Jacob Klein pointed it out[6]), the story of Theseus
that is cited at the beginning of the dialogue provides a mythical framework for the entire dialogue. Just as Theseus freed himself and fourteen
youths and maidens from the Minotaur, Socrates frees himself and the
fourteen disciples gathered around him from the fear of death. Socrates
exhorts his disciples to seek the truth about death. He confesses, however, that he himself is hardly in a position to be objective. He is eager to
make himself believe what might not be true, that death is a good thing
(91b), for only in and through this belief can he himself attain the virtue
of courage. The task he faces is practical rather than theoretical. The real
goal is to become good, to achieve victory over the fear of death, victory
over oneself. For this reason Socrates says he is "contentious," though
with himself rather than his interlocutors (91a). This is not to suggest, of
course, that he has suspended his interest in finding the truth. But if the
truth is to be sought, it is to be sought in the faith that it itself is good,
with the realization that truth provides a firmer foundation than fiction.
As long as the truth remains concealed, those fictions are to be chosen
that help propel us toward the best possible understanding of reality. The
Phaedo is a rhetorical tour de force masquerading as an exercise in logic.

The poetic and rhetorical dimensions of the *Phaedo* have (at least
among philosophical hermeneuticists) been thoroughly excavated. It is
not obvious, however, that this accomplishment is enough to justify my
own contention that Socrates, as he was about to take leave of the world,
was simultaneously striving to root himself securely "in" the world. To
bring this more fully into view, I will focus on the way even these hermeneutic readings of the dialogue remain entrapped within the framework
of a certain logicality. The hermeneutic fixation on words fails to do justice to the silence that is artistically interwoven into the fabric of the dialogue (*Phd.* 79d, 84c, 95e, 116b, 117e, 118a–b). The importance of this
silent dimension even has a quantitative measure: for a conversation that
was supposed to have taken place between dawn and sunset, the *Phaedo* is

surprisingly brief—a shorter dialogue, for instance, than any out of the *Theaetetus* cycle, each of which was supposed to occupy only a morning or an afternoon.

The point is not meant to be subtly "irrational." Indeed, we might begin with Socrates's own warning: what triggers irrationalism (or misology as he calls it) is an exaggerated (and irrational) trust in the power of reason (89d).[7] Although he himself clearly wants to guard against skepticism and actively nourish a trust in reason, he does so by emphasizing that one must begin with an awareness of the limits of reason. Arguments serve an important need. They are the charms with which one draws the soul (both of oneself and of others) closer and closer to the moment of vision. But they are to be appropriated critically to the degree that they are incapable of doing more than entertain speculative possibilities. Reason is a daemon, not a god. It offers the soul a kind of guidance, but without freeing it from the necessity of finding its own way.

The limitation of reason is itself more a function (and failure) of insight than of logic. By making this assertion, I want to distance myself from the prevailing belief that each of the arguments the *Phaedo* provides for establishing the immortality of the soul is fundamentally flawed. It would be more proper to maintain that the arguments *appear* to be flawed, given the deeply entrenched presuppositions of the present age.[8] Arguments themselves, as long as they offer an apparent plausibility, can be neither definitively confirmed nor refuted.[9] The crucial question is whether we ourselves possess sufficient insight to follow them into whatever claim they are making (90d). The general assumption, for instance, that Socrates could not have been serious when he advanced arguments based on the idea of reincarnation provides a case in point. Viewed through the lens of a Christian and post-Christian worldview, it is, of course, difficult to buy into the argument's most basic premises. This says more, however, about our way of looking at reality than about the rationality of the argument as such. There is, moreover, no methodical way out of this dilemma. Premises might be secured, for instance, by their compatibility with "everyday language." But the acceptance of such a tribunal itself simply reflects the presuppositions of a democratic culture.

Recognizing this dilemma should not lead us to unduly privilege the insight of the great thinker. "As for you, if you will take my advice, you will think very little of Socrates, and much more of the truth. If you think anything I say is true, you must agree with me; if not, oppose it with every argument that you have" (91c). Insight philosophy is always, because of the intensity of its commitment to truth, painfully aware of the profoundly personal nature of all thinking. The demand this places on us is great: given the inadequacy of what alone really matters—our level of insight—we are forced to take up a kind of project that is different from those offered by the prevailing philosophical schools. Rather than methodically critiquing arguments with the help of a rationally determined methodology and on the basis of the common prejudices built into the way we use language, but also rather than attempting to reconstruct, on the basis of close textual investigation of authoritative authors, the vision of someone we can trust, we have no choice but to attempt the thoroughgoing self-transformation that was the real concern of both Socrates and Plato.

To successfully initiate this project, we have to first reposition the mind itself. Rather than anchor it aloft, in either "concepts" or "texts," we have to let it gravitate to its own natural context: any mind is the mind of one who exists within a world.[10] Successful thinking occurs only on the basis of some kind of experience, either that of natural consciousness, which is mediated through the senses, or that of a higher consciousness, mediated through the visionary capacity of the mind as such. The possibility of a uniquely philosophical order of experience is what both the hermeneutic and the analytic philosopher effectively deny.

If contemporary philosophers are mistaken in this regard, it would seem that the *Phaedo* itself has prepared their way. In the brief autobiographical sketch Socrates provides (96a–100b), he relates how he first attempted to investigate the phenomena themselves, but, finding that he was never able to approach what he was seeking, an understanding of the Good (the real reason why things are as they are), he was forced to undertake his famous "second sailing" (99d). If the wind falters, one has to use the oars. If direct vision of the forms is impossible, one has to seek their reflection in concepts, undertaking the laborious movement through the *logoi*. Socrates even goes so far as to suggest that this presumably second-best way of proceeding is actually the best, for the direct path carries with it a tremendous danger: intuition may lead to blindness (99e).

The appearance that the second sailing is superior to the first derives from Socrates's account of his initial investigations. He first sought the kind of explanation of reality that is still pursued in the natural sciences: the explanation of things, even living organisms, from their material constituents. The result, though, was a "blindness" of another sort (96c), not the blindness of direct intuition, but the blindness of systematic looking away from the phenomena toward what explains them. His only "progress" was that he lost the little knowledge he once thought he had, those commonsense certainties that had initially led him to a scientific examination of nature. He had once assumed that the phenomena were more or less what they appear to be. At the same time, he assumed that a given phenomenon is a product of other phenomena. The problem, however, is that by pursuing causal investigation one keeps looking away from what one wants to understand: the appearances themselves.

What Socrates came to realize is that wholes are more than the sum of their parts. Putting together the separate limbs of a human being would yield (at best) a dead corpse—never the living being one wants to understand. Scientific analysis leads to reductionism. A is not A but the x, y, and z that gave rise to A. A thing is explained not in terms of its own form but in terms of the conditions that, added together, make possible its emergence. The same point can be made mathematically. One has not understood the number two when one regards it as the addition of one and one. It could just as easily be understood in terms of the division of one of the ones. Explaining something in terms of the process that generates it does not lead to insight into the nature of what we explain if such wildly competing processes as addition and division yield the same result. Besides, evenness has to be understood in contrast to oddness. In the same way, duality has to be understood in contrast to unity. To understand two, in other words, one has to remain within the two itself. The phenomenon of rain is more successfully disclosed in a poetic invocation of its cool wetness or its moody fickleness than in a meteorological explanation of how a certain conjunction of humidity and atmospheric pressure will "trigger" its occurrence. For this reason, the hermeneutic act of understanding must have priority over the reductive act of explanation. Even Anaxagoras, with his conception of mind as the ultimate cause, was not able to satisfy this condition. Because he was a dualist, treating mind as if it were a cause operating alongside the various material causes, which from his evolutionary perspective actually preceded it, Anaxagoras was unable to escape the limitation of the natural-scientific perspective. He was unable to do justice to our immediate intuitive sense that it is we ourselves, not our muscles and bones, who are primarily responsible for the way we conduct our lives. Again, it is the idea that is of real concern. The earth is held in place by neither wind nor hidden chains, but by the fact that it occupies its proper place (98c, 108e–109a).[11]

The shift to the second sailing involves the recognition that the ideas are not something we can immediately intuit. To gain access to them, we have to resort to "hypotheses." That is, we have to name them in a *logos* and thereby invoke their presence. Because the ideas are said to be eternal structures, it is tempting to conclude, as most commentators have, that Socrates has simply abandoned the concerns that first drew him to Anaxagoras.[12] Whereas initially he hoped to find an explanation for becoming, for what determines the position of the earth and all that derives from the earth, he now shifts his concern to the unmovable heaven beyond the heavens, the realm of pure form. And because to peer into *that* would mean blindness indeed, he is left with no choice but simply to investigate the ways in which the ideas can be talked about. As I have suggested before, the hermeneutic philosopher finds here a justification for an approach that is "conversational" (entering into a dialogue with texts) rather than phenomenological (engaging the things themselves). It is this strategic concern that has lent so much prominence to Socrates's "second sailing."

Against this reception of the doctrine, I want to argue that the second sailing is not the primary and only mode of doing philosophy but one that we are forced into by virtue of the fact that our moments of real vision are few and far between. In other words, it really is the second-best avenue of approach, one that has as its purpose the preparation for the kind of insight that Plato alludes to in the *Seventh Letter*: "After practicing detailed comparisons of names and definitions and visual and other sense perceptions, after scrutinizing them in benevolent disputation by the use of question and answer without jealousy, at last in a flash understanding of each blazes up, and the mind, as it exerts all its powers to the limit of human capacity, is flooded with light" (344b). The primary sailing that is depicted in Socrates's autobiographical statement looks to the "wind" of sense experience and of authoritative texts (that of Anaxagoras). This wind is not enough. One does have to "turn to the oars" by relying on one's own power of insight. Because of the darkness that permeates the human condition, one has no choice but to take up argument and dialectics. But such rationality, insofar as it is something we can seize on to propel ourselves forward, is intrinsically limited. It is not a rationality that could illuminate the nature of reality for the very reason that, rather than engulfing us, along with whatever else truly exists, it places itself at our disposal as a kind of instrument. It is for this reason that the second sailing has to be understood as a propaedeutic: its purpose is to prepare the soul for the true wind, which blows neither through things seen nor through things heard, the wind of Spirit itself.

One does not grasp the "two" through a mechanical manipulation of the "ones." The very idea of the idea is that direct seeing is possible. A human being is not the sum of its body parts. Nor is two simply the sum of one and one. When one "gets" the idea, the two is itself unveiled. But peering at the thing itself does carry with it the danger of blindness. Only when standing at the threshold of death, on the verge of having every one of his senses annihilated, can Socrates leave behind the fear of such blindness. He may once have responded to the danger by "fleeing" into the *logoi* (*Phd.* 99e); if so, he has now reached the point where flight is impossible. That he demands silence once he drinks the hemlock (117d–e) bespeaks his readiness to face what has to be faced. If he has been diligent in his practice of death, he already knows something of the light he is about to encounter. As the allegory of the cave reminds us, gazing at the sun is not something we need to avoid forever. If we succeed in finding and exercising the proper organ, we can pass beyond the attempt to perceive the sun "through reflections." Strengthened by the right kind of practice, we can venture moments of direct intuition (*Rep.* 516b).

The second sailing brings with it the assurance of authenticity. True thinking is always first and foremost the interior dialogue that the soul carries on with itself (*Theaet.* 189e). This is the reason for Socrates's insistence that his interlocutor state his real belief; it is why he refuses to "teach." The external dialogue with others plays a secondary role, serving the purpose of freeing thought in the mind of anyone who encounters it. The dialogical movement of thinking is, however, a frustratingly piecemeal affair. Baptized in a prebirth vision of form and totality, the mind contains all that it needs to know. But washed ashore onto the rocks of finitude, the same mind has forgotten what once it must have known. This "forgetting" yields the condition for achieving an articulate understanding of reality, for articulation proceeds through rupture. The mind that knows can give birth to its knowledge only through the agency of the mind that has forgotten, the mind that, anchored in the very element of its finitude, body and soul, concentrates itself into a question, growing thereby into the willingness to sacrifice itself completely for the sake of a wisdom that it must have but can never embrace. The moment of sacrifice comes when the strongest wind begins to blow. The wind that carries us to truth is the very wind that casts us into death.

It is still too early, however, to throw ourselves entirely to the wind. We have to heed the advice of the philosophical midwife: say it and you will lose it; say it and you will fall into contradiction; indeed, you must understand that you are already in contradiction and that you have no choice but to gather yourself into the pain of that contradiction in the hope that the tension of not knowing can grow powerful enough to give birth to a word worth hearing.

One last observation on Socrates's autobiographical sketch is in order. Socrates's personal struggle recapitulates the early history of philosophy in Greece. From the materialism of the nature philosophers, he proceeds through the dualism of Anaxagoras. The flight into the *logoi* appears, in its turn, to reflect the idealism of the Eleatics. Instead of answering Cebes's question about the cause of the soul's incarnation in a body, Socrates appears to abandon all concern for the realm of becoming. Buried in the *logoi* are reverberations of forms that are elevated above all change. To explain something through the new formal cause that Socrates introduces is to resort to tautology: x is what it is because it is what it is. This procedure works only to the degree that reality is good, insofar as goodness effectively silences the question concerning the origin.[13] If the appearance of being is experienced as profoundly problematic, the Parmenidean assurance that it is "because it is" will do nothing to still the question "why." Reason itself, and the principle of identity on which it is based, is the endowment of a health that is far from being universally enjoyed.

If health is the "silence of the organs," the standpoint of Eleatic idealism and its silencing of the tortured "why?" will seem the epitome of good health. But the silencing is too forced to take root: the material realm continues to assert itself; the sense organs refuse to be tamed. The thesis that reality is form brings with it the denial that matter is real. The *bellum omnium contra omnes* of metaphysical possibilities is the dialectic of assertion and denial, the internal struggle that pushes us inexorably toward higher insight. Socrates must ultimately arrive at a standpoint that does justice to each of the stages he has traversed. Materialism, dualism, and idealism have to come together in a vision that so accommodates them that they are freed of any need to assert themselves. Each must be perceived as a manifestation of a higher wisdom that, in its freedom, withholds itself even as it shows itself. Socrates is a midwife because he himself has no fruit to bear: thought has already struggled sufficiently to find its way into its formal alternatives. All that remains is a wisdom that, like the wind that bends the tree, refuses to be caught.

Socrates's own refusal to provide us with answers testifies to the deep accord between his own spirit and the elusive spirit of a wisdom that pushes us relentlessly into an ever-growing awareness of our own ignorance. The alternative ways we have of conceiving reality coalesce only because none of them reaches high enough to do justice to that principle of being that is itself so sublime that it has constituted all of the alternatives by remaining pure of contamination by any of them. Matter is born out of the vacillating attempt of the void to touch the fleeting shadow of coy divinity. The form that can be grasped, the form that shows itself in the reflection of the *logoi*, is the mirror image of what it reveals. The determinate boundaries of cognizable form are the objectification of what can never be fully objectified.

The idea, in truth, takes shape in the inchoate sea of indeterminacy. We are referred, after all, to the path of becoming. Indeed, if it is freedom we seek, the highest imperative is that we see through that which first cast us into chains. Cebes's question about why we got stuck in bodies is a legitimate one. But the mind that knows the answer is mute, enshrouded in an ignorance of its own, living beyond the possibility of articulating its knowledge—or of hearing whatever articulation might be possible. It finds its mirror only in its other, a very human mind, one that has achieved awareness at the price of losing wisdom. Locked in by too much knowledge of what is contingent and unknowable, such a mind fails to satisfy the heart's frenzied desire to know. The Father begets the Word, as does Socrates through his philosophical midwifery, not by pronouncing it himself, but by evoking its articulation from the darkness that has such need of it. Through the word, if ever it can be spoken, a moment of recollection unfolds.

The word that recalls forgotten truth is myth. Socrates has spoken mythically throughout the dialogue. The world of bodies serves as a reminder of a higher world of the spirit.[14] We ourselves are cast into bodies in order to learn to love what they denote rather than what they themselves are. To love bodies (rather than wisdom) is to bring on oneself the punishment of getting what one loves: this is the key to the Socratic doctrine of reincarnation (*Phd.* 81b–e). As in the Indian doctrine of Karma, justice must involve more than the call for liberation, for the prisoner is responsible for his own imprisonment: what he suffers is the lesson he himself must learn (83a). The philosopher alone has suffered enough (although in some forgotten life) to glimpse the truth: the body is a path, a conduit to something higher, a crystallization of desire that, like all desire, reaches beyond itself toward the Good that it seeks. The purification of desire is the acceptance of its proper object, the eternal light from which the soul always first recoils in fear (81c–d). Fear of blindness must give way to love of the very light that blinds. The philosopher's courage, unlike the courage of a soldier who fears punishment and disgrace, is never determined by any kind of fear (68d). Fear itself, by being confronted and accepted, is transmogrified into love. Once this is fully achieved, the philosopher is freed from the pain of rebirth and is elevated into the divine world of light (82c): Nirvana.

The elevation of the philosopher is itself the resurrection of the body. The fear that has to be overcome is the fear of being alive. The truth that has to be recognized is the truth that there is no escape from the circle of life (107c). Suicide, as Socrates pointed out to Cebes in the very beginning, is not a viable option (61c–62e). Yet insofar as fear is what generates the illusion of world (which attains the semblance of reality through the dialectic of pleasure and pain [83c]), the acknowledgment that there is no escape involves a kind of escape.

The philosopher is the one who has learned the art of dying. We can let go of what binds us only when we have understood that we are like the earth itself, held in place by neither chain nor vortex. Until that deep realization (the capacity to levitate) has been fully accomplished, the *logoi* enable us simultaneously to hold reality at bay and to prepare ourselves for the moment of final acceptance through which darkness gives birth to light. The same death that casts those who love only the carnal into the imprisonment of their renewed incarnation serves to liberate the philosopher. With gods as companions and guides (light perceived without fear is divinity), the philosopher attains the realm in which true vision is possible. There, where the form of the idea itself can be disclosed, Socrates lets fall a remarkable word: the idea itself, it seems, is the earth—or as he proceeds to describe it—the true earth (108c).

The disclosure was anticipated in the initial explanation of the second sailing. After witnessing the collapse of his attempts to understand, Socrates felt the temptation simply to return to the salutary narcosis of everyday consciousness, submerging himself in the stream of sense experience. But he feared that this would be to acquiesce to ignorance. This much, of course, is not very surprising. The critique of sensuality is the critique of the shadows on the cave wall. Astonishingly, however, this is not the case. To look at things through the eyes is to look at them more directly than the scientist does, for the scientist works behind the shield of explanation. To look at things through the eyes, without this shield, can be blinding, for behind the sensually perceivable things, indeed, at their very heart, lies the dazzling display of the forms. The eclipsed sun is dangerous, because one thinks one is looking only at the moon. Looking at the world of bodies is equally dangerous, for one thinks one is looking only at the physical. It is, in fact, this assurance that obscures the possibility of real wisdom. A body caught in a world of bodies does not have to attend to anything beyond the pursuit of pleasure and the avoidance of pain, for its life is ephemeral. In the end, it passes away. Socrates's insight is not that there is a supernatural beyond, for the sake of which one has to withdraw from the world of bodies, but, on the contrary, that there is a supernatural *within*, for the sake of which one has to undertake the purgatory of disciplining the body, of freeing it from the puppet strings of pleasure and pain, so that it itself, thus purified, is able to step into the realm of light.

The myth of the true earth tells the story of how the ensouled body is born and how it dies—and how, through the catharsis of its suffering and death, or, more accurately, through the philosophical recognition of the necessity of this catharsis, it finally achieves salvation. In other words, Cebes in the end receives the answer to both of his most urgent questions: how does the allegedly "simple" soul enter into the confusion of body? and what way better than suicide can lead us out of the darkness? The point of Socrates's myth is not to present yet another possible explanation of the ultimate nature of reality. It is not to offer any more of the putative "knowledge" that blinds the understanding. Instead, its purpose is to help us with the only project that makes any sense, the project of discovering how to live.

Socrates unfurled the sail of his myth with the confidence of one who has learned to trust the wind. The myth of the true earth is his last word, but, oars now cast aside, he has placed himself in the trust of another, presumably the god who is about to guide him through his death (*Phd.* 108c). Placing his trust in the unseen god, he has broken out of the peculiar circle of the first sailing, whereby the recognition of what something is derives not from what it in fact is but from a "hypothesis" about what it might be. Having through a lifetime of philosophy discovered how the clarification of hypotheses leads to the progressive purging of their content, Socrates is prepared to embark on a new voyage, using the vehicle of what in fact exists to carry him across the sea of death. The myth reveals that what is, is always the possibility of transformation and transcendence. Facing the blackness of death, Socrates seeks identity with light. To gain that identity he summons to his aid the energy and power of the earth itself, on which he has long since planted his feet (61d).

The true earth, Socrates says, is held in place by nothing more than the perfection of its position in the center of the heavens themselves. The true earth is pure; it itself is heavenly; it is as large and expansive as the sky (109a–c). The earth in truth, or idea, is not an "abstraction": whatever it is, it is "more." It is larger; it is more colorful; it is more radiant with light. Our own realm is a narrow crevice, filled with air and water, what Socrates calls the sediments of ethereal light. Locked in a cave, we have convinced ourselves that we are inhabitants of the real world. Not so. Beyond the visible horizon lie mountains that tower high above the sky itself. We have imprisoned ourselves in narrow confines because of our terror of space, openness, and light. True mountains, gigantic and free, have the transparency of gems. The true body glows with its own inner light. True vision peers into an openness without end. There, on the true earth, an extension of heaven itself, are sacred groves and temples in which the gods really dwell (111b).

In considering this powerful vision with which Socrates closes off his life, I suggest that we reflect one final time on his enigmatic insistence that his grieving disciples answer his death by seeking after a wise man, *even among the barbarians* (78a). Who are the strangers Socrates had in mind? A possible answer to the question presents itself once one recognizes in the myth of the true earth the outlines of a much older myth, the Persian myth of the emerald city. Inspired perhaps by the great snow mountains that tower above Tehran, Persian seers told stories of a great emerald mountain that, positioned on the base of the daytime sky, rises into the heaven beyond the heavens.[15] On that mountain stands the great city of light. Whether Socrates himself encountered the Persians directly or only heard their stories (perhaps from far-traveled Alcibiades) is, of course, more than I can say. But the myth is Persian. A Socrates suspected of sympathy for Sparta was a Socrates capable of sympathy for Persia. Teachers of wisdom can even be strangers from the land of our enemies.

Be this as it may, Socrates leaves us with a vision of a celestial nature that he imagines as a world teeming with life, culminating with a humanity more refined than our own, a world as tantalizingly near as the far side of the horizon into which we immediately peer. The key to the vision is given in the very forms that, with a more Platonic twist, are understood as antipodal to body and nature. But consider, if you will, the way the antipodes bind opposites together. If the heaven of forms is the "heaven beyond the heavens"—or the "true heaven"—then to it must correspond a "true earth," of which ours is but a lowly, silt-filled crevice. The celestial earth is the earth as it really is: mountains higher, colors more vivid, with "trees, flowers, and fruits, that are proportionally more beautiful" (110d) than anything in our god-forsaken valley. Instead of vanishing in the face of the forms, the earth rises to its true stature. In its lofty regions, people live longer, are healthier and happier. They gather at temples that are inhabited not by sculptures of the gods, but by the living gods themselves. By the power of our understanding and our attachments, born in the element of fear, we have reduced the earth to a realm of shadows, rendering it familiar and predictable, an object that can be known and controlled. In contrast, by the power of philosophical ignorance, brought fully alive through the proximity of death, Socrates releases the earth into the enormity of its truth. Having stood in his fear, he has no need to retreat into what stands below him.[16] Having transformed fear into love, he has found the wind that can carry him, newly winged, into the ever-growing expanse of true reality.

The proof of Socrates's conquest of fear is his willingness to plunge into the depths. In the minutes before his own death, he calmly narrates the fate of the unpurified soul. In the myth he unfolds, the earth itself is as pure and expansive as the heavens, but its elements congeal and decay and fall into ever darker regions of internality. Four great subterranean rivers flow into the abyss, from which their movement reverses, so that they flow back toward the surface (112a–b). The whole earth is thus a living body that sustains itself with a beating heart and the steady rhythm of one who breathes (111e). Through the fashioning of his myth, Socrates is gathering together the folds of his own corporeal interiority. Purity of soul shows itself not in withdrawal from the physical but in the ability to penetrate its darkest folds. Intent on such inner penetration, Socrates revisits even the gates of hell. He describes without flinching the lava flows of Pyriphlegethon and the black waters of the Styx, waters that flow down into Tartarus, which, like a great colon, expels the unredeemable (113e). Each of the four great rivers depicted by Socrates makes its way into Tartarus, whence it reverses its motion and flows upward to light. Like a tantric yogi who reverses the flow of his semen, or like Joshua reversing the flow of the Jordan (Josh. 3:13–17), Socrates enters into the pit of Tartarus ready to ride its waters backward and upward into the field of light.

Philosophical humility, achieved through a thoroughgoing purgation of the soul from every pretense of knowledge, overcomes the barrier that separates the spirit from the true earth. Socrates's Persian myth bespeaks the completeness of his union with earth and body. One way of seeing this more clearly is to reflect on the kinds of crime that, according to his myth, lead to banishment in Tartarus. Of all crimes, murder and the violation of the filial bond are the most serious (113e–114a). Both crimes evince a will to separation. In murder, the autonomous will seeks to abolish any barrier that stands before it. In an act of violence against one's parents, one tears at one's very roots, the sacred bonds that attach us to the earth. Through the family, we belong to city and nation—and ultimately to the great womb of earth itself. Salvation is not the denial of origin but its full and open affirmation. To successfully ride the stream of life beyond the necessity of incarnation, one has to turn not away from the body but into it. The world of bodies melts away only when it is fully and completely embraced. To fear any aspect of it is to bind oneself to it. Release requires movement and life, the fulfillment of tension rather than its elimination. Devotion to ideas provides purpose and direction. Real movement requires something more, the soul's ability to cleanse itself in the fire and water of its own ignorance, to humble itself by reentering the cavernous darkness of its first emergence.

In other words, real movement, the possibility of transformation and release, requires nothing short of death. Socrates completes his myth by expressing the hope that his own soul will soar into the transparent luminosity of the Absolute beyond (114b–c). He then bathes himself, rejoins the family circle (116a–b), and emerges again only when it is time to drink the poison. He assumes a reclining position, breaking for the first time the bond of his legs with the earth, but only after they had become first heavy and then numb (117e). The heaviness he feels is the return of the disintegrating body to the earth, the waning of the life force through which the body holds itself aloft. Crushing, oppressive heaviness dissolves itself in numbness, not through division, but through unification. The deepest stage of the myth is reenacted in Socrates's very act of dying. Becoming earth, he is earth no longer but swims in the waters and fluids that now reverse their downward spiral. As the slowly rising movement of the poison frees his stomach from its churning frenzy, Socrates speaks his very last words, asking Crito to sacrifice a cock to Aesculapius, god of good health: for freedom from the swirling waters means the release of spirit in good and holy death.

Achieving release through unification rather than separation from the elements is a highly paradoxical affair, and Socrates does no more than evoke it as a possibility. He leaves completely unaddressed the ontological status of the philosophical soul that gains final release from imprisonment, leaving us free to contemplate the riddles. The path into the beyond seems to lead inward rather than outward. The spell of embodiment is dissipated only by being fully embraced. Release from the awful mechanism of return is made possible only by return itself.

The truth is not that there is no truth but that truth is depth and lives out of mystery and concealment. The hell of cyclical return without the possibility of escape bespeaks the ontological necessity through which nature is eternally posited. The idea that a self must therewith endure the unbearable weight of infinite existence is a truth too awful to articulate, apart from the realization that it holds only for the moments, fortunately fleeting, in which it is felt and taken to heart. The released soul knows no more than the present that, held gloriously aloft from any relationship to past or future, is freedom and light. Eternal life is life unbound, life that, belonging to no one, belongs to everyone. Spirit itself is pure; the last of the forms is open and unformed; knowledge is ignorance and holy wonder. If the soul lives forever, it is only by dying completely. Consciousness does not so much *have* space and time for its conditions as it itself *is* space and time. Philosophical enlightenment is an event, the emergent awareness of what is and always is—what, as this simple present, lives only by dying. World and self live, but only by incessantly dying into one another. The spirit of Socrates is alive and well only where philosophy is alive and well. Philosophy lives in vision and insight, not in words and arguments. The moment of philosophical reflection is an eternal possibility with which the spirit eternally wrestles. To live the life of the spirit is to open oneself to the horror and solace of simple awareness.

Systole and diastole. Within and beyond. Empty and full. Socrates assured Crito that by dying, he would go on living. But, living through dying, he would never be easy to catch (*Phd.* 115c). If Socrates were not a riddle, if he were in fact easy to catch, then understanding him would require a great deal less *effort* on our part. The project of understanding Socrates cannot be completed without engaging one's full and complete self. Philosophy is not simply an affair of the mind. To understand Socrates one must, in some very significant sense, set out to become Socrates. But Socrates's is a subtle spirit, as empty as the empty space that formed a home for the world. In taking on that spirit, translucent as it is, one emerges not as an echo chamber of Socratic beliefs and ideas or of Socratic projects and engagements: one emerges quite simply as oneself. And if it comes to that, there is no crime in stepping forth from the conventional order and defying the very institutions that provided one with discipline and direction, for the only justification of a culture is its capacity to give rise to free individuals. The resurrection of the spirit of Socrates is the ongoing conversation that we call philosophy, and as we all know, philosophers are renowned for their spirited disagreements.

But the feast of words should not be my final word. What in the title of this chapter I have called the resurrection of the body may itself be the actual breakthrough to wisdom: the disclosure of the true earth. In the light of this disclosure, it becomes possible not only to reach for the blossom, as word-enamored as we might be, but to fall to our knees in celebration of earth transfigured. Nothing in that transfiguration belies the fact that when the earth but trembles, entire great cities can be smashed to ruin. Heraclitus spoke the truth: *phusis kruptesthai philei*—nature loves to hide.[17] Hiding with her deepest concealment, she sinks back into dark death, swallowing much that has life. But even so, in the face of just this mystery, it remains fitting that we not simply embrace, but kiss the earth, for what brings death brings also life. The phoenix does indeed rise from the ashes.

Epilogue

It is the stillest words that bring on the storm. Thoughts that
come on dove's feet guide the world.
    —Friedrich Nietzsche, *Thus Spoke Zarathustra*

The metaphysics of the "supernatural within" leaves us standing, finally,
nowhere else but where we've always stood: on the earth. Socratic wisdom
resolves none of the riddles, but it does give us hope that we can stand
firmly in them. Standing firmly ultimately requires that we jettison every
metaphysical assurance—including the assurance that the earth must
remain solid beneath our feet.

    Thinking arises in trauma, just as assuredly as false consciousness
arises in the attempt to hold trauma at bay. It is thus fitting that I recall
one last time the Kobe earthquake, the uncanny occasion for writing this
book. Its power is what delivered me from the pieties of conventional
scholarship, so deeply opposed to the spontaneous word that illuminates
darkness only in the flashing forth of actual insight. What might appear
as arrogance and hubris on my part shows itself differently to me, as the
simple realization that there is no longer any need to pretend, either for
me personally or for us collectively. As for myself, the rewards for compli-
ance have lost their allure. My career is what it is—and I have never been
bothered by the Faustian dread of the "bed of sloth." As for humanity,
the illusion that life will someday be protected on all sides by the completed edifice of science, a world made stable and enduring, is just that:
an illusion. The only way to overcome death is to embrace it as the very
heart of life.

    I would not be offended if one were to decide that what has re-
sulted is an illegitimate fusion of self-help sermonizing with serious philosophical scholarship. Justifying the project is the figure of Socrates himself. It was Socrates who was humble-arrogant enough to teach us how to
laugh at pomposity—not for the sake of disrespecting others, but for the
sake of helping them to find and give birth to themselves. So laugh, if you

will, with the assurance that I will join in the laughter, all of which pales in the face of the laughter that nature herself has in store for all of us.

Remembering nature's "last laugh" may be likened to the wisdom of a fool. Recollecting finitude is both painful and liberating. Incarnation is not the graveyard of the spirit, not as long as earth continues to bear fruit. The death of what is finite is the life of the spirit, whose words flash forth from the heart of darkness. In the silence of Socrates (even into death) was forged the poetry of Plato, poetry that lets the silent Socrates speak, while the word-gifted Plato takes his turn at silence. Friendship can prevail, even among strangers.

Acknowledgments

I would like to acknowledge that the *Southern Humanities Review* published versions of "Socrates in Japan" (which appeared in the fall 2001 issue) and "Socrates and Alcibiades" (which appeared in the fall 2003 issue). I remember how grateful I was when the journal honored both contributions with its Theodore Christian Hoefner "best essay" award.

In addition, I want to express my gratitude to the College of the Holy Cross for years of steady employment, complete with sabbaticals and faculty fellowships. Important for this book was the one-year leave of absence that enabled me to teach in Japan. Among my many friends at Holy Cross (I have particularly in mind all members—past and present—of the Philosophy Reading Group), I think it is appropriate to single out Bob Cording, Jim Kee, Chris Dustin, and Jeff Bernstein. Over the years, the four of them have endured more of my writing than anyone else I know. In addition to being generous with their criticisms, they have shown how well they understand that loyalty to a friend is a virtue worth preserving even in the context of a professional world founded on the principle of competition. Similarly, Thom Quinn, Steve Dowden, and Nancy Billias, who studied with me many decades ago at the Universität Tübingen, have shown just how long-lasting such friendship can be.

That roll call ended, I trust that everyone will agree that friendship's true miracle, even beyond loyalty, is the way it is continuously renewed by the arrival of young people on the scene. When dedicating this book "to my students" I provided the real reason for my gratitude to the College of the Holy Cross: the opportunity it has afforded me to teach the young men and women who study there. Among my current students, I am grateful to Timothy Nowak for letting me insert his name when he knows how many others I would like to add. In a similar way, I hope my former students forgive me if I single out Phil Fournier and Luiza Mouzinho to represent all of those who have learned that, although I still respond to the name "Professor," at a certain point I really do prefer to be called "Joe."

Even so, I can't stop there. With the pride of a teacher, I want to thank Maria Cimitile, Joe Bulbilia, Bob Dobie, Ann Cahill, Angela Smith,

Danielle Haug, and Tim Jussaume for showing (along with others), and despite my complaints about the state of the contemporary academy, how happy I am when former students fight their way to a Ph.D. and an academic post. I am glad as well that Andy Jussaume, Teresa Fenichel, Jack Pappas, and Sean Gleason are poised very soon to follow them. As for the rebellious ones who ended up choosing law school over philosophy, I appreciate the way Patrick Tinsley and Molly Mahan have persisted in reminding me that Themis is, after all, the sister of Apollo. And with regard to the rest of you, scattered in so many directions, remember Socrates and his assurance that all that really matters is that we continually examine our lives.

Before closing, I want to thank Jason Wirth, David Jones, and Michael Schwartz for bringing this book to the attention of Northwestern University Press by suggesting that it be included in the series they are editing on behalf of the Comparative and Continental Philosophy Circle. I also owe a tremendous debt to Burt Hopkins and Charles Bambach for sharing with me the reader reports they prepared. I tried my best (with many failures) to rise to the standard of their suggestions and criticisms. Finally, with regard to the Northwestern "team," I want to thank Anne Gendler not only for guiding me through the process but also for handing the job of copy editor to Carolyn Brown, in whom I quickly recognized a kind and kindred spirit.

But the book began of course in Japan. For twice bringing me to Kwansai Gakuin University in Nishinomiya (most recently in 2009), I owe perhaps the greatest debt of all to Hideki Mine. The reason I wrote this book in the first place is that I wanted to do some little justice to the world he introduced me to. Having mentioned him, I must quickly mention (in memory of our time both in Japan and in Tübingen) Tetsuro Mori, Tadashi Otsuru, and Kisun Kim.

After such an impressive listing of best friends, I will conclude by thanking the most wondrous ones of all, my wife Elisabeth and my daughters, Nina and Silvia, for their love—and for their consistent generosity in putting up with someone as strange yet ordinary as me.

Notes

Preface

1. Little has changed since Max Weber wrote "Science as a Vocation," his famous essay on the scholarly vocation and the "value free" nature of scholarship in 1917. It can be found in Max Weber, *The Vocation Lectures*, trans. Rodney Livingstone (Indianapolis: Hackett, 2004), 1–31. Weber's essay should be read in conjunction with his more famous writing, *The Protestant Ethic and the Spirit of Capitalism*, ed. and trans. Peter Baehr and Gordon Wells (New York: Penguin, 2002). If the ethic that regards work as intrinsically virtuous produces wasteful mountains of superfluous consumer "goods," the idea that knowledge is pure only when it is divorced from the need to know produces superfluous mountains of scholarly books and articles that go unread.

2. Alexander Nehamas, *The Art of Living: Socratic Reflections from Plato to Foucault* (Berkeley: University of California Press, 1998).

3. Pierre Hadot, *Philosophy as a Way of Life*, trans. Michael Chase (Cambridge, Mass.: Blackwell, 1995).

4. Throughout this book I will cite Plato's text in the conventional manner, including an abbreviated form of the title followed by the Stephanus numbers that were devised during the Renaissance and are standard across all editions and translations of Plato. Most of the translations I use are drawn from the Edith Hamilton and Huntington Cairns edition: *The Collected Dialogues of Plato, Including the Letters* (Princeton, N.J.: Princeton University Press, 1961). When I deviate from this edition, I have generally done so in consultation with the bilingual Loeb Classical Library edition, *Plato in Twelve Volumes*, various translators (Cambridge, Mass.: Harvard University Press, 1906–1929). When I use a Loeb translation, I indicate this in a note that specifies the volume.

5. Martin Heidegger, *What Is Called Thinking?*, trans. J. Glenn Gray (New York: Harper and Row, 1968), 8.

6. Socrates confesses in that passage in the *Apology* that he has a difficult time minding his own business because he feels called to scrutinize both himself and others (38a). At the same time, he stayed out of public life and tried to keep as low a profile as he could (32e).

7. In 1987, Allan Bloom published a critique of the American academy that was far more detailed and sustained than what I have to offer. My major disagreement with Bloom has to do with his feeling that anarchy prevails because existen-

tialists and German philosophers weakened the right program of education. For myself, I am on the side of the existentialists and German philosophers. What we need is not the right program but the right spirit. Bloom sought to restore the classical understanding that some people are better than other people. His hero was Plato. I want to restore the sense that there is much that we just plain don't know. My hero is Socrates. See Allan Bloom, *The Closing of the American Mind* (New York: Simon and Schuster, 1987).

Introduction

1. Just as I use the Stephanus numbers to cite Plato, I will use the similar system of Bekker numbers to cite Aristotle. Translations are from *The Basic Works of Aristotle*, ed. Richard McKeon (New York: Random House, 1941).

2. Nehamas's *The Art of Living* starts from a similar premise, using Montaigne, Nietzsche, and Foucault as examples of thinkers who philosophized in conscious imitation of Socrates. It is inviting to interpret this as a kind of philosophical correlate of the *Imitatio Christi*.

3. Karl Jaspers, *Socrates, Buddha, Confucius, Jesus*, ed. Hannah Arendt, trans. Ralph Manheim (1962; New York: Houghton Mifflin Harcourt, 2006).

4. Even more interesting than this proclamation from Erasmus's *The Godly Feast* is his adage "Sileni Alcibiadis," in which Erasmus moves seamlessly from Alcibiades's depiction of Socrates as a Silenus figure (in Plato's *Symposium*) to a characterization of Christ as the ultimate Silenus: *The Adages of Erasmus*, ed. William Barker (Toronto: University of Toronto Press, 2001), 241–268.

5. Plato, "Epistle 2," in *Plato*, vol. 9, trans. R. G. Bury, Loeb Classical Library (Cambridge, Mass.: Harvard University Press, 1929), 402–419.

6. Alexander Nehamas, *The Virtues of Authenticity: Essays on Plato and Socrates* (Princeton, N.J.: Princeton University Press, 1998).

7. I agree with Kierkegaard's assessment of Socrates: "Truth demands silence before it will raise its voice, and Socrates was to bring about this silence. For this reason he was purely negative." Søren Kierkegaard, *The Concept of Irony*, trans. H. V. Hong and E. H. Hong (Princeton, N.J.: Princeton University Press, 1989), 210. But, I would add, this is the source of something very positive.

8. Wallace Stevens, "Notes toward a Supreme Fiction," in *Collected Poems of Wallace Stevens* (New York: Knopf, 1954), 383.

9. Hans-Georg Gadamer, *Truth and Method*, trans. Joel Weinsheimer and Donald Marshall (New York: Continuum, 1989), 297.

10. Heidegger, *What Is Called Thinking?*, 8.

11. Martin Heidegger, "Science and Reflection," in *The Question Concerning Technology and Other Essays*, trans. William Lovitt (New York: Harper and Row, 1977), 155–182.

12. *The Chicago Manual of Style*, 16th ed. (Chicago: University of Chicago Press, 2010), § 7.18, 354.

13. Gadamer, *Truth and Method*, 411.

14. See Norbert Wiener, *Cybernetics: Or Control and Communication in the Animal and the Machine* (Cambridge, Mass.: MIT Press, 1965), 12.

15. I refer again to Weber's "Science as a Vocation."

16. Apart from his saying "Socrates" where I would say "Plato," my reading concurs with that of Peter Sloterdijk, *The Art of Philosophy: Wisdom as a Practice*, trans. Karen Margolis (New York: Columbia University Press, 2012).

17. Hans-Georg Gadamer, "The Proofs of Immortality in Plato's *Phaedo*," in *Dialogue and Dialectic: Eight Hermeneutical Studies on Plato*, trans. P. Christopher Smith (New Haven, Conn.: Yale University Press, 1980). There is a deep affinity between Socrates's "as if" and Kant's notion in the *Critique of Judgment* that such ideas as God and the immortality of the soul are "regulative ideas" of reason.

18. Plato, *Phaedo*, in *Plato*, vol. 1, trans. Harold North Fowler, Loeb Classical Library (Cambridge, Mass.: Harvard University Press, 1927).

19. *Zen Flesh, Zen Bones*, compiled by Paul Reps and Nyogen Senzaki (Boston: Tuttle, 1998), 19.

20. A close reading of the pre-Socratics supports this claim. Anaximander speaks the truth of religious sacrifice in such a way that the possibility of tragedy emerges "for they give justice and make reparation to one another for their injustice" (12); Heraclitus peers into the thunderbolt of Zeus and discerns the event-structure of truth itself—frag. 64; Xenophanes (frags. 14–16) and Parmenides (frags. 7–8) find philosophy in religion's urge to break through idolatry (frags. 22 and 43). The fragments can be found in *Ancilla to the Pre-Socratic Philosophers: A Complete Translation of the Fragments in Diels, "Fragmente der Vorsokraticker,"* trans. Kathleen Freeman (Cambridge, Mass.: Harvard University Press, 1983). A strong case for the unity of philosophical and religious practice has been made by Pierre Hadot, *What Is Ancient Philosophy?*, trans. M. Chase (Cambridge, Mass.: Harvard University Press, 2004).

21. Schopenhauer evokes the distinction between philosophy and academic philosophy at the very beginning of his main work. Arthur Schopenhauer, *The World as Will and Representation*, vol. 1, trans. F. J. Payne (New York: Dover, 1969), xxvi. Fritz Mauthner has a humorous description of Socrates leading the laughter of philosophers in heaven when they hear about philosophers on earth attending a philosophical "congress." Fritz Mauthner, *Nach berühmten Mustern: Totengespräche / Verse, Narr und König (1909)* (Whitefish, Mont.: Kessinger, 2009). The book has unfortunately never been translated into English.

22. I already quoted in the preface Heidegger's assessment of Socrates as "the purest thinker of the West." The purity refers to his perseverance "right into his death" at holding himself in the elusiveness of being, the very withdrawal of meaning that leads us to question and to think. Beyond this, Heidegger remains silent about this "purest of thinkers."

23. Friedrich Nietzsche, *Human, All Too Human*, pt. 5, aphorism 263, trans. Gary Handwerk (Stanford, Calif.: Stanford University Press, 1995). The word stems from Pindar and is echoed throughout Nietzsche's work.

24. Sloterdijk, *The Art of Philosophy*, 5. See also Peter Sloterdijk, *You Must Change Your Life*, trans. Wieland Hoban (Malden, Mass.: Polity, 2013).

Chapter 1

1. Julia Kristeva's *Strangers to Ourselves*, trans. Leon Roudiez (New York: Columbia University Press, 1991), starts with this recognition. It is one of the things that separates the continental feminist from most of her American counterparts.

2. This is line 375 in Sophocles, *The Three Theban Plays*, trans. Robert Fagles (London: Penguin, 1984). The translation I use is the one commonly used in translations of Martin Heidegger, who often returned to this passage of the *Antigone*. An example can be found in Heidegger's *An Introduction to Metaphysics*, trans. Ralph Manheim (New Haven, Conn.: Yale University Press, 1959), 146.

3. A popular example of this misinterpretation is I. F. Stone's *The Trial of Socrates* (New York: Little, Brown, 1988). Stone simply ignores everything that kept Socrates in Athens, including the spirit of freedom that transforms one's followers into autonomous agents who make their own choices and their own mistakes.

4. It is Zen Buddhism above all else that has come to represent the Spartan aspect of Japanese culture. An apt example is the way D. T. Suzuki, who first popularized Zen in the West, has come under criticism for allegedly inspiring kamikaze attacks in World War II. For a balanced discussion of the issue, see *Rude Awakenings: Zen, the Kyoto School, and the Question of Nationalism*, ed. James W. Heisig and John C. Maraldo (Honolulu: University of Hawai'i Press, 1994).

5. As for the undeniable and well-documented evils, they read like an inventory of Western problems: racism, sexism, a history of imperialism, economic profiteering, and uncontrolled industrial pollution. Being black in America (or a *Gastarbeiter* in Germany) is presumably as difficult as being a Burakumin or Korean in Japan.

6. Julia Kristeva, *About Chinese Women*, trans. Anita Barrows (London: Marion Boyars, 1977).

7. A similar argument could be made, of course, for any number of Asian societies, including China and India.

8. See Weber, *Protestant Ethic and the Spirit of Capitalism*, 70–80.

9. I have borrowed this formulation from the generous review that Dan Latimer attached to the previously published version of this chapter in *Southern Humanities Review* 35, no. 4 (Fall 2001), iii.

10. The quotation is from Dogen's *Genjo Koan*, included in the collection *Shobogenzo: Zen Essays by Dogen*, trans. Thomas Cleary (Honolulu: University of Hawai'i Press, 1986), 32.

11. There is a metaphysical correlate for this feature of Japanese as well. Nishida, for instance, describes an action not as something that a subject does but as the movement of the world itself: "the world which moves by itself through contradictions, as unity of the opposites of the many and the one, always contradicts itself in the present; the present is the 'place' of contradiction." Kitaro Nishida, *Intelligibility and the Philosophy of Nothingness: Three Philosophical Essays*, trans. Robert Schinzinger (Westport, Conn.: Greenwood, 1958), 177.

12. See *Four Plays by Aristophanes*, translations by William Arrowsmith, Richmond Lattimore, and Douglass Parker (New York: Meridian, 1994), 143.

13. In doing so, I will play off the account given in Tetsuro Watsuji's *Cli-*

mate and Culture: A Philosophical Study, trans. Geoffrey Brownas (Westport, Conn.: Greenwood Press, 1961).

14. See Max Horkheimer and Theodor Adorno, *Dialectic of Enlightenment*, trans. E. Jephcott (Stanford, Calif.: Stanford University Press, 2002), 35.

15. This understanding of the conventionality of culture has, of course, its moment of truth—people are undoubtedly able to learn from one another. A European can become a Buddhist and an Asian can become a Christian.

16. See Augustin Berque, *Le sauvage et l'artifice: Les japonais devant la nature* (Paris: Gallimard, 1986).

17. In Socrates's day, of course, the Greek mountains were forested. Lacking the monsoon rains, however, they were never forested as densely as the mountains of Japan.

18. In section 15 of the *Birth of Tragedy*, Nietzsche goes so far as to suggest that Socrates was the true author of the mechanical view of nature that emerged in the seventeenth century.

19. The older alphabet of the Hebrews left vowels to the imagination. The export of that alphabet to Greece by the Phoenicians was the occasion for a transformation of fundamental importance. For an interesting and highly readable account of this event, see chaps. 3–5 of David Abram, *The Spell of the Sensuous* (New York: Pantheon, 1996).

20. See, for instance, Jacques Derrida, *Of Grammatology*, trans. Gayatri Spivak (Baltimore: Johns Hopkins University Press, 1976).

21. See Eric Havelock, *Preface to Plato* (Cambridge, Mass.: Harvard University Press, 1963), and Walter Ong, S.J., *Orality and Literacy: The Technologizing of the Word* (New York: Methuen, 1982).

22. One can imagine a Parisian intellectual who indicates an *a* with a wave of his hand while announcing: "I didn't mean *différence*, but *différance*."

23. Gadamer gives the history of the inner word in *Truth and Method*, 418–428.

24. The best exposition of Socrates's aloofness is Kierkegaard's *The Concept of Irony*.

25. A Japanese student once explained the distinction between *tatemae* and *honne* to me at some length. I discovered it again in one of the more insightful introductions to Japan, Arne Kalland's *Japan bak fasaden* (Oslo: Cappelen, 1986).

26. It is Xenophon who suggested that Socrates was old and tired of living. *Memorabilia*, trans. Amy Bonnette (Ithaca, N.Y.: Cornell University Press, 1994). This is irreconcilable, however, with the full picture painted by Plato, for if we consider all the conversations he was supposed to have conducted in the days before his death, he was clearly at the peak of his power! For a spirited defense of Socrates's vitality at the time of his trial, see Karsten Friis Johansen, "Sokrates Hos Platon," in *Sokrates i historiens lys*, ed. Egil A. Wyller (Oslo: Solum Forlag, 1985), 27–48.

27. The page numbers refer to the standard Greek text. In the *Four Plays by Aristophanes*, the parallel passage can be found on pages 38–40. For the best commentary, see Kierkegaard, *Concept of Irony*, 132–154.

28. Karl Popper, *The Open Society and Its Enemies* (Princeton, N.J.: Princeton University Press, 1986).

29. For a book that uses the Aristotelian critique of Socratic "intellectualism" as the basis for constructing a full interpretation of Socrates, see Norman Gulley's *The Philosophy of Socrates* (London: Macmillan, 1968).

30. According to Gadamer in *The Idea of the Good in Platonic-Aristotelian Philosophy*, trans. Christopher Smith (New Haven, Conn.: Yale University Press, 1986), 60, "Socrates' statement that aretē is knowledge proves to be a provocation." Once one realizes this, the Socratic paradox becomes compatible with Aristotle's insistence that virtue, though it is not identical with reason, occurs together with reason (*meta logou*).

31. Plato himself even suggested that the penalty for what we call "practicing" law should be death (*Laws* 938b–c).

32. That the education of desire is not achievable through words is made clear in any college or university where drunken parties and sexual assaults continue unabated, despite endless sermons about the necessity of treating others with respect.

33. Gregory Vlastos, *Socrates: Ironist and Moral Philosopher* (Cambridge: Cambridge University Press, 1991), 107–131.

34. *Zen no kenkyū* has been published as *An Inquiry into the Good*, trans. Masao Abe and Christopher Ives (New Haven, Conn.: Yale University Press, 1990).

Chapter 2

Epigraph: In the *Phaedrus* (in a passage I already discussed in chapter 1), it is his young interlocutor who calls Socrates *atopōtatos* (230a), referring to his seeming to be out of place outside the city. A few lines previously (230e) the same word was used to describe the "flood of Gorgons and Pegasuses and other monsters" that one confronts in mythology. When Socrates suggests that he cannot begin to think about those bizarre apparitions until first he comes to know himself, he is effectively suggesting that the self, far from being the self-evidently given, has to be understood as the result of a rupture every bit as great as the one that announces itself in the sudden apparition of a god.

1. See Slavoj Žižek and F. W. J. von Schelling, *The Abyss of Freedom and the Ages of the World*, trans. Judith Norman (Ann Arbor: University of Michigan Press, 1997), 26.

2. After fleeing Germany after the rise of Hitler, Strauss found his way to the New School and later to the University of Chicago, where he taught many years. He distinguished himself from the continental mainstream by firmly rejecting the historicism of thinkers such as Heidegger, Gadamer, and Derrida, who have also had a big impact on the study of ancient philosophy.

3. Gadamer's remarks on Strauss in *Truth and Method* (532–541) sparked a debate that has been reproduced under the title "Correspondence concerning *Wahrheit und Methode*," *Independent Journal of Philosophy* 2 (1978), 5–12.

4. The epigraph to this section is from Vlastos's introduction to *The Philosophy of Socrates: A Collection of Critical Essays*, ed. Gregory Vlastos (Notre Dame, Ind.: University of Notre Dame Press, 1980), 9. The original version of the es-

say, entitled the "Paradox of Socrates," can be found in Gregory Vlastos, *Studies in Greek Philosophy*, vol. 2: *Socrates, Plato and Their Tradition*, ed. Daniel Graham (Princeton, N.J.: Princeton University Press, 1995), 3–18.

5. To see just how historical Vlastos's interests became, consider his essays "Socrates *contra* Socrates in Plato" and "The Evidence of Aristotle and Xenophon," both of which are included in Vlastos, *Socrates*, 45–80, 81–106. See also Thomas Brickhouse and Nicholas Smith, *Socrates on Trial* (Oxford: Clarendon Press, 1989) and, by the same authors, *Plato's Socrates* (Oxford: Oxford University Press, 1994).

6. See Vlastos, *Philosophy of Socrates*, 17.

7. See the epilogue "Socrates and Vietnam" in Gregory Vlastos, *Socratic Studies* (Cambridge: Cambridge University Press, 1994), 127–134.

8. Consider the boldness of the title of the first chapter of Vlastos's *Socratic Studies*: "Socratic Elenchus: Method Is All."

9. Vlastos frames the paradox of Socrates in terms of bringing together the importance of knowledge with the realization that it can't be achieved, a paradox not meant to pacify reason but to incite it. See *The Philosophy of Socrates*, 4.

10. Ibid., 11.

11. In his last writings on Socrates, Vlastos goes so far as to suggest that Socrates believes himself actually to have *proven* "those strong doctrines of his on whose truth he based his life" (*Socratic Studies*, 18). I too believe that Socrates's virtue is based on truth—but the truth of a vision, not a doctrine.

12. Vlastos, *Socrates*, 235.

13. Ibid., 210–211.

14. See Aristotle, *Magna Moralia* II 15, 1213a.

15. Peter Singer and Jim Mason, *The Ethics of What We Eat* (Emmaus, Penn.: Rodale, 2006).

16. See Vlastos, *Socratic Studies*, 127–134.

17. See Leo Strauss, *Studies in Platonic Political Philosophy* (Chicago: University of Chicago Press, 1983), 46 and 44. Hereafter cited as *SPPP*.

18. Vlastos, *Philosophy of Socrates*, 5, 21.

19. Cicero, *Philosophical Treatises: Tusculan Disputations*, trans. J. E. King, Loeb Classical Library (Cambridge, Mass.: Harvard University Press, 1927), 5.10.

20. That Vlastos himself was worried about the implications of Socrates's decision to go to war is clear from his concluding remarks in *Socratic Studies*, 128–131.

21. Vlastos, *Studies in Greek Philosophy*, 2:15.

22. This picture of a Socrates who cares about his interlocutor is the upshot of Vlastos's description of Socratic elenchus found in *Socratic Studies*, 1–3. In his essay on irony he makes explicit the understanding that compassion is what dictates the procedure. Because he loves Alcibiades, he must let him flounder. *Socrates*, 44, esp. n82.

23. It is because Aristophanes's play seriously endangered Socrates's life that I disagree with Strauss's assertion that Socrates and Aristophanes were "friends." Leo Strauss, *Socrates and Aristophanes* (New York: Basic Books, 1966), 5. Although one might cite the *Symposium* as evidence that Socrates ultimately

forgave Aristophanes or that the two men had found another path to friendship, one cannot read *The Clouds* without taking note of the viciousness of the attack.

24. Socrates's annoyance at interlocutors who do not pronounce their true opinion is made abundantly clear throughout the *Gorgias* when Callicles repeatedly asserts that he will follow the argument through but not believe a word of it. Vlastos develops this point fully in *Socrates*, 107–131.

25. The modern self has had a long incubation. In some very important respects, Socrates was already "one of us." The entire story is told, complete with epochal shifts, in Charles Taylor, *Sources of the Self: The Making of Modern Identity* (Cambridge, Mass.: Harvard University Press, 1989).

26. Vlastos, *Socrates*, 107–131.

27. Although I insist on Socrates's power of empathetic understanding, I do not want to take it to the extreme that can be found in Nalin Ranasinghe, *The Soul of Socrates* (Ithaca, N.Y.: Cornell University Press, 2000), 11. To endow Socrates with an X-ray vision that enables him to see into souls and penetrate into secret and hidden motives is not only a romanticizing of Socrates but a dangerous one. If Socrates knew Glaucon as well as Ranasinghe pretends, then he would be quite justified in setting himself up as a philosopher-tyrant. Against this, one has to keep in mind the import of the passage I have already cited in which Socrates concedes that he cannot see that deeply even into his *own* soul. He does not know whether he is simple and good—or instead a monster (*Phdr.* 230a). Without that "I do not know" the basis for a forgiving and compassionate humanity is removed. I can find no Socratic or Platonic justification for Manichaeism.

28. The forceful nature of Socrates's preliminary encounters with the philosophically unschooled may be the explanation for Socrates's strange concession in the *Republic* that Hesiod's accounts of violence among the gods may retain an esoteric function even after they are abolished from the canon (*Rep.* 378a). The order of Zeus can tolerate patricide as little as the order of reason, but both must begin there. In a world governed by myth and convention, reason must first establish itself. Law always covers over the violence that gave it birth, which is why the cynical unmasking of the law as a power ploy by the powerful, apparently emancipatory, can be so dangerous. Slavoj Žižek, *For They Know Not What They Do* (New York: Verso, 2008). The insight is discomforting, leaving us in the final analysis with no better place to stand than our own abysmal freedom.

29. Hermann Gundert, *Der platonische Dialog* (Heidelberg: Winter, 1968), makes clear how differently Socrates responds to friend and foe.

30. Vlastos, *Socrates*, 46.

31. The long discussion begins at 258d with the question "What is the nature of good writing and bad?"

32. When Socrates insists that Phaedrus himself is responsible for his own poetic excess (*Phdr.* 238d), he ties together the familiar doctrine of philosophy born in love with the very specific situation in which he finds himself: alone, with an attractive young man.

33. Helpful for highlighting what makes Xenophon a poor commentator on Socrates is a footnote that Kierkegaard added to *The Concept of Irony*: "Were Xenophon's conception of Socrates correct, then I should have thought that in

sophisticated and fickle Athens one would sooner have had Socrates out of the way because he bored them than because they feared him" (18). Or, even more to the point, the wonderful passage in the main text: "We trust that readers will agree with our statement that the empirical determinant is the polygon, that the intuition is the circle, and that there the qualitative difference between them will continue forevermore. In Xenophon, gadding observation always wanders about in the polygon, presumably often victim of its own deception, when, just by having a good distance to go, it believes that it has found the true infinity and, like an insect crawling along a polygon, falls off because what appeared to be infinity was only an angle" (21). Although it is tempting to use this image to parody the prevailing scholarly approach to the question of the true Socrates, it would be foolish to do so, because even a modicum of humility would suggest that one might oneself be the insect.

34. The *Protagoras* passage I allude to provides good evidence that logic was not the issue for Socrates and Plato. When Protagoras points out the mistake, Socrates accepts it without argument or comment of any sort whatsoever, shifting immediately to a new question—that is, a new strategy for turning Protagoras's soul, the *only* real issue (*Prt.* 351b).

35. See Stanley Rosen, *Plato's "Sophist"* (New Haven, Conn.: Yale University Press, 1983).

36. Compare Günther Figal, *Sokrates* (Munich: Beck, 1995).

37. Reliance on this "plainly right" explains the strident character of that most popular of Straussian books, Bloom's *The Closing of the American Mind.*

38. Strauss ignores the imprudent nature of Eros even in his meticulously close, line-by-line reading of Plato's *Symposium.* Leo Strauss, *On Plato's "Symposium,"* ed. Seth Bernardete (Chicago: University of Chicago Press, 2001), 193.

39. Ibid., 221–222.

40. Strauss makes his preference for the prudent Socrates explicit in "Jerusalem and Athens: Some Preliminary Reflections," in Strauss, *SPPP*, 172–173.

41. Ibid., 44.

42. Ibid., 46.

43. See Strauss, *Xenophon's Socratic Discourse: An Interpretation of the Oeconomicus* (Ithaca, N.Y.: Cornell University Press, 1970).

44. Strauss, "Correspondence concerning *Wahrheit und Methode,*" 6.

45. Bloom, *The Closing of the American Mind.*

46. Leo Strauss, *Natural Right and History* (Chicago: University of Chicago Press, 1953), 36.

47. See Leo Strauss, *Jewish Philosophy and the Crisis of Modernity: Essays and Lectures in Modern Jewish Thought* (Albany: SUNY Press, 1997), 137–145.

48. See Leo Strauss, *Persecution and the Art of Writing* (Glencoe, Ill.: Greenwood, 1952). The argument is (in part) that the negative theology of Maimonides's *Guide to the Perplexed* (which renders problematic the statement that God exists) is hidden behind a popular work (the *Mishneh Torah*) in which Strauss discusses the laws that govern Jewish life. Presumably the political philosopher is the one who holds these two together, understanding how the political realm is opened up and justified by the absent God. See also Leo Strauss, "On a Forgot-

ten Kind of Writing," in *What Is Political Philosophy?* (Chicago: University of Chicago Press, 1959).

49. I refer to Strauss's "Preface to *Spinoza's Critique of Religion*," which is contained in *Jewish Philosophy and the Crisis of Modernity*, esp. 140–144. I want to thank Jeff Bernstein for pushing me on the issue of the religious dimension of Strauss's thought, saving me from the temptation to read Strauss as a one-sidedly political thinker. His own highly nuanced reading of the issue can be found in Jeffrey A. Bernstein, *Leo Strauss: On the Borders of Judaism, Philosophy, and History* (Albany: SUNY Press, 2015), 135–164.

50. Strauss, *SPPP*, 172–173; emphasis is Strauss's. The point is also repeated in Strauss, *On Tyranny*, rev. and expanded ed. (Chicago: University of Chicago Press, 2000), 43, where Strauss argues that Socrates was wise, not courageous. And the wisdom he has in mind is a wisdom better understood by Xenophon than by Plato. It is prudence. Hence, the decisive sentence on page 43: "The brave would take risks for the sake of freedom. . . . Would the wise take risks for the sake of freedom? Did Socrates . . . take such risks? While blaming 'somewhere' the practice of Critias and his fellows, and while refusing to obey their unjust commands, he did not work for their overthrow."

51. See Strauss, *Socrates and Aristophanes*, 314.

52. See Strauss, *Natural Right and History*, 84.

53. Although Hobbes and Locke are the names that first come to mind, the crucial step to political modernity was taken by Machiavelli's rejection of classical political philosophy, which concerned itself with the Good. Of the three figures, Machiavelli seems to be the most important for Strauss. While rejecting the Platonic and the Christian emphasis on moral virtue, Machiavelli retains a high level of enthusiasm for the Greek and Roman cult of civic virtue. See ibid., 165–251.

54. See Niccolò Machiavelli, *The Prince*, trans. Harvey Mansfield (Chicago: University of Chicago Press, 1985), 34–37.

55. See Emmanuel Levinas, *Totality and Infinity*, trans. Alphonso Lingis (Pittsburgh: Duquesne University Press, 1969), 20–30.

56. See ibid., 22.

57. See Emmanuel Levinas, "Diachrony and Representation," in *Time and the Other*, trans. Richard Cohen (Pittsburgh: Duquesne University Press, 1987), 97–120.

58. Strauss, *On Tyranny*, 27.

59. In at least one passage Strauss *seems* in fact to suggest that annihilation is the better option when he says that "nihilistic negation" would be "preferable to the indefinite continuation of the inhuman end" (which in the context of the discussion with Alexandre Kojève, included in the revised and expanded edition of *On Tyranny*, seems to refer to universal communism). In fairness to Strauss, he refers not to nuclear war as such but instead to the possibility of reducing humanity to the "primitive horde" from which civilization would slowly once again emerge (209). He is sufficiently cryptic not to say how this will happen. In fact, he is sufficiently cryptic that I have to confess I may have missed his meaning entirely.

60. Focusing so narrowly on the question of how a city is to defend itself from enemies results in a reading of Plato's *Republic* that, by excising the metaphysical heart of the work (bks. 6 and 7), presents the impression that Plato's real goal was to argue for a state ruled by its soldiers. See Leo Strauss, *The City and Man* (Chicago: Rand McNally, 1964), 50–138. In sharp contrast to Strauss's "close reading" of the *Republic*, which ends up being so close that it allows him virtually to ignore what is surely its primary intention, one might consider the exemplary close reading carried out by John Sallis, who examines the detail of the work in conjunction with a comprehensive one-page outline of the "Structure of the Republic" that makes it clear that the City of the Philosopher is meant as a radical alternative to the "purged" (or militarized) city that captured the attention of Strauss. See John Sallis, *Being and Logos: The Way of Platonic Dialogue* (Bloomington: Indiana University Press, 1996), 455.

61. They were discussing Strauss's *On Tyranny*.

62. Ibid., 191.

63. Plato, *Euthyphro*, in *Plato*, vol. 1, Loeb Classical Library, 10. In the *Symposium* (189d), Aristophanes says of Eros that he is *theōn philanthrōpotatos* (the most philanthropic of the gods).

Chapter 3

1. The entire discussion from 88c to 91a turns on the question of doubt (*apistis*) and faith (*pistis*).

2. Sarah Kofman interprets Hegel rather freely in an attempt to make this "almost" into a completely Oedipal situation. See Sarah Kofman, *Socrates: Fictions of a Philosopher*, trans. Catherine Porter (Ithaca, N.Y.: Cornell University Press, 1998), 64–65.

3. Without adding the reference to Parmenides's rejection of the visible god, Sarah Kofman's depiction (see the preceding note) of Socrates as having been the victim of an Oedipal situation is hard to accept. But one need only recall Aristophanes's *Clouds* to realize that Socrates had always awakened the suspicion of patricide by daring to question authority as he did.

4. The good effects of the right natural setting is the theme in particular of the concluding letter of part 1 of *Hyperion*, which is devoted specifically to the question of how Athenian culture could have emerged. Friedrich Hölderlin, *Hyperion: Or the Hermit in Greece*, trans. Ross Benjamin (New York: Archipelago, 2008), 102–121.

5. If the Good and the Beautiful are internally unified, they differ in this respect: the Good itself is utterly transcendent; the Beautiful is the Good in relation to that which appears.

6. The question of how we are able to learn language is clearly at issue in the famous passage in the *Phaedrus* in which Socrates describes the prebirth journey of souls around the celestial sphere and then comments: "A soul that was once human can move from an animal to a human being again. But a soul that never saw the truth cannot take a human shape, since a human being must

understand speech in terms of general forms, proceeding to bring many perceptions together into a reasoned unity" (*Phdr.* 249b).

7. I am referring to the opening sections on "Sense-Certainty" and "Perception" in G. W. F. Hegel, *Phenomenology of Spirit*, trans. A. V. Miller (Oxford: Clarendon Press, 1977), 58–79.

8. See Peter Warnek, *Descent of Socrates* (Bloomington: Indiana University Press, 2005), 84–86.

9. See Gadamer, "The Proofs of Immortality in Plato's *Phaedo*," 21–38.

10. See Warnek, *Descent of Socrates*, 57–61.

11. See Hölderlin, *Hyperion*, 104. The same problem is also implicit in Plato's *Timaeus*. Before Timaeus delivers the famous discourse about how nature was fashioned, Critias delivers a shorter discourse about history. He tells the story of how, nine thousand years in the past, Athens was at its fullest blossom, displaying the wisdom of Athena in establishing the city in that most perfect of places, where "the happy temperament of the seasons in that land would produce the wisest of men" (*Tim.* 24d). The perfect place produces the perfect city—until the inevitable fall. But why then does paradisiacal nature withdraw itself? Why is once glorious Athens now in shambles?

12. See Aristotle, *Meta.* 993b.

13. Hölderlin, *Hyperion*, 105.

14. Ibid., 104.

15. Ibid., 215.

16. Ibid., 209.

17. As Socrates himself suggests in *Tht.* 152e, Parmenides was the only one of his predecessors who was not rooted in nature.

18. See Warnek, *Descent of Socrates*, 119–140.

19. The seriousness of the need for salvation is why "just sitting" is presented as work—in conjunction with the stern warning, "*Hatarakazaru mono kuu bekarazu*" (if one doesn't work, one shouldn't eat).

20. I compiled my list with the help of Herman Sinaiko, *Love, Knowledge, and Discourse in Plato: Dialogue and Dialectic in "Phaedrus," "Republic," "Parmenides"* (Chicago: University of Chicago Press, 1965), 199–222.

21. Perhaps the best sustained attempt to show the importance of the reduction to absurdity is Kelsey Wood's *Troubling Play: Meaning and Entity in Plato's "Parmenides"* (Albany: SUNY Press, 2005).

22. See Samuel C. Rickless, *Plato's Forms in Transition: A Reading of the "Parmenides"* (Cambridge: Cambridge University Press, 2007).

Chapter 4

Epigraph: Hölderlin's "Sokrates und Alcibiades" appears, together with a translation, in *Friedrich Hölderlin: Poems and Fragments*, trans. Michael Hamburger (Ann Arbor: University of Michigan Press, 1967).

1. That the sophistic will to instrumentalize reason derives from a fear of death is a point that Socrates makes against Callicles in the *Gorgias* (511b). That

this very fear leads the sophist to establish a kingdom of death is the intuition that lies at the basis of the interpretation of the *Republic* as a dialogue taking place in Hades. The best example of this interpretation is the one in Sallis, *Being and Logos*, 312–320.

2. See Friedrich Nietzsche, *The Gay Science* (New York: Vintage, 1974), § 340, 272.

3. The modern opposition between culture and civilization (Vico versus Descartes) is in many essentials a renewal of the ancient opposition between Eros and Logos (Plato versus the Sophists), but with this important difference: Eros in its modern manifestation is dangerously enflamed by its tendency to become its own object (e.g., Nietzsche's "Will to Power"). I have in mind two recent discussions of "enflamed Eros" in modernity: Stephen Gardner, *Myths of Freedom: Equality, Modern Thought, and Philosophical Radicalism* (Westport, Conn.: Greenwood, 1998), and Richard Velkley, *Being after Rousseau: Philosophy and Culture in Question* (Chicago: University of Chicago Press, 2002). My own reason for focusing on the ancient side of this divide is the hope it affords. Bourgeois conventionality, as affirmation of the needs of civilization (the state and the market) over the needs of culture, is not the only alternative (and often not an alternative at all) to the dangers of Eros enflamed. Recovery of an older and more natural form of Eros strikes me as in every way a saner and healthier move.

4. See Martha Nussbaum, *The Fragility of Goodness* (Cambridge: Cambridge University Press, 1986), 168. Hereafter cited as *FG*.

5. Müller speaks as a philologist who has traced the way mythologies often arise out of the forgotten fragments of older mythologies. See Max Müller, *Lectures on the Science of Language*, 2 vols. (New York: Scribners, 1884), 375–376.

6. Misunderstandings sometimes play a creative role. See Max Müller, *Chips from a German Workshop* (London: Longmans, Green and Company, 1867), 5:65.

7. Heidegger, often criticized for his "incorrect" etymologies, sometimes responded in a tongue-in-cheek fashion by dangling, one after the other, clearly incompatible etymologies before his readers. In "Science and Reflection" (163–165), for example, he juxtaposes two different etymologies of the word *theōrein* (theorize), one likening it to attentively watching a theater (*thea* and *horaō*) and the other to revering a goddess (*theá* and *ōra*).

8. See Kierkegaard, *The Concept of Irony*, 47–51.

9. See Vlastos, *Platonic Studies* (Princeton, N.J.: Princeton University Press, 1981), 3–42. The theme is the subject of an entire chapter, "The Speech of Alcibiades," in Nussbaum, *FG*, 165–199. Nussbaum agrees with Vlastos that Socrates was too thoroughly turned toward universals to truly love, particularly in a sensual way, a specific, corporeal, and imperfect human being. She uses Alcibiades's speech, however, to make the point that *Plato* was perfectly aware of what such love involves. Alcibiades himself, after all, was in love with Socrates in the normal human way. She then turns her attention to the *Phaedrus* and claims that there, rather than in the *Symposium*, one can find the authentic Platonic view: love does not force us to abandon our lovers, whom we may even cuddle and kiss (*Phdr.* 255e).

10. See Stanley Rosen, *Plato's Symposium* (New Haven, Conn.: Yale University Press, 1968).

11. See "Plato," in Diogenes Laertius, *Lives of Eminent Philosophers*, vol. 1, bk. 3, trans. R. D. Hicks, Loeb Classical Library (Cambridge, Mass.: Harvard University Press, 1925).

12. Krüger is compelling on the issue of why philosophical monotheism (much like theological monotheism) creates the need for a mediator. See Gerhard Krüger, *Einsicht und Leidenschaft: Das Wesen des platonischen Denkens* (Frankfurt: Vittorio Klostermann, 1939), 3–73.

13. Plato, *Symposium*, in *Plato*, vol. 3, trans. W. R. M. Lamb, Loeb Classical Library (Cambridge, Mass.: Harvard University Press, 1925), 207. Each of the *Symposium* citations in both this and the following chapter are drawn from this Loeb edition (and cited according to the standard Stephanus pagination).

14. For a beautiful defense of what I would like to call a mystical reading of Plato, see Karl Albert, *Griechische Religion und platonische Philosophie* (Hamburg: Felix Meiner, 1980).

15. The same thing can be inferred from the fact that Alcibiades sometimes finds himself wishing Socrates were dead (*Symp.* 216c).

16. A notable exception is Georg Picht. See his *Platons Dialoge "Nomoi" und "Symposion"* (Stuttgart: Klett-Cotta, 1990), 429–448. That his lectures on the *Symposium* (delivered in 1968) remain fragmentary is a sad commentary on the shortsightedness of the student revolts. The man should have been heard. He—and his project—were more "on our side" than we were grown up enough to realize.

17. The full force of the recommendation that one begin the ascent by cultivating physical desire becomes clear only when we see that the kind of "disembodied intellect" that Nussbaum (*FG*, 184) associates with Socrates is not a human possibility. Indeed, the attempt to portray it as such seems to have more to do with her distaste for New England Puritanism than with Plato or Socrates. For an interpretation that emphasizes the genuineness of Socrates's passion, see Krüger, *Einsicht und Leidenschaft*. Apart from calling attention to the religious dimension of the dialogue, Krüger's big contribution was to show just how far "below"—in very physical passions—Platonic love is ultimately rooted. Coming as he does from the Heidegger school, Krüger's work can be read as an example of what Heidegger's "positive" understanding of Plato might have been had he ever elaborated it. These are issues I addressed in my essay "Commentary on Patterson: The Ascent in Plato's *Symposium*," *Boston Area Colloquium in Ancient Philosophy* 7 (1991), 215–225.

18. See Robert Lloyd Mitchell, *The Hymn to Eros: A Reading of Plato's "Symposium"* (New York: Lanham, 1993), 179.

19. As I will show with more detail below, Nussbaum's characterization in the *Fragility of Goodness* of Socrates as being encapsulated within a tightly closed sphere of perfection (184–195) represents a serious misunderstanding.

20. See the epigraph to this chapter. The line plays a pivotal role in Heidegger, *What Is Called Thinking?*, 20.

21. Plutarch's description of Alcibiades can be found under the title *The Rise and Fall of Athens: Nine Greek Lives by Plutarch*, trans. Ian Scott-Kilvert (London: Penguin, 1960), 245–285.

22. See Picht, *Platons Dialoge*, 368.

23. The mistake of turning Socrates into a "busybody" is common among Straussian interpreters. An egregious case of it can be found in the first chapter (entitled "Glaucon's Republic") of Ranasinghe, *The Soul of Socrates*, 1–27.

24. The name "Callicles" is not mentioned by any writer besides Plato, which is rather odd because he was so determined to make a political career (*Grg.* 515a). For this reason Georg Picht suggests that we are simply supposed to reflect on the meaning of the name ("one who is known for his beauty") to make the connection to Alcibiades (*Platons Dialoge*, 369). Whether Picht is right in his assumption that Callicles was intended as a mouthpiece for Alcibiades is probably not that important, for Callicles clearly desired to live Alcibiades's life (and in accord with Alcibiades's principles). In the *Gorgias*, Socrates puts the two together: "If you are not careful, they will lay hands on you and on my friend Alcibiades" (*Grg.* 519a).

25. In the *Republic*, Thrasymachus initially played the role of the devil's advocate. But when (like Callicles) he grew weary of the argument and acquiesced before he had arrived at a real understanding, the role was taken over by Plato's older brothers, Glaucon and Adeimantus. Socrates's response was one of elation: precisely his *friends* had grasped the importance of forcing justice to defend itself against the argument of the devil (*Rep.* 386a–c).

26. The need for the *advocatis diabolis* can send the philosopher to the strangest places—and into the most dubious associations. For a full development of this interpretation, see Sallis, *Being and Logos*, 312–345.

27. See Vlastos, *Socrates, Plato, and Their Tradition*, 15.

28. Ranasinghe, in an act of real inspiration, describes the gallery of speakers in the *Symposium* in terms of the six transformations of Proteus as a bearded lion, a snake, a leopard, a savage hog (Aristophanes!), running water, and a tree with towering branches. Ranasinghe, *The Soul of Socrates*, 118–148.

29. Nussbaum, *FG*, 184, 195.

30. Ibid., 190.

31. Ibid., 195.

32. Ibid., 180.

33. The parallel between Socrates and Homer can be found in Picht, *Platons Dialoge*, 399.

34. The transition to an inner sense is a central and generally ignored point. A similar claim can be found in L. A. Kosman's "Platonic Love," first included in *Facets of Plato's Philosophy*, ed. W. H. Werkmeister (Amsterdam: Van Gorcum, 1976), 52–69, and reprinted in *Eros, Agape, and Philia*, ed. Alan Soble (New York: Paragon House, 1989), 149–164.

35. For this crucial passage I have followed the translation in Plato, *Symposium*, trans. Alexander Nehamas and Paul Woodruff (Indianapolis: Hackett, 1989), 59.

36. Aristotle, *De Anima*, 431b20.

37. The "night in which all cows are black" is the famous parody of Schelling's philosophy of identity from Hegel's preface to the *Phenomenology of Spirit*, 9.

Chapter 5

1. Gadamer puts the point well: "The beautiful disposes people in its favor immediately, whereas models of human virtue can be only obscurely descried in the unclear medium of appearances, because they have, as it were, no light of their own. Thus we often succumb to impure imitations and appearances of virtue" (*Truth and Method*, 481).

2. That beauty shows forth an inner essence is something we can experience when we look at artificial flowers. The artificial garden in Disney World, even when it is momentarily experienced as beautiful, becomes quickly something repulsive. As Kant points out in his "analytic of the sublime," once one discovers the artificiality of flowers or of "carved birds on the boughs of trees, . . . the immediate interest that he previously took in them would disappear at once." Immanuel Kant, *The Critique of Judgment*, trans. J. H. Bernard (New York: Prometheus, 2000), 178.

3. Thus, although generally appreciative of Heidegger's well-known attempt to replace an artist aesthetic with one that focuses first and foremost on the truth of the work itself (and so decisively that the word "aesthetic" no longer suffices because it reintroduces a relationship to either the creator or the observer of the work), I will fault him for a certain polemical excess. The truth displayed in art is always also the truth of any subject that becomes engaged with it. See Martin Heidegger, "The Origin of the Work of Art," in *Basic Writings*, ed. David Krell (New York: Harper and Row, 1977), 149–187.

4. For books devoted to the need for ever-renewed descent, see Sallis, *Echoes: After Heidegger* (Bloomington: Indiana University Press, 1990), and *Chorology* (Bloomington: Indiana University Press, 1999). The idea of descent plays a crucial role in two other works as well. An older book is his *Delimitations* (Bloomington: Indiana University Press, 1986). More recent is his *Transfigurements* (Chicago: University of Chicago Press, 2008).

5. By emphasizing the living nature of philosophical discourse, I want to reverse the thesis of H. J. Krämer's *Arete bei Platon und Aristoteles: Zum Wesen und zur Geschichte der platonischen Ontologie* (Heidelberg: Carl Winter, 1959). The existence of a Platonist school is undeniable, as is the inference that Plato must have been teaching some kind of "system." But the notion that Plato himself was dogmatically attached to that system is untenable, for it contradicts the spirit of everything he was doing in the dialogues. A reading of the *Sophist* should make clear to what degree Plato had a system—and to what degree he maintained an ironic distance from it. That his students did not always understand the importance of that irony is not surprising. The entire history of philosophy represents a series of creative attempts to begin the project of thinking anew and the degeneration of those attempts into one form or another of scholasticism.

6. Not only Leo Strauss insists unduly on an absolute separation between "Athens and Jerusalem." The same point is made just as emphatically from the perspective of Protestant Christianity in the classic work of the Swedish theologian Anders Nygren, *Agape and Eros*, trans. Philip S. Watson (Philadelphia: Westminster, 1953). I have already entered into an implicit dialogue with Nygren's

contrast. I will explain my understanding more fully once I have completed my own interpretation of Eros. As for the general relevance of the prodigal son motif, I believe it is of very great importance that one understand it as constituting the essence of religion as such rather than pretending that Christianity alone has loved the sinner. For an effective use of the story by a Zen Buddhist, see Kitaro Nishida, *An Inquiry into the Good*, 172. A much fuller discussion of the relationship between Buddhism and Christianity can be found in the work of Nishida's student Keiji Nishitani, *Religion and Nothingness*, trans. Jan Van Bragt (Berkeley: University of California Press, 1982).

7. The failure to take seriously this very well marked division in the text made it possible to collapse the Platonic conception of Eros into the romantic conception. This is what stands behind the spurious critiques of both Nygren in *Agape and Eros* and Vlastos in *Platonic Studies*. For a masterful presentation of the romantic conception, see Denis de Rougemont, *Love in the Western World*, trans. Montgomery Belgion (1940; New York: Harper and Row, 1974).

8. The way I am interpreting the *Symposium* stands in sharp contrast to the interpretation that Herbert Marcuse drew on in constructing his vision of an "Eros without Thanatos," the happy world (of universalized suburbia I am tempted to say) in which pain and unwanted death have all been overcome. Herbert Marcuse, *Eros and Civilization: A Philosophical Inquiry into Freud* (Boston: Beacon, 1966), 222–237. The narcissism of a generation that embraced this vision has, with the passage of many years, become fully manifest. The Marcuse who should survive is not the utopian but the Socratic realist and gadfly. For that dimension of his thinking, see Herbert Marcuse, *One-Dimensional Man: Studies in the Ideology of Advanced Industrial Society* (Boston: Beacon, 1964).

9. The idea of Christ as the incarnation of Dionysus is worked out in full in Schelling's philosophy of mythology, the introduction of which now exists in English translation. See F. W. J. Schelling, *Historical-Critical Introduction to the Philosophy of Mythology*, trans. Mason Richey and Markus Zisselberger (Albany: SUNY Press, 2007). The best contemporary assessment of the entire Dionysus revival is Manfred Frank's *Der kommende Gott: Vorlesungen über die neue Mythologie* (Frankfurt: Suhrkamp, 1982).

10. It is significant that Nietzsche borrowed the quotation from Sophocles's last play, *Oedipus at Colonus*. Sophocles, *The Three Theban Plays*, trans. Robert Fagles (London: Penguin, 1984), 358. Although he was right to depict the quotation itself as constituting the most horrific of truths, he neglected to mention what makes the work of Sophocles a part of Greek mystery religion: Oedipus is finally released from his suffering by death—but also by transfiguration, insofar as his body is mysteriously dissolved into light (381). One could go so far as to speak of the "redemption" of Oedipus's sufferings. Indeed, what does it really mean that Sophocles depicts the spirit of Oedipus as chosen already by Theseus to guard over Athens. Precisely what sufferings have been redeemed in the beauty of the Parthenon?

11. Nietzsche develops the notion of morality as constituting the "will to power of the powerless" in *The Genealogy of Morals*, trans. Walter Kaufmann (New York: Random House, 1969). The primary argument is, of course, the old one

that Plato put in the mouths of Callicles and Thrasymachus. If justice is always the "interest of the stronger," then democracy represents a kind of perversion whereby the weak have combined to gain power over those who are strong by nature, the victory of *nomos* over *phusis*. For Nietzsche, of course, the revolution of the weak was intensified by the emergence of Christianity, whereby priests used the fiction of hell as a device for emasculating the strong altogether.

12. See especially the concluding section, "General Observations on the Whole System," of Schelling's *System of Transcendental Idealism*, trans. Peter Heath (1800; Charlottesville: University Press of Virginia, 1978), 233–236.

13. In the *Phaedo*, this discovery is placed in the mouth of Socrates, who is giving his disciples an account of why he grew dissatisfied with natural science: "I once heard someone reading from a book by Anaxagoras, who asserted that it is mind that produces order and is the cause of everything. This explanation pleased me. Somehow it seemed right that the mind should be the cause of everything. . . . It was a wonderful hope, but it was quickly dashed. As I read on I discovered that the fellow made no use of mind and assigned to it no causality for the order of the world, but adduced causes like air and aether and water and many more absurdities" (*Phd.* 97c–98c).

14. A proper account of the organic nature of unity would demand a long discussion of Plato's *Parmenides*, in which the "universalizing" thrust of the "doctrine of forms" is subjected to a rigorous and sustained critique. This would involve an exercise in real philosophy, something that stands far above what can be accomplished in the present work.

15. The allusion is to the preface of Hegel's *Philosophy of Right*.

16. For a wonderful attempt to grasp the elusive personality of Socrates himself in the light of this "suddenness," see Wyller's "Sokrates—Skikkelsen, en presentasjon," 9–22.

17. Nygren, *Agape and Eros*, 210.

18. Fyodor Dostoevsky, *The Brothers Karamazov*, trans. Richard Pevear and Larissa Volokhonsky (New York: Farrar, Straus and Giroux, 1990), 256. The biblical reference is to Rev. 7:4–8.

19. Meister Eckhart, *Selected Writings*, trans. Oliver Davies (London: Penguin, 1994); sermon 13 (158–164) is exemplary.

Chapter 6

The epigraph from Plato's *Symposium* follows the Nehamas and Woodruff translation, 72–73.

1. I will discuss Hegel's commentary later in this chapter. It can be found in *Lectures on the History of Philosophy*, vol. 1: *Greek Philosophy to Plato*, trans. E. S. Haldane and F. H. Simson (Atlantic Highlands, N.J.: Humanities, 1968). For commentary on that commentary, I can already now refer the reader to Sarah Kofman, *Fictions of a Philosopher*, 66–68.

2. Leo Strauss indicates that there is something comic about an old man such as Socrates comparing himself to Achilles (*SPPP*, 44). This is because he

accepts Xenophon's impression that Socrates was an old man who knew he was soon going to die in any case. Plato's Socrates had a good deal more life in him. Not only does he have two very young children, but in the days immediately preceding his trial, we find him engaging in exceedingly long and complex conversations with Theaetetus and the Athenian Stranger. There was also the famous encounter with Euthyphro. The defense speech itself is a masterpiece of both reasoning and spontaneity. The conversations in the *Crito* and the *Phaedo* indicate the same thing: Socrates was more alive than ever. He himself refers to his renewed vitality, likening his words to the song of a swan, which attains its ultimate beauty when death draws near (*Phd.* 84e–85a). Impending death, not youth, is also the most important key to understanding the godlike vitality of Achilles.

3. See Immanuel Kant, "What Is Enlightenment?"; the 1784 essay can be found in *Kant: Selections*, ed. Lewis White Beck (Englewood Cliffs, N.J.: Prentice-Hall, 1988), 462–467.

4. Dostoevsky was the greatest master of the dialectic whereby freedom is viewed as the gift of the absent God. I once again have in mind the "Grand Inquisitor" chapter of *The Brothers Karamazov*, 246–264.

5. If one were to object that this is just not Socrates's problem (that is, if one were still unconvinced by the claim I have repeatedly raised that Socrates saw beyond the problem of the city), then let me answer by referring to the *Timaeus*. Although Socrates is not the one who poses the question of the abyss and the riddle of the beginning, he listens in wonder as Timaeus speaks about these greatest of mysteries. Something like that rapt attention is foreshadowed in the text we now have before us.

6. For the strange dilemma of needing wings to find one's wings, see Sallis, *Being and Logos*, 153–159.

7. The classic illumination of the relationship between the two gods is contained in Nietzsche's *The Birth of Tragedy*, ed. Michael Tanner, trans. Shaun Whiteside (London: Penguin, 1993). For a detailed philological demonstration of Nietzsche's fundamental insight, see Walter F. Otto, *Dionysus: Myth and Cult*, trans. Robert Palmer (Bloomington: Indiana University Press, 1965).

8. The figure of Socrates is discernible throughout Hegel's section on "Morality" in the *Phenomenology of Spirit*, 365–374. It is after all Socrates who first challenged what Hegel calls "ethical substance"—the rule of convention in traditional Greek society. Although the section culminates in a presentation of the Kantian concept of duty, it begins with a stress on self-consciousness and individual conviction that is clearly aimed at Socrates.

9. Ibid., 452–453.

10. A worthy project would be an investigation of the Socrates motif that operates implicitly in Hegel's *Phenomenology of Spirit*, *History of Philosophy*, and *Philosophy of Religion*, with regard specifically to the relationship between Socrates and Christ.

11. In *Lectures on the History of Philosophy*, Hegel introduces the trance to present the image of a self-encapsulated "internality" that is then interwoven into the entire discussion of Socrates (1:390). Finally, when discussing the mean-

ing of Socrates's *daimonion*, Hegel returns to an explicit discussion of the trance (1:424), which he likens to a cataleptic state.

12. G. W. F. Hegel, *Science of Logic*, vol. 2, trans. W. H. Johnston and L. G. Struthers (New York: Macmillan, 1929), 460: "the self-certainty of the subject is always simultaneously a certainty of the irreality of the world." The ultimate consequence of this sense of irreality is the epochal fight between man and nature. For this reason, Socrates represents for Hegel the annihilation of pagan religion, which is always essentially the worship of nature (463).

13. In addition to the Nehamas and Woodruff translation of the *Symposium*, I consulted, as always, the translation by Michael Joyce that can be found in the Edith Hamilton edition of the *Collected Dialogues* and the translation by W. R. M. Lamb that is given in the Loeb Classical Library edition. See also Plato, *Symposium*, trans. Robin Waterfield (Oxford: Oxford University Press, 1994), and *Plato's "Symposium,"* trans. Seth Benardete (Chicago: University of Chicago Press, 1993).

14. Hegel, *Lectures on the History of Philosophy* 1:390, 424.

15. Ibid., 1:424.

16. Ibid., 1:384–388.

17. Consider in particular book 10 of the *Confessions*, in which the interiority of the confessional act merges with the interiority of the God within ("You are the power of my soul"). Before developing a theology of creation in books 11–13, Augustine first discloses his God as the foundation of anamnesis. Saint Augustine, *Confessions*, trans. R. S. Pine-Coffin (London: Penguin, 1961), 207–252.

18. The hidden problem of obeying laws, the possible complicity in an act of injustice, is discussed in the *Crito*. Socrates's acceptance of his own execution can also be regarded as an act of complicity. In his defense, Socrates asserts that the rule of law is so important for a society that it should not be undermined because of an isolated case of poor judgment. Individual human lives are simply not that important: "the really important thing is not to live, but to live well" (48b).

19. Dante, *Inferno* 3.9. Schelling refers to the passage in his famous 1821 lecture "On the Nature of Philosophy as Science," which can be found in *German Idealistic Philosophy*, ed. Rüdiger Bubner (London: Penguin, 1997), 218.

20. How could the Greek philosopher who discovered God go down to Piraeus to worship the devil? That this is scandalous was pointed out in the fourth century by the great Father of the Church, Athanasius of Alexandria. See the opening of Saint Athanasius, *Contra Gentes*, ed. and trans. Robert W. Thomson (Oxford: Clarendon Press, 1971).

21. Sallis begins his interpretation of the *Republic* in *Being and Logos* by pointing out that the entire narration describes what took place "yesterday," so that it effectively begins within hours of the completion of the actual conversation. The concluding myth of Er thus sets the tone for the whole. Eric Voegelin made the same observation in his *Plato* (Baton Rouge: Louisiana State University Press, 1966), 54–55. Eva Brann is a third writer who has called attention to this mythical framework of the *Republic*. Her long article "The Music of the *Republic*," *Agon: Journal of Classical Studies* 1 (April 1967), 1–117, deserves careful study. The essay eventually grew into an entire book, *The Music of the Republic: Essays on Socrates' Conversations and Plato's Writings* (Philadelphia: Paul Dry, 2004).

22. See Robert F. Brown, *Schelling's Treatise on "The Deities of Samothrace"* (Missoula, Mont.: Scholars, 1975).

23. See A. E. Taylor, *Socrates: The Man and His Thought* (New York: Doubleday, 1952), 73–88.

24. Ibid., 82.

25. Although written years before I first encountered John Sallis's *Chorology*, this section constitutes the basis for why it claimed my full attention. If at this late date I were to break open this section and write it anew, then I would explore in much more detail the idea that lies at the root of the *Timaeus* and was first fully unfolded in Schelling's *Philosophical Investigations into the Essence of Human Freedom*, trans. J. Love and J. Schmidt (Albany: SUNY Press, 2006). For an exploration of the relationship between Plato's text and Schelling's, see John Sallis, *Chorology*, 154–167.

26. See Nietzsche, *The Twilight of the Idols*, trans. Duncan Large (Oxford: Oxford University Press, 1988), 13. On Nietzsche's reading, dialectic is a form of revenge, the knife taken up by an intelligent but weak man who lashes out at others.

27. I. F. Stone's *The Trial of Socrates* is an example of a "purely political" approach to understanding Socrates that is decisively not Straussian. Stone's underlying assumption is that politics represents the only path to freedom and happiness, so that the highest form of human existence conceivable is the achievement of a democratic state in which everyone is able to represent his or her interests. Stone's hero is Pericles; his villain, Socrates; his project, the demonstration that the Athenians' decision was right and good.

28. And Socrates was educated by women. Diotima initiated him into the mysteries; Aspasia taught him rhetoric (*Menexenus* 235e). As a self-declared "midwife," Socrates was a womanly man. Indeed, the entire tradition of metaphysics flows out of Parmenides's poem on Being, itself a revelation of a "goddess." As decisively as politics reduces itself to the will to power, a notably male obsession, philosophy reduces itself to the attempt to find a home in the world. "Homemaking" was traditionally considered a womanly art. Where the political man or woman discerns a male-female "opposition," a philosopher might discern a male-female "polarity." What that involves can be illustrated with the example of a magnet. Detach one of the poles and one will discover that its "opposite" is contained within it. A worthwhile study would apply this great principle (most beautifully displayed in Leibniz's *Monadology*) to the relationship between philosophy and politics. The language of glaring "opposition" is itself a product of what contemporary feminists have rightfully criticized as "dualistic" thinking.

29. Nietzsche, *Thus Spoke Zarathustra*, trans. R. J. Hollingdale (London: Penguin, 1969), 46. Martin Heidegger makes effective use of this image in *What Is Called Thinking?*, 64.

Chapter 7

1. I disagree with Eric Voegelin's assertion in his *Plato* that the *Hermocrates* would somehow have been a "superfluous" dialogue (182). He defends his

remark by saying that the *Critias* would have "exhausted" the theme before the *Hermocrates* begins because it was to deal with the evolution of human society after the *Timaeus* portrayed the creation of nature. He fails to see that the human is not the ultimate. The point can be clarified by using a temporal sequence. The *Timaeus* describes nature as the origin. It discloses the existence of a "receptacle" that existed "even before creation" (*Tim.* 49b, 50c). If then the human community represents the "present," the *Hermocrates* must refer to what comes "after" everything passes away. Its topic is thus clearly that of "death and the Absolute."

2. The picture of Socrates as a skeptic, introduced by Cicero, is shared by both analytic philosophers and Straussians. The former are quite willing to openly proclaim the fact, while Straussians tend to regard it as an esoteric truth, to be shared only with those who are willing to endure long and wearisome "readings" of the dialogues. Gregory Vlastos is to be applauded for finally extricating himself from this understanding (*Socrates*, 4–5).

3. Indeed, there is a good reason for asserting that the doctrine of ideas has more to do with Socrates than with Plato. In the *Parmenides* the doctrine is attributed to the youthful Socrates and then subjected to a devastating critique by Parmenides, who can be understood as the mouthpiece of Plato himself. For those who resist the notion that a "late" dialogue might have anything at all to say about Socrates, reference to the *Euthyphro* should suffice as a reminder that the "ideas" also come into play in securely "Socratic" dialogues.

4. The Straussian interpretation of the *Phaedo* is well represented by Peter J. Ahrensdorf, *The Death of Socrates and the Life of Philosophy* (Albany: SUNY Press, 1995). Ronna Burger's *The Phaedo: A Platonic Labyrinth* (New Haven, Conn.: Yale University Press, 1984) also tends in this direction. Burger's interpretation strikes me as the superior one, insofar as she focuses her attention more closely on what Socrates and Plato might have believed than on the psychological needs of Socrates's disciples. In other words, she is less enamored of the necessity of the lie and more concerned with the real question of truth than Ahrensdorf is. To this extent, her reading has some affinity with the Tübingen school of Plato interpretation, which was led by Hans Joachim Krämer. Like the Straussians, members of the Tübingen school spoke of a "secret" or "unwritten" doctrine. But instead of seeing that as political, they regarded it as metaphysical, effectively suggesting that Plato already anticipated the metaphysics of Hegel. Burger never goes so far. In fact, in her reading of the *Phaedo*, she seems to assume that the moderns have it right: death is dissolution—and nothing more. Plato's view (like Hegel's) is more interesting than that.

5. In addition to Ahrensdorf's *The Death of Socrates* and Burger's *The Phaedo*, I have found very helpful the commentary of Kenneth Dorter, *Plato's Phaedo: An Interpretation* (Toronto: University of Toronto Press, 1982). Most illuminating, however, are Gadamer, "The Proofs of Immortality in Plato's Phaedo," 21–38, and Jacob Klein, "On Plato's *Phaedo*," *College* (St. John's College) 26 (January 1975), 1–10.

6. Klein, "On Plato's *Phaedo*."

7. In contrast, Ronna Burger asserts that misology is "the inevitable result of a misconception of wisdom as direct contact of the pure psyche with the 'be-

ings themselves'" (*The Phaedo*, 10). Socrates says the problem is that we believe too naïvely in the power of argument. Burger says the problem is that we believe wisdom is some kind of direct intuition.

8. A good example of someone who gives meticulous attention to both the arguments and their dramatic context can be found in Dorter, *Plato's Phaedo*, 88–90.

9. My statement may appear to go too far. I mean by it, though, nothing different from what Aristotle says at the end of the *Posterior Analytics*: "Now of the thinking states by which we grasp truth, some are unfailingly true, others admit of error—opinion, for instance, and calculation, whereas scientific knowing and intuition are always true. . . . There will be no scientific knowledge of the primary premises, and since except intuition nothing can be truer than scientific knowledge, it will be intuition that apprehends the primary premises" (*Post. An.* 100b5–12). *Posterior Analytics*, trans. G. R. G. Mure, in *The Basic Works of Aristotle*, ed. Richard McKeon (New York: Random House, 1941).

10. In his comments on the *Phaedo* in *The Question of Being* (New Haven, Conn.: Yale University Press, 1993), Stanley Rosen provides an excellent description of Socrates's attempt to philosophize from the vantage point not of a theoretical construction of reality but of life itself. The description is based on an interpretation of Socrates's autobiographical remarks in the *Phaedo*, the very ground I am covering (too briefly) here. Rosen wants to show that Plato not only anticipated Heidegger's best insight but that he remained truer to it than Heidegger ever did. My only criticism of his interpretation is that it need not have been so polemical in relation to Heidegger. I am hardly the first erstwhile Heideggerian who has lived to find a better master in Plato. The reason, I believe, that Rosen has such a difficult time reconciling Heidegger and Plato is that (true to the tradition of Strauss) he understands the "vantage point of life" in a narrowly *political* fashion. Rosen's real problem with Heidegger is not that Heidegger falls back into metaphysics but that he has essentially religious concerns—and a weakness for what Rosen calls "Oriental kitsch," a remark that discloses, however, Rosen's own weakness. As Socrates himself pointed out (Thracian schooled as he was), one who is genuinely searching will look in every direction for help, giving special attention to "foreigners" who espouse exotic doctrines (*Phd.* 78a). Heidegger does little more than call for a dialogue between East and West. Plato, by contrast, was already immersed in such a dialogue. The view of death in the *Phaedo* comes closer to that espoused in the *Tibetan Book of the Dead* than to any contemporary Western view. Consider first the extensive discussion of reincarnation (*Phd.* 70c–72d). Second, consider the remarkable passage that describes the fate of souls immediately after they die (*Phd.* 80c–84b). Any commentator who, like Rosen, is allergic to "Oriental kitsch" will see right past these passages, regardless of how committed he or she might be to pursuing a close reading.

11. A full development of the point would, in another context, be of some interest. For what it means is that, even in the *Phaedo*, by appearance the most "transcendent" of the dialogues, the conception of form that is presented is fully as "immanent" as what we find in Aristotle. The earth needs no new Atlas to hold

it in its place because its place is where it belongs, its form. What Socrates failed to find in Anaxagoras's conception of "mind," a kind of immanent natural teleology (*Phd.* 97c–99d), is what Aristotle later offered. Although Socrates seems to have abandoned his own search by taking up the "second sailing," the myth of the true earth shows that his ultimate aim remained unchanged.

12. Even Ronna Burger, whose reading of the *Phaedo* is delightfully idiosyncratic, is sometimes guilty of rather conventional readings. In any event, she does assume that Socrates backed quickly away from Anaxagoras. See Burger, *The Phaedo*, 138–142.

13. Compare explanation through formal causes with what Heidegger has to say in *The Principle of Reason*, trans. Reginald Lilly (Bloomington: Indiana University Press, 1991), 35–43. Heidegger opens the dimension whereby the question "why?" falls away through a discussion of a poem by the seventeenth-century German mystic Angelus Silesius: "The rose is without why; she blossoms, because she blossoms / she pays no attention to herself, does not ask whether one sees her or not." To understand reality from the perspective of the Good implies then that the question of its origin ("why is there something and not just nothing?") falls away.

14. Unlike the *Meno*, which traces out a mathematical conception of recollection, the *Phaedo* focuses on images, traces, and reminders. We think of our lover when we perceive his lyre. The transparent structure of a priori rationality gives way to the veiled structure of erotic longing. Sallis notes much the same thing in *Being and Logos*, 84–90.

15. Henry Corbin makes the connection in *Spiritual Body and Celestial Earth: From Mazdean Iran to Shī'ite Iran*, trans. Nancy Pearson (Princeton, N.J.: Princeton University Press, 1977), 96. I have written more extensively on the connection to Socrates in "Plato Encounters Zen—Atop the Mountain Peaks of Iran," *Comparative and Continental Philosophy* 1, no. 1 (2009), 119–141.

16. And what reality does modern science permit us to consider beyond that which stands below us? The study of angels has given way to the study of atomic particles and molecular interactions.

17. Heraclitus, frag. 123, in *Ancilla to the Pre-Socratic Philosophers*, 33.

Index